Safeguarding Your Teenager
From The Dragons Of Life

Other Works By Bettie B. Youngs

BOOKS

Stress In Children

Is Your Net Working? A Complete Guide To Building Contacts And Career Visibility

Friendship Is Forever, Isn't It?

Problem Solving Skills For Children

Getting Back Together: Creating A New Relationship With Your Partner And Making It Last

The 6 Vital Ingredients Of Self-Esteem And How To Develop Them In Your Child

Goal Setting Skills For Young Adults

The 6 Vital Ingredients Of Self-Esteem And How To Develop Them In Your Students

Self-Esteem For Educators: It's Criteria #1

You And Self-Esteem: A Book For Young People

Stress Management For Educators: A Guide To Manage Your Response To Stress

Keeping Your Children Safe: Promoting Physical, Emotional, Spiritual and Intellectual Well-being

Managing Your Response To Stress: A Guide For Administrators

A Stress Management Guide For Young People

AUDIOCASSETTES

The 6 Vital Components Of Self-Esteem And How To Develop Them In Your Child

Helping Children Manage Anxiety, Pressure And Stress

Developing Responsibility In Children

Helping Your Teenager Deal With Stress

How To Raise Happy, Healthy, Self-Confident Children

SAFEGUARDING YOUR TEENAGER FROM THE DRAGONS OF LIFE

A Parent's Guide To The Adolescent Years

Bettie B. Youngs, Ph.D., Ed.D.

Health Communications, Inc.
Deerfield Beach, Florida

Library of Congress Cataloging-in-Publication Data

Youngs, Bettie B.
    Safeguarding your teenager from the dragons of life: a parent's
guide to the adolescent years / Bettie B. Youngs.
       p.   cm.
    Includes bibliographical references and index.
    ISBN 1-55874-264-6
    1. Adolescence. 2. Parent and teenager — United States. 3. Teen-
agers — United States. I. Title.
HQ796.Y5825   1993   92-38946
305.23′5—dc20   CIP

©1993 Bettie B. Youngs
ISBN 1-55874-264-6

Publisher: Health Communications, Inc.
                3201 S.W. 15th Street
                Deerfield Beach, FL 33442-8190

Cover design by Bonnie Rheault

DEDICATION

To parents and their teenagers

ACKNOWLEDGMENTS

Over the past 20 years I have conducted numerous courses and workshops throughout the world for parents and children, professional educators, psychologists and pediatricians. I have listened to and learned from many parents, watched and learned from their children, taught both adolescents and adults and have had the privilege of being a parent myself. As I shared with others, they shared with me. They helped reaffirm in me that it all begins in the home. The quality of the parent-child relationship is quite central to wellness in childhood and adulthood as well. To those parents and their teenagers, then, this book is a giving back.

The special ability of teenagers to be astute social critics never ceases to amaze me. For that I thank the many teenagers who actively participated in formulating the thesis for this book. In particular, I thank my own daughter, Jennifer. This loving young woman continues to expand my life in many ways. As usual, when I begin to write a book, she worries about my sleep, fiercely protects our time together, and steps up her own crusade of helping by being extraordinarily responsible for her share of home and family responsibilities as well as for her own activities.

I gratefully acknowledge Jeremy Tarcher who conceived this work years ago when he asked me to write a book for parents on ways to help their teenagers manage stress. This book came about one beautiful day in May when I was speaking at a conference in West Palm Beach, Florida. There descended upon me three wise men from the East (of West Palm Beach!): Peter Vegso, Gary Seidler and Michael Miller from Health Communications. As always when you have adults assembled, conversation eventually turned to our children. As we talked about the enormity of our adolescents' challenges and our concern in helping them find meaning, purpose and direction, this book was reborn. Though it had been brewing for some time, by noon that day this book not only had a name, but a potential table of contents as well. So to Peter, Gary and Michael, a sincere thanks for your vote of confidence in me and your belief in this work.

I wish to acknowledge the able staff at Health Communications: Barbara Nichols, Editorial Director, for her leadership and Marie Stilkind, Senior Editor, for her sensitive editing on this work, and for making this project both easy and fun. I would also like to thank Eleanor Rawson of Rawson & Associates and Davis Perkins from Westminister John Knox Press for their permission to use ideas from my books with them as they relate to the chapters on self-esteem, chemical use and assisting our children in their roles as learners.

Experts in the behavioral sciences have produced an enormous amount of research and tested ways to help adolescents make meaning of their lives. I acknowledge the contributions of the many highly specialized researchers and practitioners for their insightful and useful prevention and intervention strategies that have proven useful in helping teenagers traverse adolescence safely. Some have become well known for their work, others remain unsung heroes who make a significant difference in the lives of young people every day. Both groups generously gave support, advice and expertise. Thank you.

To my own parents, for their years of parenting when I was oblivious to just how much effort it takes to raise teenagers (they had six!), and for their abundant packages of unconditional parental loving and caring for my well-being (— still), and for the ways they remain important anchors for me.

I lovingly thank the many friends who called often to see when I could come out to play, and for not losing faith that at some point I could. A warm thank you to long-time friend Mary Louise Martin, to Jill Scott, Bill De Leeuw, Brad Winch, Joanie Marks, Debbie Bush, Roger Norman, Steve Pinson, Bob Nightingale, Tommy Groff, Cathy and James Jones, Valerie Preiss and Harry Cooper, Mel Davis, Sandy Shapery and Rochelle Swanson, Bill Locke and Nayda Munoz-Locke, Wendy Bunster, Mary Lou and Don Mars, John and Julie Wingo, Larry Maybee, Craig Grosvenor, Dale and Gracie Wilson, John Konstanturos, Tom Dixson, H. Stephen Glenn, Jenny Hawkins, Dale Halaway, Jimmy Higgenbotham, Steve Lorber, Lynn Fox Nafzieger, Colleen Morey, Susanna Palomares, Stephen Covey, Pam Fawaz, Burton Cohen, Dee Acker and Jan Seahorn. Thanks for all the ways you stay tuned in and insist that our friendships stay tuned up.

And finally to Phil Salley, whose charisma, friendship and endless hours in the role of listener were a most special gift. His constant reading and critiquing of this manuscript provided wonderful insights and nourishing conversations. Phil remained positive and encouraging throughout the energy and attention I devoted to writing this book, and best of all, kept me centered on a balanced agenda that included time for play.

CONTENTS

PART
ONE

Understanding The World Your Teenager Lives In

Kids Just Aren't Like They Used To Be!

 A woman in my neighborhood — a loving mother and a bank vice-president — is visiting with the police: Her 17-year-old son, Larry, was expelled for bringing a gun to school. It turns out that Larry "borrowed" a gun from a friend and took it to school to threaten several fellow students who had been heckling and teasing him. When the boys began to call him "Nerdo" on a regular basis, he'd had enough. A gun, he thought, would certainly show the other boys what a tough guy he was and cause them to leave him alone. One morning when the hecklers started in, he lifted his sweatshirt and flashed the gun he had tucked into the belt at his waist. Needless to say, he was ushered out of school by school officials, turned over to local police, booked and released on $5,000 bail. Six days ago, frightened of an upcoming juvenile hearing, he ran away from home. No one knows his whereabouts — or at least no one is revealing where he is.

I've known Larry and his family for a number of years. Larry has always been a trustworthy and considerate boy, pleasant, a great guy to hire for odd jobs and yard care. He fits the profile of what we would typically call "a good kid." Until now he hasn't caused his mother an inordinate amount of stress, and he genuinely likes his stepfather. Because they are neighbors, attend the same high school and sometimes share a ride to school, my daughter and Larry have become friends over the years.

Just Your Average Sort Of Kids . . .

Right now three guests are at my house visiting with my 18-year-old daughter. Lisa is Larry's girlfriend. At 16 she is a model with a local agency in town and lives with her 20-year-old brother in his apartment. Lisa attends Sunset School, a facility for youth who have been removed from the traditional public school setting because they could not deal effectively with its formal structure or abide by its rules and regulations. She is essentially on her own, since her brother rarely checks up on her. Lisa's mother asked her daughter to leave their home for what she called "repeated lying." Translated, her mother said "Out!" when she learned that Lisa had been skipping school and not going on the modeling jobs that had been lined up for her by her talent agency. Her discovery that Lisa had once again started to use drugs was the straw that broke the camel's back; two years ago Lisa completed an expensive drug rehabilitation program.

With Lisa are two boys — David, 18, and Shaun, 17. David's mother struggles to make ends meet for herself and four children; David's income as a supervisor of 38 kids with paper route deliveries is needed — basically, he is the head of the household. David works nearly 35 hours a week in addition to being a senior in high school. Keeping up with these responsibilities means that he gets up at dawn and is seldom home before 9:30 each evening.

Shaun, on the other hand, is a junior in high school and has never had to do a day's work — or anything else on his own. He drives a new car, his second since turning 16 less than a year and a half ago. His friends are in awe of him — he is the first to have the latest of everything. His parents provide for all his expenses, including a credit card with the instructions that he is not to put more than $850 on it each month! He has many friends, several of whom "need" him for transportation; he has a lot of time on his hands and is always available to act as chauffeur for his friends.

Larry's four friends are feeling pretty forlorn right now. They have gathered here on Larry's behalf to exchange information on his dilemma; they all give their rendition of what he should do. Like so many teens, their outward appearance — good looks, youthful health, trendy haircuts and stylish clothing — belie the insecurity, fears and strains that usurp their energy and undermine their self-esteem. I overhear their conversations: Their voices are animated, their words indignant as they reveal the secrets they harbor. The nature of their lives and that of their friends weigh heavily upon them. Larry isn't their only friend in trouble and needing, as they say, to "chill out." Lisa reveals that until this moment, no one but she and Larry know that she is four months pregnant. She had an abortion seven months ago; the two have decided, she says, to keep this baby. She asks the others for their opinion on this: The teens discuss whether to "keep" or "not to keep" the baby, and put it to a vote. By a show of hands, the baby wins the right to keep its life. They agree that having this baby is a good decision, but advise Lisa against telling her mother or brother. Other secrets are unveiled; mysteries discussed.

THE SECRET SOCIETY

The lives of this odd assortment of friends look and sound like the lives of many youth today. Their plight is representative of the complexity of the web teens spin within the hallowed sanctions of the sacred cocoon commonly called *adolescence*. To capture the essence of what it's like to be a teenager is to feel a surge of invincible, raw, youthful power; yet it is also to feel trapped by the limits of seemingly too many external boundaries — all perceived as beyond the teen's control. Many adolescents suffer from delusions of uniqueness, having no idea that what is most personal is also most general.

The life of the adolescent is more private and off limits to adults than many of us would like to believe. Like so many parents, Larry's mother does not know the extent of her son's troubled life, yet she and her son are "close." To Larry, like other *troubled* teens, life seems overwhelming. Because he shares his woes only with young people — many of whom are themselves troubled teens — he holds himself hostage. He is unable to unlock his own door, all the while believing it is others who hold him captive.

PARENTS ARE USELESS UNLESS . . .

It's more than membership in a secret society and a natural immaturity that hinders teens. Unfortunately many adolescents believe that few if any adults can possibly assist them in owning less confusing lives — after all, the lives of their parents are complex in their own way, their problems so dramatically different. Teens believe parents couldn't possibly relate, let alone empathize with their needs and concerns.

Many teens are unwilling to bring adults in the picture for other reasons. They believe, many from experience, that the adults will blow the whistle and shatter their lives or the lives of their friends who are intimately involved in forbidden and secret activities — experimenting with drugs, alcohol or sexual activity, or exploring dark mysteries, such as rituals and cult activities.

The fact that many teens don't genuinely admire too many adults doesn't help. Forty-five percent of children between the ages of 12 and 18 said they didn't believe their parents were in mutually satisfying relationships, but were simply going through the motions. Sixty-five percent said they know of no adult who enjoys his or her work. Forty-seven percent said they possess a great deal more sensitivity and spirituality than do the adults they know. Less than half said they believed their teachers were neither very interested in teaching them nor all that interested in what they would make of their lives.

ALL TEENAGERS ARE EASY PREY FOR TODAY'S DRAGONS

Why do so many more of our young people seem to have such complex and risky lives? "At risk" is a common expression used by schools, social service agencies and the criminal justice system to denote potential risk factors in those young people most likely to fall prey to destructive activities. Once, or so it seemed, only certain adolescents were at risk for becoming involved in destructive behaviors. Not so today. When we aren't paying attention to the emotional life or physical whereabouts of our teenage children, they are all at risk. Without our attention and good parenting, we are likely to see the increase in self-destructive behavior continue.

Destructive behaviors are increasing among all children — not just the ones we label as "at risk" because they are economically deprived, or emotionally or physically abused. The attendant symptoms — drug involvement, pregnancy, dropping out of school, disrespect for adult authority (and seemingly little concern for peers as well), apathy, violence and other such maladies — show us how much young people are in need of added protection from what I call the *dragons* of modern-day life.

THE EVOLVED DRAGONS

As evolution would have it, the offspring of yesterday's dragons look different than their ancestors. Recently my daughter Jennifer asked, "Mom, when I was little and you thought about me as a teenager, did you ever think that just as you had to advise me on protection from becoming pregnant, that you would have to teach me how to protect myself from dying of AIDS?" I had to shake my head. When she was born, AIDS had not been diagnosed.

AIDS is a new and life-threatening danger, far worse than teenage pregnancy or venereal disease. Using crack cocaine is much more dangerous than smoking cigarettes or marijuana. Like me with my daughter, you too are faced with keeping your adolescent safe from today's fire-breathing dragons. Violence in the school, drive-by shootings, crack cocaine and synthetic drugs, dress-for-success values — it's a tough, more violent and less forgiving world than the one we knew. Adolescents need to know how to protect themselves from these and other dragons. Helping your teenager circumvent the dragons — avoid the devastating experiences that can alter his or her life forever — takes much effort on your part.

Helping your teenager get out of scrapes he is already in is another. Luckily, there is help. Even though centers to help teens cope with the new dragons of life are steadily increasing in numbers, *you* are your child's first choice as a solid and meaningful anchor. Stay with the process.

TEENS NEED PROTECTION FROM THE DRAGONS

We parents want to nurture our children, not just "raise" them. We want to show our teenagers our love, and to be loved and respected by them in return. Because the physical, emotional and social needs of adolescent children are so different from those of younger children, these needs are often misunderstood. Unprepared for the marked changes that suddenly occur in the stages of adolescent growth and development, and sometimes unsure of how to decipher the emotional upheavals of teens in a time of dynamic social change, we parents lose confidence in ourselves and in our abilities to parent teenagers. *It's difficult to be sure we are the steadfast anchors our adolescents need as they come to grips with their new and changing selves and find their place in a rapidly changing and technological world.*

Knowing what to do isn't always easy. I remember hearing my eight-month-old daughter cry years ago, when I was a new parent. I had been told by a pediatrician that if an infant cries for no apparent reason, the parent should not always run to her child's side. Doing so would teach the infant that "needless" crying could elicit attention. So there I was, sitting on the floor outside my daughter's room, crying in frustration because I wanted so much to hold and soothe her, yet fearing that I might thwart her emotional growth if I did so. Luckily, after a time, my instincts overshadowed my fears, and I responded to my needs and those of my infant's by going to her and holding her. I realized eventually that holding and soothing my daughter did not make her overly dependent on me, as I had feared; instead, it gave her a feeling of security that allowed her to grow and become independent.

In the same vein, parents of teenage children can find themselves "outside the room," listening to their children crying out — for parental affection, human warmth and nourishing life skills. *Adolescence is a period when parents and their teenagers can become estranged even when they want and need each other very much.*

Apparently, we parents have been sitting outside for too long. The number of adolescents who do not understand their intense feelings or how to cope with them continues to increase. According to psychologist Barbara Massey:

- Teen suicide is at an all-time high.
- Every eight seconds of the school day a student drops out.
- Every 26 seconds a child runs away from home.
- Every 47 seconds a child is abused.

- Every seven minutes an adolescent is arrested for a drug offense.
- Every 30 minutes an adolescent is arrested for drunken driving.
- Teen abortion is at an all-time high.

It is very saddening to read these statistics. Clearly, our adolescent children are experiencing a great deal of stress, they have many fears and anxieties, they worry more than we might suspect and they wish they were happier. It is very depressing to find out that in their desire to escape from pain, teenagers take routes such as alcohol and drug abuse, truancy, delinquency, sexual promiscuity, aggression and violence and running away from home — routes that lead them into problems more overwhelming than those they were trying to escape. Such behavior can make us feel that forces outside ourselves exert a stronger influence on our children than we do, but we must recognize such actions as cries for help.

PARENTS AS USEFUL: HELPING YOUR TEENAGER SLAY THE DRAGONS

What do these young adults want and need from us? How can we best help them prepare to live purposeful and joyous lives now and in future years? How can we help our young people *desire* a life characterized by purpose, meaning and joy; come to know and value productive and meaningful work based on inner desires and talents; grow capable of satisfying and loving relationships; place a supreme value on good health and sustaining wellness; become personally and socially responsible; care for their emotional well-being; learn to be compassionate people; nurture and sustain the warmth of friendships; and set and achieve *worthwhile* goals? How can we safeguard our teenagers from absorbing incongruous and harmful values from outside influences? How can we best use our parenting time to help our teens and ourselves make it through these turbulent teen years — and do so with a measure of joy and family harmony?

These are important questions. We parents must address them if we want to keep our teenagers safe from today's dragons.

Don't give up. Stay with the process of parenting your teen, even when the going gets rough, as, inevitably, it will.

LOVING OUR CHILDREN IS NOT ENOUGH

Even though I have extensive formal education and training and some 20 years of experience in working with parents, youth and childcare professionals, I have learned as much, if not more, from simply living with my daughter. It's this day-to-dayness that gives us the best clues as to what is going on in our teenagers' lives.

We are not perfect, and we may not always do everything right. I'm certain that some things I did have served my daughter very well, while other things I did, all with good intentions, have hurt her. In some areas I was unable to influence her in the way I would have liked to, and perhaps I will be able to go back and try to correct these when she is older and has a different perspective. Or perhaps I will have to wait until I am older and have a different perspective! In some areas my skills are deficient. I will need to acquire new ones in order to strengthen our relationship and to nurture its growth.

It won't always be smooth sailing — you can count on that! But, we parents and our adolescent children need not be estranged: The wear and tear, the psychological damage, the sheer loss in time — the substance of our lives — is too high a price to pay. If we parents are willing to turn the spotlight on our parenting actions, commit to do the high-intensity parenting that the adolescent years require, then we are more likely to prepare our children to be successful as people. In the process we will create a higher level of joy between our teenagers and ourselves, thereby making harmonious living and a sense of personal fulfillment possible.

Loving our teenage child is not enough. Helping our teenagers become healthy and whole people who look forward to experiencing life and are interested in growing capable of taking on its challenges is an awesome responsibility. We will need to be aware of our own feelings about the child-as-adolescent, and about our perceptions of our abilities to help our teenagers deal effectively with the realities and dream-making aspects of their lives. We parents shoulder the responsibility for guiding and supporting our teens in these and other endeavors.

MEET TODAY'S DRAGONS

In many of the arcade games our kids love to play, they need to cross the bridge without letting the fire-breathing dragons attack them. In the same way, you'll need to help your child traverse adolescence without being attacked by the dragons. And just as in the arcade games, where dodging some obstacles are worth more points than others because of the nature and severity of impending danger, in real life some of the lurking dragons are merely dangerous, while others are downright lethal. Some problems will merit your undivided attention and parenting time, while others are simply a matter of observing from a distance. Helping teenagers internalize a sense of respect for their bodies and wellness (including safeguarding them against drugs), for example, is *urgent and important;* teaching them to care for their body's tone and strength, while *important,* is less urgent.

The following goals are supremely important and must take priority in our parenting actions:

- Maintaining a family unit that provides the teenager with a high degree of physical safety, emotional security, belongingness and skills for living harmoniously with others.
- Understanding the stage of adolescence and providing parenting leadership at this crucial stage of development (and meshing it with your parenting partner).
- Helping your child develop a healthy and whole sense of self-regard.
- Keeping your child drug free.

- Helping your child achieve success in learning and in school.
- Helping your child acquire a healthy attitude toward intimacy and the know-how to safeguard her sexual health.
- Helping your child cultivate an attitude of personal and social responsibility.
- Providing your child with appropriate experiences to foster self-efficacy.
- Providing stimulating experiences to help your child recognize his innate talents and gifts and desire their fulfillment through meaningful and purposeful activities.
- Providing a base of universal truths and spiritual principles so that the teenager might understand her mission and purpose in life and evolve spiritually.
- Transmitting *your* own essence in such a way that your child might *feel* your loving actions and *assimilate* them because your child loves and respects you.

My goals in this book are several:

- To help you understand better this stage of life we call *adolescence.*
- To delineate pivotal characteristics unique to this stage of development and to increase your practical understanding of them.
- To help you put into practice ways of helping your child develop the inner resources needed for becoming a happy, healthy self-confident teenager.
- To help you feel confident that you can help your teenager strengthen the skills she needs to manage life and its challenges successfully and joyfully.
- To realize that each of these goals works with the other to help your teenager feel secure and nourished in the journey through adolescence.
- To help *you* meet the challenge of transmitting a core of parenting that can create physical, emotional, spiritual and

intellectual wellness in your child, and do so in a way that your teenager might feel your loving actions and assimilate them.

All these add up to one big goal: to help your child come closer to the true meaning of fulfilled adulthood. To this end, this book is written for you, the parent of that irritating, demanding, confusing, challenging, perceptive and cherished young person — your teenage child.

"The Times, They Are A-Changing." What *Does* That Mean?

 More than just two decades separates teens from their parents. Teenagers and parents are light-years apart in experience and reasoning ability. They have different ideas, beliefs and expectations about themselves and each other and what they want. That's always been true. But parents raising teenagers today face additional challenges. Parenting a child in the adolescent phase is always a challenge; providing guidance and direction in helping the teenager surmount life's challenges is laborious; raising a happy, achieving, chemical-free and self-confident child in today's times is an achievement. Times have changed *quite a bit* since you were a teenager.

IT'S A BRAVE NEW WORLD OUT THERE

Even though the biological changes of puberty affect the adolescent in many stark and important ways, social and environmental forces exert an equally important influence. At a time when teenagers enter a dramatic life stage — a time when they must normally search for and examine the various dimensions of self and come to grips with their expanding and changing inner world — they face an ever-changing outer society that is filled with inconsistent messages about what it means to be a fulfilled person.

For instance, my parents worried that if I dated the "wrong boys," I might get pregnant, so they restricted dating. In parenting my daughter, my concerns are a bit different. I worry that my daughter may contract AIDS from any source, including boys! It's unlikely that restricting her dating activities will teach her to become sexually responsible. In helping her internalize a respect for her health, I've had to help her do a number of things in order to ensure a measure of protection, such as helping her store her own blood for use in an emergency, and informing her of the necessity to exercise caution in medical and dental procedures. What worked for my parents will not be enough to keep my daughter safe. Let's look at a few of the realities that our children have inherited.

HOME-BASED CHANGES

For starters, the family unit is different. Major changes have taken place in the ways we live together. In 1955, 60 percent of the households in the United States consisted of a father who worked outside the home, a mother who was a housewife and two or more school-age children. In 1980 that kind of family unit existed in only 11 percent of our homes. In 1986 the figure was 7 percent — an astonishing change. Nearly 74 percent of women are in the work force, and that percentage will undoubtedly increase. Of our 97 million-plus households, almost 23 million consist of one adult and one child, with adolescents making up 16 percent of these children. There is evidence that the trend will continue. According to the census, 61 percent of the children born in the United States in 1990 will live with only one parent before they reach the age of 18; this now becomes the *normal* childhood experience. Of every 100 children born today:

- 17 will be born out of wedlock
- 48 will be born of parents who divorce before the child is 18
- 16 will be born to parents who separate
- 6 will be born to parents of whom one will die before the child reaches 18
- 13 will reach age 18 "normally."

We often underestimate just how much adolescents need a stable homelife with a responsible (and stable) parent providing guidance and direction. At a time when stability in the home can help teenagers feel less chaotic, today, ironically, they are likely to get less support. It's been estimated that on the average, parents of children ages 4 to 18 spend less than five minutes of meaningful conversation time each day with their children. Meaningful conversation is different from, "Did you take out the garbage?" "Did you get your homework done?" "Did you make your bed?" or "Did you feed the dog?" Yet children equate our time with our love and want our love more than anything else. In their report on the wellness of children, the 1991 National Commission on Children (NCC) confirmed that today's adolescents are desperately in need of focused parental attention: "If we measure success not just by how well most children do, but by how poorly some fare . . . children at every income level lack time, attention and guidance from parents and other caring adults."

Not spending enough focused time with our children is reflected in the alarming incidence of delinquent behaviors seen in adolescents today. Last year over a million kids ran away from home. Some sarcastically said their parents wouldn't notice. Sadly, many said their parents didn't care. That was hard to believe. Yet when some 34 percent of these children were located by child-find agencies, which attempted to return them to their homes, many parents refused to take them back. Not to be wanted physically or emotionally is a terrible feeling. The response to parental indifference is anger, and today there are many angry children — both out there and in our homes. *Today we spend less time with our adolescents, yet they need us more.* It's not just a question of finances. Money does not ensure that parents will care for their children's physical or emotional needs, or teach them the skills they need to grow and prosper in a healthy and functional way.

WORKPLACE AND SOCIETAL-BASED CHANGES

There's a good chance that the society your parents prepared you to enter was relatively stable and predictable. Your parents believed, perhaps, that your life would take a fairly precise and constant course. Not so today. We are living in the midst of a profound revolution. Young people will enter a very different world. For example, today's workplace is characterized by innovation, change, speed, newness, competitiveness, diversity, stress and pressure. It requires a greater degree of personal autonomy, self-reliance, independent judgment, self-management, personal responsibility and self-direction. In such an environment, the more choices and decisions a person needs to make, the greater the need for a healthy and whole sense of self, and a sense of fairness and equity in dealing with others. The possession of a healthy regard for self and others in adapting to an increasingly complex and competitive workplace is more than just a nicety. Aside from its supreme importance to individual and social well-being, the health of an individual's self-esteem has enormous implications for your child's ability to adapt to an increasingly complex and competitive world.

Arthur Combs, a prominent humanist, warns us that other challenges abound. Enormous social, economic and political forces are at work in the larger society, much more so than even a decade ago. These create new expectations and anxieties. Let's look at these new realities.

1. The Information Explosion

Most of us are aware that technological advances have created banks of extensive information. What is more difficult to comprehend, however, is the extent of the increase in available information. An explosion of information has occurred in every profession, field and endeavor. Science has provided us with marvelous techniques for the dissemination of that information via satellite, radio, television, movies, computers, recordings and more, placing vast amounts of information in the hands of almost anyone quickly and efficiently. What happens in another region of the world airs on the six o'clock news at home and is then subject to our immediate feelings about it. Consider the Rodney King decision and how it affected people in hundreds of cities within minutes of being relayed. The information explosion has transformed the nature of the world in which your teen will live.

2. The Increasing Pace Of Change

The speed of communication, transportation and computation and the amount of power available to us has increased phenomenally. There are some 107,000 different occupations in our society, and the number increases yearly. Students graduating from college are told they will have to change professions (not jobs) eight to ten times. In short, the future is not the stable predictable one we once thought we knew.

An increase in the rate of change affects not just our adaptation to new work demands, but the mission and structure of entire professions. As an example, consider how it must transform the educational profession. Once upon a time, the teacher was the smartest person in town, the fountainhead of knowledge. The teacher dispensed knowledge and students were tested on their retention and recall of a specific body of information. They were labeled "smart" or "dumb" accordingly. Today teachers find that many of their students know more than they do in certain subject areas.

The information explosion, the pace of change, new social mores and the needs of the workplace have all made the recall of a set body of knowledge fairly useless. Hence the new goal for educators is not to teach blocks of information, but to teach young people to *learn how to learn*. Today's young people must know how to access, retrieve and process information in order to compete in the world.

While you and I have seen vast amounts of change — consider the last ten years alone — our teens have known only a world of incessant change. Can you grasp the full significance of living in a world of such rapid change and what it must mean to adolescents? For them, change simply is what *is*. The possibilities — and responsibilities — are endless.

3. A World Characterized By A
New Urgency Of Social Problems

The world into which our young people have been born is characterized by a new urgency of social problems. We live in the most interdependent, cooperative society the world has ever known. The more complex and technical the world becomes, the more each of us depends on thousands of people we do not know and have never seen. To live and function successfully in our community and in the world, we must all look out for each other — we must be our brother's keeper.

Such an ideal depends on a sense of moral, ethical and social responsibility. The major problem we face has to do with learning to live effectively with ourselves and others. We now have the knowledge and the technology to feed, clothe and house the entire world, only to find ourselves faced with a new problem: how to use this knowledge and technology for the general welfare. Problems, such as poverty, ecology, pollution, overpopulation, food distribution, use of energy, peace, health, crime, violence and human rights, are all essentially social. Will our children learn to be personally and socially responsible?

4. Personal Fulfillment As Being Increasingly Important

Not only are we thoroughly dependent on other people, but all of our technological advances make the world an ever smaller place in which the power of individuals is immensely increased. Technological advances make all of us — countries, careers, jobs and people — interdependent. But even if personal fulfillment were not so essential for the safety and welfare of future societies, it is destined to become an increasingly important motive for everyone. More than ever, societies of the future will need caring, responsible citizens willing and able to pull their own weight. People who feel frustrated and alienated are a danger to everyone, as we observe when we watch youth inflict harm on those in positions of authority and on each other, as well as noting the increasing incidence of unwarranted police brutality or as can be seen in nearly every hospital emergency room in the nation.

5. Self-Esteem As A Valued Commodity

The shift from a manufacturing society to an information society, from physical labor to intellectual work as the dominant employee activity, the onset of a technological society magnified and accelerated by continual scientific and technological breakthroughs, and the emergence of a global economy characterized by rapid change, increasing choices and options — all demand new levels of skill, education and training. These developments inherently require a healthy self-esteem.

The level of our children's self-esteem will affect their success in the workplace. Preparing our children to get into, assimilate and achieve in the workplace will take some doing. We have been told, for example, that our children have entered an era in which, for the first time, children will not overtake their parents' educational level, lifestyles or earning potential. Our children will not know "the good life" as we know it. Our children have been told this, and it has taken an enormous toll on their motivation to want to excel. After all, why pay your dues when you can't join the club?

6. Self-Knowledge As Fundamental

We hope that our young people both *desire* and *live* a life characterized by purpose, meaning and joy. That our young people are able to do so means they must possess a great deal of *self-knowledge.*

Young people who are secure in themselves learn to trust and to be caring, considerate and compassionate with themselves and others. They develop a healthy sense of individuality and believe in their worth as human beings. They have a realistic sense of their aptitudes and interests and will neither blow them out of proportion nor make slight of them. They can accept areas of weakness without undue harsh evaluation and focus on areas of strength and lead from them. They take responsibility for their actions and will own up to them. They have identified those things that are of value and want to pursue them.

This sense of direction means they can not only set goals, but follow through on achieving them. When faced with obstacles, people with self-knowledge are more likely to generate alternatives that allow them to continue working toward that which is of purpose and value. Their interests and intuitive aptitudes have a likelihood of becoming their chosen work. They have an inner knowledge, an inner joy — a whole sense of self.

TEENS NEED STABILITY AMID FORCES OF CHANGE

Unfortunately, the teenager must face these challenges while dealing with other obstacles. Let's take a look at some of them.

1. A Shortened Period Of Childhood

"There's no place for teenagers in America today," says David Elkind, author of *All Grown Up And No Place To Go.* "[In past years] it was generally recognized that young people needed time, support and guidance in learning how to become adults." Today, however, teenagers are thrust into a new role of premature adulthood and expected to confront adult realities. Many facets of life once regarded as being for adults only are no longer off-limits to children. In part, the new age of television and video has erased the dividing line between childhood and adulthood since it does not segregate its audience, but communicates the same information to everyone simultaneously, regardless of sex, age or level of education. Have you noticed that children on television are depicted as small adults? "What we see is a projection of the adult child — a new kind of person with an obsessive need for immediate gratification, a lack of concern for consequences and an almost promiscuous preoccupation with consumption," says Neil Postman, author of *The Disappearance Of Childhood.*

This new transformation makes the behaviors, attitudes, desires and even physical appearance of adults and children indistinguishable: clothing styles copy those designed for adults; games are becoming sports that are supervised and played with adult rules and regulations; language once reserved for adults and not even to be uttered in the presence of children is now commonly used (and accepted) by teens; young people are now committing crimes once attributed to adults only.

Premature adulthood has its problems. It forces teenagers to leapfrog the activities of teenhood that prepare them for adulthood and to play adult games for which they are ill prepared. Trying to cope with demands required in managing successful adult life naturally is very stressful.

2. Stress Overload

Because society expects a child to metamorphosize instantly into an adult, parents tend to treat teenagers as smaller versions of adults. This can have dire consequences. If we feel helpless or assume that teenagers are adults who need minimal direction and support, we impair their ability to construct a secure personal identity. This leaves teens more vulnerable and less competent to meet the challenges that are inevitable in life. Coping with an abundance of freedoms, the lessening of adults as anchors, loss of a sense of security about what the future holds, today's teenagers experience debilitation and an inordinate amount of stress.

3. Conflicting Signals

Adolescents often receive mixed and somewhat inconsistent messages. For example, we urge our teenagers to learn about relationships and love, but to do so mostly without touching. We often remind young people how bold and entrepreneurial we were at their age. When we were young, we say, we hit the work force as active, self-assertive youths.

"Be true to your feelings," we say in one breath, and "Do whatever it takes to succeed," in another. Too often we glorify youths who have found ways of growing up fast without any of the conflicts so many of today's young people inevitably feel as they contend with their confused sense of what it means to be a fully functioning, healthy and whole person leading a balanced life.

4. Option Overload

Having too many options can be as frustrating as not having enough. Today's adolescent is often confused by the wide variety of options in ideologies, careers and lifestyles from which to construct a future. More options don't necessarily mean better choices; in fact, it contributes to ambiguity and option overload.

5. An Uncertain Future

In addition to the difficulty of college entrance, career choice and employment options, teens face an uncertain future that is further clouded by possible annihilation through overpopulation, pollution or ozone layer deterioration. Many young people harbor a sense of hopelessness in making decisions premised on a future they cannot foresee. We adults often look at young people and assume they should know how fortunate they are to have their whole lives ahead of them. What we forget is that the teen doesn't know what the future holds. As one teenager so aptly put it, "If childhood is the happiest time of my life, adulthood must be awful."

6. Parents With Busier Lives

In this age of uncertainty, teenagers need added assurance and support from their parents. Instead, today's parents are busy reshaping and retooling their own lives, sorting a relationship in turmoil, trying to make ends meet, starting a business, tending to a job or career, or worrying about being fired. At a time when teenagers need quality time from parents, they are often left to cope alone.

THERE IS NO BLUEPRINT FOR RAISING TODAY'S ADOLESCENT

With so much that is new in the home, at work and in the world, we really have no blueprint for raising our teenagers. Luckily, even though the context of society differs with each passing generation, life's goals remain quite similar: raising healthy, happy, whole people.

The best chance we have for raising happy, healthy and self-confident children and keeping them safe and on track toward worthwhile goals is to care for their needs and provide a positive influence by modeling what we want them to emulate. Like younger children, teenagers need to know that we love and respect and accept them, and that we are serious in our resolve to help them prepare to live interdependently in the world. If our adolescents are to be functional people now and in adulthood, we must set appropriate expectations and consistently encourage and motivate them in living purposefully. We must *actively* help our teenagers acquire a solid foundation of self-esteem. We must not assail our children with contradictions or sabotage their formative years with actions that are devastating to their mental, emotional, physical and spiritual growth.

To prepare our children to manage their lives both now and in the future, we will need to help them develop a wide and diverse array of skills — some of which we ourselves may still be seeking to master. We must help adolescents gain self-understanding, and teach them to recognize and maintain their distinctness from others without fear, shame, anxiety or regret. Our children must come to see themselves consistently as successful in managing life and its challenges, adept at finding and using their own resources. They must gain a deep sense of personal responsibility. Conversely, they must become socially responsible — willing and able to care for their fellow companions. This is no easy task in contemporary society.

Though the adolescent's journey toward adulthood is marked by change and upheaval, it need not be fraught with chaos or deep pain. Despite the biological events of puberty and the enormous social and environmental forces at work today, we can help our teenagers acquire the necessary insights and skills to meet life's challenges. Let's do so in a way that lends itself to joy and well-being for all.

PART TWO

Your Teenager And You: Are *You* Ready?

"For Better Or For Worse:" The Parent-Child Relationship Is Forever

 Does it seem to you that parenting your teenager takes almost as much time and attention as parenting a younger child? When my daughter was an infant, I looked forward to a time when she would be able to play independently. (Even when she could, she looked around to see if I was watching!) In junior high her abundant activities required multiple bandages and a daily carpool. I looked forward to a time when she could drive a car. Now that she is nearly 18, her need to know her place in the world, to experience the dynamics of relationships and to understand her feelings sometimes makes me feel like a clinical psychologist, with her as my entire caseload!

Though she is older, my parenting actions are as crucial now as when she was small. Of course I must parent from a distance now: Though I still want to protect her from as much as possible — such as being devastated in a relationship — she must learn such lessons firsthand.

"TEENAGERS SHOULD LEAVE HOME WHILE THEY STILL KNOW EVERYTHING!"

Yesterday I saw a bumper sticker that read, "Teenagers should leave home while they still know everything!" Though most adolescents assume they do know pretty much everything, aren't you sometimes surprised by what they don't know? My daughter is a very bright young women with a great deal of common sense. Just as I am thinking I can soon hand over the baton — it's getting time for her to run this next leg of the race without my constant coaching — something happens to remind me of her inexperience. This makes me wonder what else I've not taught her.

Jennifer's friend's cat went into labor and had three stillborn kittens. My daughter and her friend expressed their dismay, but were excited that other kittens would be born, because they could feel unborn kittens within the mother cat. My daughter said she was optimistic that the other kittens would be born alive — after all, the mother cat had gone into labor nearly thirty hours ago, and now that the cat was rested she could resume her labor! I informed her gently that if the cat had not had them by now, she probably wasn't going to and that the cat needed a vet's care immediately. She thought I was exaggerating. I counseled the girls to call several animal hospitals and get "an informed opinion." Alas, some parenting is never done.

The need to parent is an ever-present one.

PARENTS ARE LIFETIME ANCHORS

My daughter will encounter life and learn from each event with or without me. She won't always be asking for my opinion, or calling on me for advice, but she will always need me as an anchor, a base from which to draw deep emotional sustenance. Parents are *anchors*. Anchors are people we *need* because they provide assurance and validate intrinsic worth at times when we feel unable to summon it ourselves. They are among the few people who love us unconditionally — no strings attached.

I was reminded of this several months ago as I was preparing for a business trip to Russia. Less than 30 hours before flight time, the galleys for a new book were unexpectedly delivered from my publisher with the instructions to please read, edit and return them within the week! In addition, several business contracts lay on my desk, needing my undivided attention, and several proposals for keynoting conferences needed review and decisions rendered. My long stay out of the country meant that my staff needed additional time and instruction from me — something I had postponed for today. My daughter also was dealing with a crisis that needed my attention. And I still had not packed. How would I ever cover all these bases adequately?

Momentarily overwhelmed, I reached for the phone and called to "check on" my parents. My parents live 2,000 miles away. Because my five brothers and sisters and their families all live within a five-mile radius, my parents are always within the bosom of a loving and active extended family. I had talked with my parents not more than a week before I placed this call. *Why* did I call? In a moment when I was overwhelmed by the tasks that needed my attention in an impossible time period and feeling the momentary pressure of having so many people depend on me, I was reaching out to a steadfast anchor in *my* life. I simply needed to connect with a source that provides a deep level of serenity, inner strength and emotional nourishment: my loving parents. After a brief conversation with them, I was able to roll up my sleeves with confidence and a restored sense of order and set out to do what needed to be done.

A crucial element in parenting the adolescent is to help our teenager *feel* that we are steadfast in our love, a stable force in her life — always there to fall back on, if only emotionally. Being an anchor is one of the most important roles of parenting the adolescent. It is a vital and necessary ingredient in helping teenagers believe in themselves and withstand their adolescent fears and insecurities.

Parents aren't our only anchors, but they are quite possibly the most important. Functional or dysfunctional, the relationship is long-term — it's for life. How we are supported by our anchors in our first 20 years of life greatly influences our sense of self as adults. The areas in which we have had our sense of self undermined or eroded, causing different parts of our *selves* to become wounded or lost, are those areas where we most need to learn to love ourselves back to health. We literally need to recover (reparent, rebirth) — replacing, if only in our mind and heart, the anchor that wasn't provided from the most primary of all our relationships, our parents.

Yes, Teenagers Do Want Their Parents

Many parents are surprised to find out just *how* important they are to their children, especially as children get older and seek the friendships of others. Though we know they still need us, sometimes it's easy to question if our teenagers want us. Rest assured, they do.

When children are asked to list the five most meaningful people in their lives, both girls and boys name parents as number one. The first person they list is their "favorite" parent — this generally ends up being their same-sex parent; the second person they name is most generally the *other* parent, even in cases of separation or divorce. Sometimes a stepparent will show up here, especially if the teenager considers the stepparent fair and supportive. The number three spot goes to a favorite educator —

the teacher the student considers to be the "best listener," although this spot is sometimes shared by a stepparent, school custodian, bus driver or someone the child develops a liking for. For the child, the attraction is that the attention is unconditional. Perhaps it's the neighbor who asks, "Hey, did you get that bike fixed?" or "Hey, who are you taking to the dance?" It's a show of interest, of considering the teenager's life as important. The child gets a sense of respect and an affirmation of intrinsic worth. This person teaches that just being a human — alive, functioning in the world — is valid of recognition.

The fourth person named is the instructor whose teaching style matches the child's learning style, and who persistently encourages the adolescent to develop her own strengths, attributes or talents. This educator is often firm but fair, sending the message that the child is worthy and *will* be held accountable for developing these identified strengths. Sometimes this educator provides the only source of structure in the teen's life. Students refer to this person as that teacher who won't "get out of my face!" I hope your teenager is lucky enough to have an educator care so much and demand excellence!

In fifth place, girls list their grandmother, followed by a sibling (male or female), and anyone else who might help them feel emotionally secure. Boys list an uncle, a grandfather and then a sibling (they'll list a brother first), in that order. Who is listed and in what order is generally based on recognition of being competent or the development of competency.

Here's the part that may surprise you: Peers rarely show up in the top five until children are at least 15 or 16.

It's Unlikely You Will Be Replaced By Your Teen's Peers

Some parents erroneously believe that their teenager's friends are *more* important to them than the parents are. Friends are important; but it's only when parents are physically or emotionally distant that children will turn to their peers for acceptance and belonging at any cost. Not to belong is a lonely experience for anyone, especially for children. This is when peer groups become the most influential, and potentially the most dangerous. In the absence of parents, teachers or other significant adults, kids will pay almost *any* price to belong.

Is there a parent in the world who hasn't had this experience? Your child comes out wearing a new sweater and asks you your opinion. You say, "Oh, you look so cute in that!" and see only the dust as the teen runs back to change. Even if you were wise enough to choose an adjective other than "cute," chances are your opinion, if it carried any weight at all, was a negative factor. (If you like it, it must be awful.) But let your teen model that same sweater for a friend and hear, "Radical!" and you won't be able to pry that sweater off him for a week! In short, your opinion is beginning to matter less, that of peers, more.

A number of studies have shown that as children begin puberty, parents feel great concern and helplessness. One problem is that they see themselves as having less influence on their children than do peers. The children, however, consider their parents to be the greatest influence on them, although they also say that they do not know their parents' views on a number of topics.

Research confirms that many parents feel poorly equipped to deal with the biological, psychological and social changes of early adolescence. Whatever the underlying reasons for this insecurity and weakening of parental authority, when accustomed parental guidance is withdrawn, the young person is thrust toward uncritical acceptance of the peer group as a model and a major coping resource. While this allegiance to the peer group may be useful in alleviating immediate anxieties, it has serious limitations. It is not a substitute for parental guidance. The peer group at this stage is usually too shallow and rigid to afford the necessary direction for growth and development. When the peer group is organized around drugs or acting-out behaviors, other fears are realized.

Parents Versus Peers: Who Is Number One?

Peer pressure, in and of itself, has no power. The peer group is powerful only when teenagers turn to their peers to fulfill needs not met at home. Fourteen-year-old Dee, an only child of divorced parents, felt lonely. Her mother worked until nearly six o'clock each night, and Dee got home from work at three. When her mother was home, she would spend a considerable amount of her time with the man to whom she was now engaged. Seeing her mother so happy and in love made Dee feel even more alone, and she longed to belong to someone too. She turned to her peers and would go along with any antic as long as it meant she would be accepted. Her mother was shocked and outraged when the school called and alerted her to Dee's role in setting two fires in the girl's restroom. Said Dee, "We did it the first time as a joke. My friends dared me to do it again and said I wouldn't be invited to the after-school party if I didn't. I thought, why not, at least I can still belong to the group."

This example shows a negative peer group influence. However, when children are able to assert themselves without feeling intimidated or fearing recrimination, then the peer group serves as a constructive experience. Peer groups help shape the common experiences of the adolescent culture, thus determining the framework for the adolescent to gain appropriate experiences. What is acceptable? What is not? Some of the adaptive tasks for which positive peer support can be especially valuable include:

- Feedback on self-image that is not criticized.
- Appraisal and reappraisal of opportunities of new situations, including learning about new roles.
- Preserving reasonable emotional balance by having dependable sources of reassurance and comfort in distress.
- Same-age resources for reduction of tension by encouragement to express feelings freely.
- Obtaining new information; development of new perspectives, new alternatives for dealing with situations;

learning from the pooling of information with others; having someone of his or her own (belonging).

- Learning about behavior, seeking role models whose behavior can be adapted or adopted.
- Obtaining feedback about behaviors, plans, goals; modifying level of aspirations.
- Acquiring and practicing social skills.
- Validation of identity.
- Identifying a supportive group for engaging in hobbies, sports or recreational activities that are unfamiliar or seem difficult.

The influence of peers is closely tied to learning how to socialize. Youngsters are joined together by participation in a fad of clothing and language. The coming together, customs and rituals are all signals that one belongs to the group. Today television and the media have influenced youngsters the world over to look and sound more alike.

Moving from childhood to adolescence creates a culture shock for your teenager. Once friendships were so easy. A child who was good at baseball found acceptance in the sports group. If you had a bicycle, you were a part of the street fun. Now that your child is an adolescent, the rules among friends have changed. Initiation rites as well as acts of rejection and exclusion can be devastating to all young people. The need to belong is a human need. Your teenager will need a strong sense of self to avoid becoming a victim of negative peer influence, as did Dee.

THE FABRIC OF YOUR CHILD'S FRIENDSHIPS

When was the last time your teenager came home and asked you, "Is it okay if I go to the concert with my peer group?" Wouldn't you find it difficult to keep a straight face if your adolescent brought home a youngster and said, "I'd like you to meet a member of my peer group, Don." "Peer group" can seem such a cold, clinical term. Teenagers almost never use such a term; they simply talk about their friends.

There is no doubt that peer friendships play an important role in the life of an adolescent. Normally, these friendships fall into two categories: internal and external. Delineating the distinct elements of each of these categories can help you assess the value placed on friendships by your teenager and provide insight into the skills she will need to interact with friends.

External friendships are based on the following:

Proximity. The closer the proximity, the greater the accessibility to each other. This availability increases the frequency of interaction and provides friends with opportunities (mostly of convenience) to "use" one another in times of need. This "situational friendship" is used in times of need, but may not possess the elements necessary for building a deep relationship. An adolescent who plays street soccer or shares a wardrobe with the adolescent down the street or shares a fifth-hour French class may also ignore and offend the same friend when in a groups of friends belonging to the internal category.

Cooperation Versus Competition. Adolescents, like adults, tend to like others who cooperate with them in their attempts to attain personal goals and rewards. Likewise, they tend to dislike those who hinder or contradict their quest for self-fulfillment. It is not uncommon for an adolescent to develop a friend for the duration of a project and to drop him as quickly as the project is over. Baffled by the change from being needed to discarded, neither friend will be able to articulate what has happened.

Esteem Fulfillment. Teenagers side with those who "like" them, see them in a positive light and "promote" them (talk well of them). This tells adolescents that they are functioning in a logical and acceptable manner. This does not mean that the friendship is mutual however. The friendship helps the teen develop self-esteem.

Internal friendships are characterized by mutual feelings in each of the following areas:

Respect. Friends respect each other in the sense of assuming that each exercises good judgment in making choices. "I'll check with Natalie. She always does what's best."

Trust. They share mutual trust in the sense that each assumes that the other will act in light of his or her friend's best interest. This promotes a loyalty. "I know that I can count on her. She never lets me down, just as I would always be there for her."

Understanding. They have a sense of what is important to each other and why the friend does what she does. They are not puzzled or mystified by each other's behavior. "I can usually figure out what's wrong when he's upset."

Enjoyment. They genuinely enjoy each other's company, even in times of working through difficulties. "I always feel so good when I'm with him."

Acceptance. They accept one another as they are, without trying to change or make the other into a new or different person. "He appreciates my style. He appreciates me."

Confiding. They share experiences and feelings with each other. "She tells me things about herself that no one else knows."

What Do Our Children Want From Us?

Remember when your young child would call out, "Watch me, Mommy! Watch me, Mommy!" or "Watch me, Daddy! Watch me, Daddy!" No matter what your child's age, he wants you to notice. Even adult children sometimes want parental recognition. Though teens may want less time, they still want and need your time and attention, and are pretty good at deciphering when you are observing them from a distance or ignoring them. "My dad is always too busy to go with me to a game, yet he doesn't miss a golf game with his buddies," chided Max. "Yeah," chimed in 15-year-old

Stephen, "My dad is always telling me what he does for me," he said in a tone riddled with sarcasm. "I wish he'd bother to do some things *with* me."

Have you ever wondered what teenagers (this differs from say, 9-, 10-, and 11-year-olds) really want and need from us? I've asked the question of young people across the country. Here's what they listed in order of its importance:

- I want my parents to be my friends and give advice like a friend would (and in a *tone* a friend would).
- I want my parents to think I'm somebody special.
- I want my parents to like me (to be as friendly to me as they are to those who phone or come to the door).
- I want my parents to be concerned about me.
- I want my parents to know the "me that nobody knows."
- I want my parents to be open to *wanting to understand me.*
- I want my parents to value that I am capable of making some important decisions that are good for me.
- I want to get to talk about what's important to me (and have those views be valued because *I* have learned from *my* experiences, too. I'd like my parents to want to know what I have learned from those experiences).
- I want to choose my friends and have my parents understand why they are special to me (and to know my friends are okay).
- I want my parents to be happy, and I want to be part of a happy family.
- I want my parents to "lighten up" and *to want to have fun* with me, to think that I am *fun to* be with.
- I want my parents to learn more about my feelings and emotions, as *I* see and feel them.

This list makes it clear that teens focus primarily on internal needs, not just on getting or having things. Unfortunately, too many parents become frustrated, disinterested or simply less involved in the caretaking chores as their children get older. Some parents substitute money and things in place of time and attention.

Many lose faith, erroneously believing their influence is less than the impact of their children's friends or peers. Others become easily intimidated and back off from providing the solid guidance that is needed when adolescents begin testing the boundaries of the very rules put in place to protect them.

WHAT DO *YOU* WANT FOR YOUR CHILDREN?

In his book *What Do You* Really *Want For Your Children?* Wayne Dyer reports on what hundreds of parents said they wanted most for their children. Here's what they listed:

1. I want my children to value themselves.
2. I want my children to be risk-takers.
3. I want my children to be self-reliant.
4. I want my children to be free from stress and anxiety.
5. I want my children to have peaceful lives.
6. I want my children to live in the present moment.
7. I want my children to experience a lifetime of wellness.
8. I want my children to be creative.
9. I want my children to fulfill their higher needs and to feel a sense of purpose.

To these nine wants, I would add a tenth: Parents want their children to want these things for themselves, too, and they feel enormous tension when they suspect these attributes may not be desired by their children.

AS CHILDREN GET OLDER, THEY SOMETIMES FEEL THEIR PARENTS LOVE THEM LESS

You know that you would overcome more obstacles and face more barriers than Indiana Jones ever dreamed of in order to be there for your children, but do they *feel* that committed dedication? Though your older children may need less physical attention, they still need your bond to be a powerful one. Just because your adolescent doesn't run across the room for a hug, jump into your lap or wait at the window for you to come home doesn't mean she wants to be ignored.

Sometimes it's easy to think you've lost the role of being the source of hugs and kisses, and now you are only the Keeper Of The Car Keys.

"It's amazing," lamented 16-year-old Rochelle. "Only three years old and Brenda gets all the attention. I have to beg and plead for three days to get my parents to come see me in the class play, and all that kid has to do to get attention is act cute and smile!" Rochelle, like most children, equates her parents' attention for her as a sign of love. Even the 15-year-old with impossible hair, a bad complexion, weird clothes and an attitude problem needs you as her number one fan.

(HEALTHY) LOVE BINDS

Robert Frost's famous line, "Love is the irresistible desire to be irresistibly desired," is true for all us. We all need a person or two to love us irresistibly. Teenagers need at least one parent to love them unconditionally. Love and respect combined is the glue that binds parents and their children together, providing essential emotional sustenance, buffering the teenager against the ravages of stress and peer pressure, and preserving emotional health. A parent's love helps teens feel loved and is a powerful source of inner confidence. They are not alone: They have support even in the face of adversity, criticism and relentless change. Parents are a potent source of feeling protected, shielded, included and needed, of not feeling alone in the world, regardless of our age.

IN THE ABSENCE OF LOVE, GROWTH IS THWARTED

In the absence of loving caretaking, growth and development may be thwarted. Researchers were studying cholesterol deposits in rabbits. Though all rabbits were fed the same diet, it was discovered that several of the rabbits had markedly reduced cholesterol deposits. Initially, the researchers had no explanation for this occurrence. On further investigation they learned that a night lab worker had grown fond of some particular rabbits and he would play with them as he cleaned out their cages. The "pet" rabbits were the ones who developed lower cholesterol deposits. Baffled that attention could account for the lowered cholesterol count, the researchers repeated the study, giving certain rabbits more attention than others. Once again, the rabbits that received special attention, such as petting and stroking, showed lower cholesterol deposits than those without the special attention.

Just as the rabbits responded to the added attention in caretaking, so do our teenagers. We as parents may feel that we are expressing our love by giving our teenagers "things," material objects we think will make them happy. But a new outfit, a CD, a car or a telephone line of their own is no substitute for our time and caregiving. Love is exchanged between people, not between people and things. Unfortunately, too many of today's children have a lot of *things*, but very little human interaction with adults whom they love and want to be loved by. Even adolescents struggling to gain a measure of their own independence need consistent doses of love and attention.

CREATING A BETTER BOND WITH YOUR TEEN

What are you doing to help your adolescent feel your special bonding? A busy parent sometimes needs to be creative. My daughter, a tremendous athlete, goes from one sports season to the next. I sometimes go up to school just to watch her in practice sessions. Why? Because even though I can't always make all of her regular games, I know the most important connection is for her to feel that I'm interested in her, not just whether the team wins. My presence at these practice times represents interest in her. She doesn't have to be a star to get my attention. I make it clear to her that *she's* worthwhile. I need to show her that even though I'm a busy person, she counts in my life. Show your teenager that you want and expect a mutually loving and respectful relationship.

The building blocks for creating and sustaining a positive relationship with our children are real basic. Essentially, the way we treat our children is the way they will treat us. We reap what we sow. The adolescent stage can be a trying time for parents, for adolescents and for our parent-child relationship as well. This makes your behavior even more important. Be careful that you don't assail your teenager with contradictions, or resort to ridicule, humiliation or physical abuse as a means of control. Teach your teenager to embrace a code of conduct for becoming a capable and loving adult by learning the skills necessary to act responsibly both on a personal and social level. Clearly articulate boundaries for your teen's safety, nourish a sense of order, set stimulating and expansive expectations and, of course, love your child — purple hair, tattoo and all. The following suggestions are a good beginning for creating unity.

Talk About Your Bond

Are you talking *with* your teen or are you talking *at* your teen? Does your communication run along the lines of, "Take out the trash," "Don't pick on your little sister," "You watch that attitude"? How are the two of you doing? In what areas does your teenager want more attention? When was the last time you asked, "How's it going?" "Do you need my help on that one or do you feel you can manage?" "How can I be of help?"

Participate In Your Teenager's Life

How much we participate in our children's lives tells them how important they are to us. If you don't feel you are participating enough, your child probably has the same idea.

Keep Commitments

Don't make promises you can't keep. Your children need to learn that they can trust you to keep your word, even when doing so may be inconvenient.

Demonstrate Your Love And Caring

Don't simply assume your teenagers know you love them, show your love. Don't say, "Of course I love you. I'm your mother, aren't I?" All children want to know they are worth loving, not just because parents are supposed to love their children. You can express this love in many different ways, verbally or nonverbally. You can just tell your children you love them. Say the words directly, don't hint. There's no need to be coy or cute, or to worry that you'll embarrass them (as long as you don't get mushy in front of their friends). Say, "I love you. You mean everything to me," as often as you feel it. Remarks such as, "You're a wonderful son, Tom," "Have a good time, Carol, and take care of yourself for me," "You're so important to me, Roger" or "I like to be with you, Chris," are significant statements to our children because they show connection. More important, our teenager gets to learn *how that feels to us.*

Nonverbal Expressions Are As Important As What You Say

Your facial expression and body language communicate your love and bonding almost as directly as your words do. Touching, for example, is a very powerful way to show your feelings of love and acceptance. Patting your child's back, straightening a collar or simply touching your teen's arm all express your love and pride.

Tell Your Children They Are Special

I say to my daughter, "You are so important to me, Jennifer," followed by *here's why* statements: "I enjoy your friendship so much," or "I can always count on your support," or "You make me feel so happy and proud that you are my daughter." Such statements are more meaningful than the overused, "I love you." (But if you rarely tell your children, "I love you," by all means say that!)

Talk About The Fun Stuff In Parenting

You want your teenager to feel special because of the bond you share in being related as parent and child. "Jennifer, I love being your mother because you are such a loving daughter. Being your mom has been one of my greatest joys. It has been fun to watch you grow and to watch you learn how to do things. I have really enjoyed loving you, getting to know you inside and learning what is important to you." Parenting the teenager is hard work, and teens see the joys and anguish they cause. Let them know that the joys of the relationship outweigh the problems.

Keep Your Perspective

Squabbling and bickering can be expected; it's more common during adolescence than during any other phase of childhood. The good news is that arguments between parents and teenagers rarely undo close emotional bonds or lead adolescents and their parents to reject one another. Though most families experience stress in the adolescent years, rarely is it remembered.

You are the most powerful force in your child's life in every way. By observing what you do and how you do it, your attitudes and viewpoints will influence how your teen views people, events and the world as it is and can be. What you do, or don't do, will leave an impression. How much you're there, or not there, will be remembered. The way you treat your child and others, the way you lead your life — all will serve as a framework for how children go about living their own lives. Children do learn what they live, and they generally live out what they have learned.

No matter what they say or how they act, teenage children wish to have a close, loving relationship with their parents. Decide that you will help your children feel confident and competent to stand on their own two feet in the world. Teenagers who feel sure of their parents' love are more likely to value their parents and embrace their teachings. Empower your teenager to meet life's challenges.

Your Teenager And Your Marriage Relationship

 Remember when you tucked your baby into bed, leaned over the crib and said, "He looks just like an angel when he sleeps"? Recall the swell of pride you felt when you watched your child on the practice field, prepared for her first date or discussed what he would like to do in life? Parenting produces cherished memories, but it can also produce stressful ones.

Children are constantly adapting to the tasks and demands of each new stage of growth and development.

We adults have to adapt at the same time to our new parenting roles, while simultaneously passing through our own stages of maturing. That's in addition to pursuing our own career and work demands, tending to and nurturing adult relationships, socializing and being with friends, making time for leisure activities and maintaining our own health and well-being.

That adults have busy lives filled with responsibilities is accepted. That adults undergo their own inner life stages is nothing new, though it is often taken for granted. Regardless of the stage of development — infancy, puberty or adulthood — the various cycles are complex. Each requires a special set of skills to adapt successfully at each of the stages.

Inevitably, there will be times when the nature of the parents' and children's developmental stages will conflict. Whenever change occurs, whether in a child or a parent, there will be a period of stress as both adjust. For example, children entering adolescence must focus on establishing autonomy and an independent identity. They try to separate from parents, yet must still depend on them for physical daily care and support, as well as for guidance on important things such as understanding aggressive and sexual impulses and learning appropriate ways to express them. At some level, adolescents recognize and perhaps resent this dependency. Parents are left to adjust to this stranger as best they can.

PARENTING ISSUES: ALLOWING INDEPENDENCE WHILE SETTING LIMITS

During a child's adolescence, parenting issues hinge on being able to allow the adolescent independence while setting limits. A parent has the difficult task of providing experiences that keep the parent-child relationship healthy at a time when the adolescent is screaming for autonomy but still needs guidance. Added to this already difficult situation is the fact that parents are going through their own stages and changes. How can parents deal with the budding sexuality and sexual curiosity of their teenager at the same time they are facing the end of their own childbearing years? It's difficult to counsel on love and intimacy when you are reassessing your own relationship. How can you feel comfortable telling your crying teenager that "Nobody is worth crying this much about or being this miserable over," when you are going through relationship turmoil or are estranged from your spouse? Teenagers are looking for absolutes; they would like to believe that you are emotionally resistant to life's strains and challenges.

ADOLESCENCE CREATES *EXTRA* STRAIN ON A COUPLE'S RELATIONSHIP

Your marriage undergoes radical changes during each stage of your child's development. Just as parenting a newborn takes major adjustment, so does being a parent in the adolescent years. In fact, stress in parenting adolescents is said to be a major cause of marital discord.

In *Creative Marriage* Mel Krantzler identifies and examines six natural passages of "marriages within a marriage" and delineates the many special demands made on the marriage by children throughout the various stages of childhood. I strongly recommend this book. Couples who are aware of the demands on parents and the ensuing dynamics in their marriage are better equipped to fortify themselves and the marriage relationship and are thereby more likely to be of help to the adolescent.

THE STRENGTH OF A COUPLE'S RELATIONSHIP IS AN ASSET IN PARENTING THE TEENAGER

The strength of the marriage is an integral part of a happy family and an important asset to each member of the family, especially to the adolescent who is watching closely to see what love and intimacy are all about. Couples who enjoy a happy marriage are more apt to like and value themselves as individuals and as a couple. Each can respect and credit the other's differences in facets of parenting and can feel that what the other has to offer is important. The parents stand together to face the adolescent and are better able to provide solace to each other as the adolescent begins the process of gaining autonomy. One picks up when the other is incapacitated.

Your marriage serves as a model for your teenager, who will emulate similar styles and patterns of interactions in intimate relationships. If you have a happy marriage, you are able to anticipate crises and needs, work together to help your child. You are able to hold firm when such a stance is appropriate and to let go when such action is helpful. As you see your adolescent gain greater decision-making ability, you give him greater latitude. Because you are trusting and secure, you give your child greater responsibility when that becomes appropriate.

Because you and your partner enjoy being with each other, because you enjoy your lives separately from your child, your child learns to enjoy life, to become a separate person without going through outbursts of guilt and self-recrimination. You make it easy for your child to move toward adulthood.

STRENGTHENING YOUR RELATIONSHIP

Because teenagers naturally have their own ideas about what they want to do and when they want to do it, and often feel fearless in carrying out these plans, there is naturally going to be strain between teenagers and parents. This can also mean strain between the parents. Here are some ways to protect your marriage relationship.

Support Each Other In The Values You Hold Important

Part of the emotional stress of parenting the teenager arises out of the parent's concern for the child's physical and emotional safety and well-being. It's easy to become anxious and frustrated when we don't know the whereabouts of our teenagers. Parents often fear that their child may be in an unsafe situation (perhaps with friends who feel that they drive better after "just a few beers") or will be treated unfairly by others (for example, ridiculed for being the tallest girl or shortest boy in the class). Whether you are married, separated, divorced or stepparenting, decide on those values you hold constant for the teenager, such as physical safety, emotional security, achieving in school. Then decide on the measures to put these into practice, such as a time for curfew. Next, support each other in making sure the teenager follows the rules that have been set up. Presenting a united front helps the teenager assimilate the values you are trying to teach and adhere to the boundaries that ensure protection, and leads to good behavior.

Don't Over-React – Stay Focused On Working Together

When our teens challenge the boundaries, it's sometimes easy to reach the limits of our own coping abilities and to react in ways that aren't always rational. Remember that feelings and emotions are a direct and automatic reaction to self-talk, to what you are telling yourself about the situation. When the parent's self-talk in a situation is sensible, the reactions and feelings that follow are also sensible. Effective problem resolution results from sensible self-talk, as shown in the following examples:

> *Situation:* Teenager slams the door to her room.
> *Nonproductive Self-Talk:* "That kid is obstinate!"
> *Sensible and Productive Self-Talk:* "My daughter is really frustrated."
> *Nonproductive Feelings and Reactions:* "If you slam that door one more time, I'll . . . !"
> *Sensible and Productive Feelings and Reactions:* "What seems to be the problem? Can you find a better way to express your frustration without destroying the door to your room?"

Just as this concept applies to the child/parent relationship, it is also useful in parent-parent conflicts:

> *Situation:* Teenager is an hour late for curfew.

Nonproductive Self-Talk: Parent 1: "That kid of yours is late again."

Nonproductive Self-Talk: Parent 2: "My kid! Why is it that when he does something right, he's your kid, and when he does something wrong, he's my kid?"

Sensible and Productive Self-Talk: "Our son is an hour late. Lately he pays very little attention to his curfew. I believe it's because we haven't been able to agree on his curfew time. Our indecision is confusing to him. I notice he doesn't take our threats of consequences seriously. Let's work toward some agreement on this."

Nonproductive Feelings and Reactions: "Your 'boys will be boys' attitude may have worked for you, but it's not what I want for my son!"

Sensible and Productive Feelings and Reactions: "Let's talk about what our son is learning, and about how we can teach him to be responsible in keeping with the time we have set up."

Communicate, Don't Shut Down

Parenting the adolescent can cause fears and apprehensions for both parents. You may not express these to your parenting partner for fear that he or she will think you are not a good parent. Or you may meet with resistance from your partner about discussing these fears, or find that you both back off from talking at a deeper level because your values are different. Your ability to discuss your differences and preferences is a good part of the success of your parenting efforts. Talk, listen and face the problems. They won't go away if you ignore them. Express yourself clearly. No one is a mind reader. Don't assume the other person knows what you are thinking. Good communication is a two-way street. It requires listening skills as well as the ability to state your needs clearly, in a way that will help your parenting partner understand your needs. Effective communication is a key ingredient in keeping your relationship working.

Consider Counseling, Individually And As A Couple Or Family

A professional who is skilled and objective can help you examine your issues and frustrations about parenting your adolescent. A professional counselor can also be of immense help at a time of crisis, whether between you and your child, or between you and your parenting partner.

Remember The Relationship

Keep the relationship and its well-being foremost in your mind. One of the most important factors in maintaining intimacy, and strengthening and sustaining a relationship, is time. It takes time to have fun together. It takes time just to be together. The quality of attention you give your children is important; it's necessary for your love relationship as well. Home-based parenting doesn't last forever. What do you fantasize about in those quiet moments when it's just the two of you together? Are you looking forward to a time without children, time to be together, just the two of you, to travel? Your kids will grow up and leave home. Think of your partner as your best friend and treat each other accordingly . . . with courtesy, respect and affection. This is your lifelong companion. Value the relationship accordingly.

Lighten Up And Have Fun!

All too often couples focus on the work and obligations, and lose the vibrancy that keeps a relationship alive. Fun is the lifeblood of a good marriage. Be sure to take time for fun as regularly as you schedule work commitments or your other obligations.

Spend Time With Other Parents Of Teens

Just as you probably enjoyed being with parents of newborns when your child was an infant, don't forget to take time to be with other parents of teenage children. Talking with other parents of adolescents and finding out how they are coping with the challenges of raising their teens can be a good support system. A word of caution: Choose to be with those parents who are positive and enjoying their children. The goal is to enrich your own parenting experience and to enhance your joy in parenting during the adolescent years.

Keep Learning And Growing

The field of psychology as it relates to family and couples has grown in scope and depth over the past few years. Keep learning and growing, and working toward building healthy family relationships.

His, Hers And Theirs: 5
Parenting Teenage
Stepchildren

 If parenting the adolescent is stressful for birth parents, it is doubly difficult for stepparents. One of the major stress-producing differences between blended families and biological families is that in stepfamilies the parent-child relationship has preceded the new couple relationship. In first marriages couples have a period of time in which to be together and assimilate values before making the necessary adjustments in becoming a new family. In remarriages the natural parent-child relationship may be strong, while the new couple relationship is more delicate and requires adjustment and compromise. The presence of a teenage child with loyalty and protectiveness toward both biological parents, and who may be secretly wanting a bigger piece of all this new affection and intimacy, can add a dimension of turmoil that corrodes rather than strengthens family harmony.

Ron had two boys, ages 12 and 13, from a previous marriage. After his divorce Ron spent weekends and vacations with his children, enjoying sports of all kinds. Ron dated Nicole only when his children were not with him. After Nicole and Ron were married, Ron and the youngsters continued their usual activities together. The children tried desperately to be the focus of their father's attention, even to the point of asking that Nicole not join in activities Ron had planned for the whole family. Both boys resented Nicole and would often sulk when she was along.

Parents And Teens Have Differing Views Of Remarriage

A child's view of remarriage is very different from an adult's view. While the new couple may be happy and excited about providing a youngster with a "family life" again, for a teenager there exists a new set of realities. His hope that his biological parents will get together again is dashed. He wonders if he will ever again see the absent parent, and if so, whether that parent will feel that the child has "sold out" if he express feelings of caring toward the new parent. An only child may acquire stepsiblings, or a youngest or oldest child may be replaced by a stepsibling who appropriates a coveted position. While the parent now has a new bond of love and friendship, the teenager experiences new losses. He now needs to share his remarried parent with another person and often other children as well — none of whom he has chosen.

Here's how 15-year-old Charles described his experience:

When my mother and I lived alone, we were so happy. We were friends. We did things together. Sometimes John — that's her new husband — would come along, but we used to discuss it and decide if we wanted him along. Mostly my mother dated him when I had activities, like play practice or something.

I know that my mom is happy now, but I miss her — us — so much. I never thought she would marry. I never thought I could miss my mom so much — and we still live in the same house! Now she spends all her time with John. I used to be the man of the house. Mom even said I was. Now John is. Mom has changed, you know. Decisions she once made are now made by the two of them, and sometimes she lets him decide.

John has a seven-year-old son who also lives with us on the weekends. Since we only have three bedrooms and one has been made into a study, he has to sleep in my room. I hate it. I hate him. He's such a brat. John spoils him, and my mother fusses over him like he's her own. It's sickening. I want my old life back. Mom said life would be better for us, that we would be a family again, but Mom and I were a family, and it's the one I want. Then our life worked. Now it's compromise after compromise, and I'm the one who always loses. Mom always decides in favor of John's kid. She thinks that I should understand and accept it. But I don't think it's fair. She sold out on me! I want John to go away.

UNREALISTIC ASSUMPTIONS

Many blended families seem to start with the unrealistic assumption that the new parent and the stepchildren will come together and love one another from the start. After all, the child loves her parent, the parent loves the new partner, and the new partner loves the parent, so all should love one another. This unrealistic expectation can lead to deep disappointment and guilt in the family and stress for parents and adolescents. In the following example, Mary can certainly relate to this:

Just two weeks after our wedding, two of Jim's three young-sters, ages 14 and 16, came to live with us. Both of our families had established different behavior patterns. My two children, ages four and seven, were used to my firm rules, but Jim's youngsters were accustomed to little if any structure. The first year was the hardest. Since the teenagers were at that breaking-away stage, they had no interest in forming a loving bond in a new family. Negotiating rules and coping with their jealousy and resentment were the most painful aspects. You have to be flexible, get used to each other's rules and then negotiate on the important ones.

Mary is right. Caring has a better chance to develop if there is less pressure placed on feeling "instant love."

THE TEENAGE "TRAITOR"

For teenagers, to love and care for a stepparent often seems disloyal to the absent, idealized parent. Sara, for example, encour-aged her mother to date, but changed her attitude when her mother remarried 18 months later. A child may have to hear from the biological parent that loving a stepparent doesn't take away from the love of the absent parent. Whereas children in biological families may try to keep their parents together, children in stepfamilies feel a strong loyalty to their natural parent and may either try consciously or unconsciously to drive the new couple apart. Loyalty to the biological parent is a very strong emotion, and adolescents feel compelled to show it.

Teenagers fare best when they are free to develop their own relationships with both parents. It is important that, where pos-sible, the teenager continue to see both biological parents. The more courteous the relationship between the divorced spouse and the stepfamily, the more easily this sharing of children is managed and the less strain there is for all concerned.

Even when the adults in both households are able to work together with regard to the children, feelings of competition and insecurity are very difficult to avoid. Children living in two house-holds may find themselves on continual emotional ups and downs. "I'm thrown back and forth between two houses," says Weldon of his natural parents. "It's really hard to shift gears and remem-ber what the ongoing saga is in each house. It's hard to get into a family routine. Besides, it's inconvenient, but no one seems to take my inconvenience seriously."

Adolescents, experiencing normal conflicts about their own identity and place in the family, have a particularly difficult time in managing loyalties between biological families. The question of "Where do I fit in?" is more acute for teenagers than for their younger siblings.

Teenagers are particularly susceptible to overt sexual displays. Aware of the sexual relationship between the newly married couple, some may feel as Donna, who said, "If Mom had treated Dad like that, they would still be together."

As the number of divorces in this country continue to rise, so will the number of remarriages. Every year in the United States a half-million marriages occur in which at least one partner has children from a previous marriage. Each day nearly 100 teenagers will become stepchildren. Sometimes the impossible does happen: Everyone gets along well and learns to love one another. All too often, however, the predictable happens: Children do not adjust well to the new lifestyle, and they experience significant stress.

If you are a stepparent who has been resented and shut out by children, or a natural parent who has seen your normally polite teenager turn churlish, you have lived through this same experi-ence. Happily, even a situation as anxiety ridden and seemingly inflexible as this one can be changed. Ron and Nicole did so in an intelligent, planned manner. The result was a lessening of their teenagers' stress and the happy coincidence of the lowering of their own anxiety levels at the same time.

Ron and Nicole began to plan periodic weekend trips to a fa-vorite family resort. While they were there, Ron and the boys went off hiking together. At other times both the adults and the children would swim and play together. While Ron and Nicole shared private time together, the teenagers entertained themselves. In this way new relationships formed, former relationships were preserved and family integration began to take place. The children began to feel less "dumped on" and more accepting of their new stepmother. Their manners improved as their stress lessened, making a cycle that fed on itself and made everyone more comfortable.

GUIDELINES FOR SURVIVING STEPPARENTING

You can help lessen the stress your children feel as a result of gaining an instant expanded family, and help them adapt to the stress caused by the need to share your love. The following suggestions are a place to start.

Listen

When your child tells you of his feelings about his new parent or sibling, listen. Let him talk as long as he wants and get it all out. Don't make him feel guilty about saying negative things. Don't you sometimes say negative things about his friends? You may have learned to love his best buddy with the tattooed cheeks, but no doubt you had a few things to say about him first.

Provide Reassurance

When you had your second child, you probably spent a great deal of time with your first child, reassuring her that you still loved her just as much. Now that your teenager is a "young adult," you may unrealistically think that she knows how much you love her and that nothing will ever lessen that love. Don't underestimate her need for reassurance. Don't you still get a twinge of fear when your spouse stares at an attractive person for just a little too long? Imagine how much worse that feeling of insecurity is when the person is brought into the family unit. Keep talking to your child; tell her over and over how much you still love and support her.

Point Out The Advantages

Teenagers are in the "me" stage. They want to know the bottom line: "What's in it for me?" Point out the benefits of having another parent: "Just think, Paul, I'll have someone else to nag besides you; you won't get picked on as much!" Let him know how good having a new sibling can be: "If you play your cards right, Susan would probably be willing to clean your room in exchange for your taking her to the movies once a week." Take the time to sit down with your teen and tell him, in terms that mean something to him personally, how the new family members can support and help him, too.

Help Your Teenager With The Change Process

Usually it's not the differences that cause problems, but rather getting used to the change. Change is never easy for any of us. However, change is considerably easier when members of the new family can see the benefits of changing and are encouraged and supported in changing.

Communicate

Talk about feelings. Parents as well as their teenagers often pine over the loss of the once close relationship between them. When the situation is openly discussed, solutions are more likely to be found. Discuss your feelings about how each of you is faring. Often, stepchildren will offer complaints to just one parent. "Mom, he always introduces me as his daughter," complains Shelley. "But I'm not his daughter. My real father is the only one who can call me his daughter. I wish he would stop."

Strive For Consistency With Your Co-parent

Parents must be willing to talk to each other in private and arrive at an agreement on troublesome issues. A mother may say, "It's okay with me if it's okay with John." But when John, the stepfather, says "No," he becomes the bad guy. Another mother may tell her new husband that she wants him to discipline her young son, but when he does, she objects, saying, "Leave my kid alone." Good communication skills can alleviate sending these confusing and double signals.

Seek Assistance If Necessary

Blended families have become so complex that the Stepfamily Association of America offers counseling referrals, support groups and educational publications with advice on legal, financial and practical ways of lowering the stress of stepparenting. Additionally, the resource section lists a number of excellent references for parents and adolescents.

Passage Through Puberty: Understanding The Adolescent Years

Do You Remember Adolescence?

 Some years ago, while I was Teacher-Of-The-Year, a reporter interviewed one of my high school students and asked him, "What makes Dr. Youngs a good teacher?" The simple answer given by the student was memorable: "She knows what it's like to *feel alive*."

Teenagers are like that: they *feel alive*. While adults are busy producing and achieving results, and rightly so, teenagers quite often derive an intensely intoxicating rush from their rapture of aliveness. Do you remember the time when a pervasive feeling of *aliveness* shored up and embedded your essence? Do you still bask in that feeling of *beingness?* Does the feeling linger or is it evanescent? Does it contribute a sense of zest, zeal and gusto to your day? Is it the lifespring that feeds your producing and achieving? Can you *sense* the blood pulsing through your veins? Does the *feel* of your skin create a fondness of you being *you?* Do the eyes looking back in your mirror send challenging and energizing messages that say, "It's wonderful to be alive; have at it; get to it; you can do it; just do it"?

I can. I can still feel that mysterious and empowering forcefield within me.

TEENS LIKE TO BE WITH ADULTS WHO EMBODY "ALIVENESS"

Teenagers need adults who remember the ambivalence the adolescent feels — to feel so alive and yet to be stifled by an arbitrary framework of boundaries. They need adults who embody *aliveness*, who remember what it's like to be an adolescent. They also need adults who will assist them in constructively channeling their own feelings of aliveness. Some parents offer their children more aliveness than others do. Maybe it's because they remember what it was like to be an adolescent.

DO YOU REMEMBER ADOLESCENCE?

There he is, standing outside the door of the classroom, shaking like a leaf, palms sweating, his heart pounding and his stomach playing the *1812 Overture.* "It's just a dumb school dance," he tells himself. "Yeah, but everyone will think I'm a nerd! Does my hair look okay? I know it's too short. I'm too skinny. You might know I'd get a pimple right on my chin where everyone will have to notice it. I don't know why I wore this outfit; I look like a geek. Everyone is going to laugh at me. No one is going to want to dance with me. I'll just die if Terry comes over to talk to me. I'll just die if no one comes over to talk to me."

Good grief, who is that poor kid putting himself through all that trauma and drama? Surely he is maladjusted and neglected. Look again. That tormented soul was *you* just a few decades ago, going to your first dance, enjoying "the best days of your life." Ah, for the "good old days."

All of us who have "grown up" vaguely remember what it was like to be an adolescent. Yet we also forget. Time blurs the difficult side of human experience, leaving mostly a certain nostalgic glow as we reminisce about the exhilarating and unforgettable moments of yesteryear. Sometimes we even long for days irrevocably gone, when we were happy, endlessly energetic, carefree and full of hopes and dreams — or so we thought. Needless to say, we were also — and maybe predominantly — plagued by uncertainty, confusion, ambivalence and moody introspection. We were filled with anxious moments of despair and frequent episodes of stress.

The period of adolescence often represents a special time of stress for both parents and teenagers. Research shows that the teen years are without a doubt among the most confusing and stressful times of life because the developmental tasks are so great. Most youngsters characterize their adolescent years as the most "unhappy and turbulent" in their lives, despite being told by adults that the teenage years are the happiest time of life. What is it about this phase of life that produces what teenagers describe as the "most unhappy and turbulent," and what parents refer to as the "most trying" of times?

"I'm strong," says Robert. "I'm capable of living independently, yet my parents treat me like a child. I'm watched and questioned. I just wish I didn't need them."

"It's like needing a loan from the bank," explained 16-year-old Karen. "It's awful to have to borrow, because there are strings attached, but you do need the loan. Adolescence is like that. You hate to live under someone else's conditions, but you have to be there."

Seventeen-year-old Dean expressed it this way:

You're just trapped in a no-win situation. For instance, my dad wants me to become a lawyer like he is, eventually going into practice with him. It's *his* dream, not mine, and I don't share it. He feels I'm ungrateful, telling me that if his father had offered him a position, he would have taken it and been thankful. I can't get him to respect my feelings about what I want to do with my life. It wouldn't be so bad if he didn't want to do my thinking for me. He tells me he knows how it feels to be a teenager. How can he know? He's not a teenager in today's world. Parents expect you to value their decisions just because they are older. I've got news for them — older is not wiser! My parents remind me that I'm grown up — that is, when it's convenient, like when they want me to assume more responsibility — but they don't really believe it. They treat me like I'm an overgrown child. They tell me they've given me so much, and they want so much for me. I feel like a $120,000 investment, and I'm often reminded that that is what it will cost to get me out the door!

They tell me they love me, but I don't think they know who I am. I want to work part-time with a friend who is a builder. He offered me a job, but my dad said, "No, get your education. I want you to concentrate on school." Then in the same breath he tells me how hard he worked to rise up and build a business for himself. "I never had time to feel sorry for myself, mope around, ask for a car and clothes like you can," he said. Yet there he was, out working when he was 15 and married at 18. "I kept at it, sacrificing time with my young family, working full-time and going to college too!"

It's ironic that my dad was boasting about what he did at 18, when he was my age. I always wondered if he enjoyed his life and if he still felt good about the decisions he made. I don't think my dad is enjoying his work, so why would he want to wish it on me?

LUCKILY, ACUTE ADOLESCENT TURMOIL DOESN'T LAST FOREVER!

Your teenager won't always be irritable, moody, suspicious and sullen, rebellious, hard to reason with and feeling that you are quite possibly a major source of this discontent! Dean, for example, is now a second-semester freshman in college. He has gained some distance on himself, is more at ease with himself, and is better able to see humor in his adolescence. His is one of the best descriptions of what adolescent stress is all about and provides insight into how it ought to be viewed by parents:

I realize now that there were moments when no matter what my parents said, I would have disagreed with them. I was determined to go my own way, and I wouldn't let anyone persuade me otherwise. But I know that I needed someone to disagree with, someone I could talk with who wouldn't walk away just because I was being a tough talker. When I have children and they grow up to be teenagers, I only hope that I'll have patience with them and not forget that it's not so much what you say, but your attitude. If you're sending signals that you care and you want to help, to be there, to stand by, that's what a teenager needs. He may try to pick a fight with you, and he may scream or cry or cuss or whatever. But he needs you there and you can't forget that. You shouldn't become passive or take abuse, just as you can't rise to every piece of bait thrown at you. I guess you have to keep remembering that with time a lot changes, and soon the person who seems completely wrapped up in himself and has no perspective gets a sense of humor about things. And the next thing you know, he's growing up. Then everybody can take a deep breath. I'm beginning to take a deep breath myself — about myself. That's when you know that you won't be a teenager too much longer. Parents just need to know what adolescence is all about.

PROFILE OF AN ADOLESCENT

An adolescent is a person who . . .

- Is leaving behind the stages of childhood and working through the stages of adolescence.
- When scared or frightened, slips back into the security of the previous stage.

- Is undergoing a rapid and intense period of physiological and psychological changes.
- Wants to be independent, but doesn't have the backlog of personal experiences to function independently in the society to which he belongs.
- Needs to express personal needs and have these needs taken seriously.
- Has not yet formed a cohesive value system that would support her in what to "live for," so this tremendously important anchor of security is not yet within reach.
- Is locked into financial and emotional dependence on the family.
- Is trying to make decisions of lasting importance — career exploration, life values, relationships.
- Vividly notices when there is a discrepancy between the rules and values espoused by adults and adult behavior.
- Has limited understanding as to what highs and lows of emotions mean.
- Has limited understanding as to how to cope successfully with the ups and downs of mood swings.
- Has a strong need for adult mentoring and guidance.
- Is constructing a sense of selfhood.
- Feels lonely and alone when parents are physically and emotionally absent.
- Needs parents to show love, acceptance and attention.
- Needs guidance and direction.
- Learns mostly by exploration and trial and error.
- Needs skills to cope with stress and the crises at hand.
- Needs adults to model healthy adult behavior.
- In the absence of effective adaptive coping skills becomes debilitated by the ravages of stress.
- When the family unit fails to provide an environment that is nurturing and supportive, turns to peers for the fulfillment of these needs.

- Is at high risk for incidence of poor health, alcohol and drug abuse, sexual abuse, family violence, sexual promiscuity, alienation and suicidal tendencies.
- Is by law a minor.

PASSAGE THROUGH PUBERTY

Sometimes we naively assume that the tension and stress between parent and teenager arises out of adolescent "rebellion." While rebellion can certainly contribute to the tension between parent and teenager, most of the stress of the teen years stems from the work of adolescence — meeting the tasks and demands the teen must attend to. These include passage through puberty: coming to grips with the newness (growing pains) of the body and mind in a time of rapid and intense physiological and psychological growth, forming a stable identity and acquiring workable socialization skills.

ADOLESCENCE IS A TIME OF CRISIS

Adolescence has been termed a period of crisis, a necessary turning point and a crucial moment when development occurs — rightly so, because several important events occur during this period. The most obvious are the physiological changes. The greater size, growth of body hair, voice changes and other outward manifestations of growing reproductive capacity all send strong signals to your adolescent that physically he or she is maturing. These new changes seem rather mystical. "Who *is* this new person?" your teenager wonders.

Most adolescents have relatively little information about what to expect, and this lack of information creates a stress of its own. For girls, the perils of puberty include height, weight, menstruation, breast development, hair growth, body shape and configuration, facial features and skin conditions. For boys, the perils of puberty include many of the same concerns as their female counterparts — height, weight, hair growth, body shape and configuration, skin condition, facial features — and other concerns such as wet dreams, spontaneous erections, masturbation and sexual fantasy. "Am I normal? Will I always look like this? Will I always sound like this? Will I ever 'feel' happy?" are all questions to which adolescents want and need answers.

HORMONES: THE BANE
OF ADOLESCENT BEHAVIOR

Hormone levels increase dramatically during puberty. They are responsible for setting in motion physical changes that transform a child's body into an adult's. The increasing levels of hormones accompanying the stage of adolescence bring out many emotional and behavioral changes. Ongoing research at the National Institute of Mental Health is uncovering the link between hormones and adolescent behavior. In an effort to "delineate the course of puberty," psychologists Edith Nottelmann, Elizabeth Susman and their colleagues are studying hormone levels and their relationship to physical development and behavioral characteristics present during pubertal years. Three groups of hormones were found to rise dramatically during puberty — a total of seven hormones, which together are responsible for the dramatic changes occurring over the adolescent years. By identifying hormonal states and fluctuations, we can more accurately predict behavioral changes and ways to offset them. Research suggests, for example, that the "rebellious" physical tension behavior is more likely in boys with high androgen levels (and low testosterone levels). Early-maturing teenage boys tend to be better adjusted. They have lower levels of adrenal androgens and higher levels of sex steroids at an earlier age. Higher androgen levels in boys are generally associated with more negative moods. Girls with lower levels of one adrenal androgen are more likely to be rebellious and feel "down-in-the-dumps."

The changes in hormone levels that contribute to mood stability are probably not surprising to many parents. As Phyllis, the parent of 14-year-old twin girls, laments, "It's good behavior one hour and deplorable behavior the next, happiness at ten o'clock and guerrilla warfare at eleven. It's hard for me to keep up with their moods. At first I was concerned with the mental health of my teenagers, but now I'm just worried about mine!" Says one of the twins, "My moods change so often, I feel like I'm going crazy. All I do is apologize for my behavior. I'm not in charge, my body is. It's an awful feeling." If the woes of Phyllis and her daughters sound familiar, take heart, for your adolescent is "normal" and is simply hard at work with the tasks and demands of puberty.

YOUR TEEN'S CHANGING BRAIN

You can see most of the changes your teenager is going through. You see his growth spurt and its effect on your bank balance in terms of clothing replacement; you watch him proudly start fingering all three of his chin whiskers. There is, however, a major change going on that you don't see. Believe it or not, his brain is growing!

Your teenager's brain capacity will increase by about one-third during these already tempestuous times. The final pound of the adult three-pound brain is "added on" when the adolescent is between the ages of 12 and 16. This growth involves further development of the nervous system and enhances the brain's efficiency and capability. The growth does not occur continuously but in sequences of short periods of rapid growth (during which the neural networks need for new cognitive functions, such as speaking and reading, are created) and longer periods of practically no growth (when the new functions are integrated into the total, or cognitive, system). On the average, children experience a rapid brain-weight increase of from 5 to 10 percent between the ages of 2 and 4, 6 and 9, 10 and 12, and 14 and 16. This growth spurt occurs during a period of about six months sometime during the two-year period, generally earlier for girls and later for boys. During the 10-to-12 growth spurt, female brain growth is about three times that of males; during the 14-to-16 brain growth period, the situation is reversed.

A NEW WAY OF THINKING

Along with physical growth, teenagers are learning to enlarge on the ways they think. Because these changes occur so suddenly, they catch both parents and their teens off guard. Such remarks as, "Did you hear what I said?" or "Oh, my God, I can't believe I said that!" are common remarks from teenagers. This is about the time the parent thinks the "rebellious streak has struck." Take heart, your adolescent is climbing one step further up the ladder to adulthood.

Now that your child is a teenager, she has a number of important learning functions to address, the most critical being formal operational thought — learning how to conceptualize "what might be" as opposed to "what is." This more abstract level of thought allows teens to go beyond the here and now, to comprehend the abstract, like philosophy, algebra and calculus, and to appreciate simile, metaphor and parody.

A New (But Not Necessarily Winning) Way With Words

There are a number of outcomes of formal operational thought and flashing a new vocabulary is one of them. I asked my teenager and her friends to share with me some expressions they use daily. I have been surprised by how quickly the slang changes. No sooner did I get down several expressions than I was told, "That's not 'live' anymore," meaning it is outdated!

One reason young people readily develop their own lingo is that it allows them to practice their new mental abilities and at the same time enables them to define their own tastes, values and preferences, in their own way. These new abilities give rise to the use of humor and wit necessary to move outside of themselves to view, examine and define aspects of themselves that are too delicate and too painful to confront in a more serious manner. This doesn't mean adolescents are fully aware of their new skills, though they, too, are amazed at their newfound wit.

Your Child, The Critic

All of a sudden your adolescent is an astute social critic as well. "That's unfortunate," you say, "because she now criticizes me too!" Since formal operational thought enables your adolescent to go beyond the real and into the possible, it opens up for her the world of the "ideal" and "perfection." The concept of "ideal" may enable her to gain a new view of her parents.

Your Teenager's Phantom

It is not uncommon for adolescents to fantasize that they were adopted and to wish that their real parents (who just happen to be extremely rich and very famous) will send for them. Just like their parents, adolescents are unsuspecting and unprepared for the behavioral changes that follow. One dad in a workshop of mine remarked:

Yesterday, I was his beloved parent. Suddenly today, nothing suits my son's tastes. The house is "dumpy," the car is "funky," we are "old fashioned," his friends are "to die for." He is "rad," "awesome," and "totally uptown." We were walking down the street and a friend of his approached us. My son introduced me to his buddy as a *friend!* When I asked about it, he said, "Geez, Dad, you're wearing cords. They went out of style years ago!"

If parents are open for attack, peers are geared for guerrilla warfare. Adolescents can be quite cruel with one another. Ridiculing comments are all too common. Obviously, such remarks are painful for the adolescent receiving them.

Learning To Argue

New thinking skills also provide your adolescent with the ability to argue. No doubt you have already learned this! During their early teens, children develop the ability to marshal facts and ideas to make a case. "Because I said so!" is no longer a logical explanation. Rather, they want to know the *reasons* they should or shouldn't do something. Your instruction, such as, "You can't have Alicia stay overnight on a school night because you have homework, and besides the house rule is 'no staying over on a school night,' " will be met by reasoned and logical response: "I study better with Alicia's help, and that dumb rule was made two years ago when I was just a kid." Such arguments should be seen for what they represent: an effort on your teenager's part to exercise her new powers of argument. You might reply, "It's good to know you enjoy studying with Alicia. Should you decide to invite her over for the early part of the evening, I'd be happy to accommodate that. But she will not be able to stay over during the week."

Delusions Of Uniqueness

Caught up with the many transformations he is undergoing in his body, facial structure, feelings and thinking powers, your adolescent quite naturally becomes focused on himself. He develops a kind of delusion of uniqueness: "No one feels the way I do about anything; no one has ever had this problem." Or "This is unbearable. You can't solve this problem. No one can." He may fear that he is not normal. Tormented by issues that seem private and personal, he has yet to learn that many fears, anxieties, doubts and needs are universally shared by all.

Identity Crisis

The adolescent phase is a time of discovering the more constant core of self among the seemingly many selves. Answers to questions such as, "Who am I?" or "What do I believe in?" are part of the search, and may lead your adolescent to adopt, at least temporarily, ideologies that are different from yours. You notice that your parent-child relationship begins to change. Sometimes a parent feels ambivalent about allowing a dependent child to become an independent adult. Parents may send mixed messages: "You're a child, but not a child; you're a young adult, but not a young adult." "Grow up," but then later, "Act your age."

That adolescence is set apart as a time of crisis is not surprising. It is an intense stage in many ways. By understanding what is involved, you can help your teenager cope effectively and in a way that preserves the parent-child relationship.

What's A Parent To Do?

Knowing about your teen's developmental stages is more than just interesting. Used wisely, this information can help you understand the teenager's needs and behaviors, and shed light on how best to provide effective guidance and direction.

But let's face it. Understanding the enormity of the changes your teenager is undergoing can help you be more compassionate and tolerant of what your child is going through, and it can also help you feel less frustrated by his seemingly erratic personality. Sometimes, just knowing and understanding isn't enough. If your child shouts an obscenity at you when you simply remind him to do chores, are you really going to stop and say, "Oh, that's all right, dear. I understand — it's just that your brain is growing"? Of course not! You're more likely to snarl back, ground him or take some other punitive action. Compassion doesn't always translate well in day-to-day situations. What does?

Expect Individuality

You can expect fewer automatic agreements now that your child is an adolescent. Ask her for her opinions on adult topics, such as current affairs, moral issues, job decisions, personal problems. Encourage her to think through her own philosophy, to give it more form and substance, to develop and put it into words. She'll need to see that you respect her, that you are helping her learn the process of decision making, evaluating the consequences and learning how to put one foot in front of the other to go forward into her life.

Expect Your Child To Question

As your adolescent unfolds, he will naturally question and challenge existing value systems, beliefs and ideals with which he has been reared. Understanding this can help you feel less anxious about their scrutiny and his occasional rejection of those things you hold near and dear. This search is often as painful and stressful for your child as it is for you. Help your child develop a sound sense of self. The adolescent phase is so rocky that discovering one's true essence — a *constant* core of self — among the seemingly many selves is difficult. Answers to questions such as, "Who am I?" "What do I stand for?" and "What do I believe in?" are part of the search. The search for identity may lead your adolescent to adopt, at least temporarily, moral, religious and political ideologies that are different from yours.

Get Information

Accurate information about what's going on can help your child feel comfortable and better accept the individual changes she may be experiencing. Because they are experts in this area, pediatricians are an excellent first source of information. Additionally, your family pediatrician knows your child will be able to talk with her about the anxious feelings she is having. School nurses are also a ready resource for parents. Read. Ask your pediatrician or school nurse for recommended reading. A number of excellent books for both parent and adolescent are also listed in the resource section of this book.

Personalize, Don't Generalize

Help your adolescent come to grips with her changing self. Don't say, "Oh, don't worry about it; everybody looks like that." Be sensitive to your child's momentary embarrassment with her changing self. One approach that I used to help my questioning adolescent gain a perspective about the changes that occur in facial features over time, for example, was to frame for her a series of my own pictures from early childhood right up to the present. Next to it I placed a similar array of the photos of her father, followed by photos of herself from birth to present. This proved an invaluable tool in helping her accept her appearance as the one belonging to her right now, and also illustrated for her the marked changes that occur not only throughout adolescence but throughout other life stages as well.

Monitor Rest And Nutrition

During this stage of pronounced growth, your adolescent has an enormous need for adequate rest and nutrition. Researchers have found that about 90 percent of teenagers do not get enough sleep, which affects their ability to function at a high level during the day. Dr. Carskadon at the Stanford University Sleep Center believes that teens need more sleep than children, and recommends that adolescents between the ages of 12 and 17 get nine or more hours of sleep each night.

Proper nutrition is essential to good health and a significant factor in our overall well-being. Studies suggest that the nutrition of teenagers is so imbalanced that they are at risk. The Department of Health and Human Services has found that adolescents consume less than 60 percent of recommended daily allowances of food nutrients. It is a well-established fact that the breakfast meal is an important part of eating habits in the health equation, yet it is estimated that well over 70 percent of adolescents go to school without eating breakfast. Habits for good nutrition start in the early years. The fitness and nutrition sections in Chapter 15 provide additional suggestions for helping teenagers. A number of excellent books for both parent and adolescent are also listed in the resource section of this book.

Set Firm, Fair Guidelines And Adhere To Them

Set guidelines that allow your teen to respect the rights of all. Parents need to offer patience and understanding, but not at

the risk of getting emotionally battered in the process. Differ-
entiate between acceptance and approval. You can tolerate un-
likable behavior or remarks without sanctioning them. Saying,
"James, I can't stop you from swearing and using vulgar language when you are away from me, though I would prefer that
you didn't. However, it is not appropriate in the house and will
not be tolerated," acknowledges his right to expression, while
demonstrating your respect for family integrity. Firm, fair and
consistent expression of your family values keeps the channels
of communication open with respect and dignity for all.

Teach Your Teens To Examine Their Thinking

Adolescents think that parents and the events in their lives cause
them to feel the way they do. Thus they often blame someone else
for their feelings of stress and emotional upset. In doing this, however, they often neglect an important factor: The way we think
determines our behavior and response to stressful situations. From
time to time, we all engage in faulty or irrational thinking. What
we say to ourselves before, during and after an incident greatly
influences our feelings and behaviors. Acting on their own faulty
thinking, they react compulsively. Help your adolescent learn more
appropriate ways to respond to stress situations.

Teach Your Teen To Be Assertive

An important reason for teaching your teenager to develop
assertiveness skills is so he may confidently confront situations
that would typically produce anxiety, frustration or otherwise
cause him to deny his own feelings and emotions. Teenagers are
often cruel with each other. Teach your teenager that it's okay to
lighten up and have a sense of humor, but that he doesn't have to
tolerate being the butt of someone's unkind jokes or ridicule.

Allow For Mistakes

Adolescence is a time of exploration and discovery through
experimentation. Teens need time to flex their newly discovered
"muscles." Be patient. Learning these skills won't happen over-

night. Remember, trial and error is the path to learning. Also remember that at each age you are dealing with a changing person, one who has not yet formed a stable sense of self. Sometimes when your adolescent puts childhood aside and moves into the adolescent stage, she experiences loss. She may become confused or frightened by the complexity of tasks and demands and (unknown) changes confronting her and slip back into the security of being a child.

Communicate, Negotiate And Remain Open To Change

Shared communication is a real key. Even if you have clear and explicitly defined rules for maintaining stability in your family, it will be necessary periodically to negotiate "new and improved" ones. Throughout children's adolescent years, parents must be oriented to the inevitable ability to modify or change. If a parent is unable to transform rules to allow for change and growth in the "new" teenager, the stress between them will be monumental. Decisions about curfew, allowance and part-time jobs are examples of issues that change as the teenager learns to accept more responsibility for his actions. Issues such as these require listening, conversing, compromise, cooperation and respect from both parents and teens.

Get Help When You Need It

Support groups can allow your teenager to share concern with others his own age, helping him gain a better sense of how the teenager's problems are common and shared by many. Check with your teen's school nurse or counselor to see what support groups are available at your child's school. If none is provided, or if you are not able to get your teen to participate in a group at his school, ask for referrals to community psychologists. Guidelines for selecting counselors, psychologists and therapists can be found in Appendix A.

Modeling Plays An Important Role

Children learn what they see. In adolescence, teachers, parents and coaches should be terrific people worth emulating. Don't assail your children with contradictions. Discipline fairly and support your child in the role of a learner. Don't forget your child's need for spiritual fulfillment and, above all, have the courage to parent. Remember, actions speak louder than words. Your adolescent is observing you, your lifestyle, your patterns of interacting — everything about you — to discover what adults and adulthood are all about. *Being* an adult is something that she wants very badly to become right now: It has her attention. It's a good time to examine what you are up to and how your professed values are expressed in your actions.

7

"Children's Play Is Their Work:" What Is The Work Of Teenhood?

 Have you ever heard the expression, "Children's play is their work"? It means that through their actions they are gaining information about the world. This is true whether the child is 2 or 12 or 17. Each stage of development presents its own set of tasks and demands, all focused on gaining self-knowledge.

A child's work at each age is pretty well-defined. The particular stage of development your child is experiencing is one of the driving factors behind her motivations and is reflected in behavior. By being aware of these developmental stages, you can understand better the work that a child must undertake at each stage (and consequently, her behavior), and thus help your child learn acceptable ways to respond to the challenges, people and events in life.

Child Development: Stages And Their Tasks

So that you can see how the child at each stage has specific tasks to do, and see how these tasks form the building blocks to growth and maturity, we'll look first at the early years. Then we'll plunge into the adolescent years.

AGE TWO: AUTONOMY

Up until the age of two, a child primarily views himself as part of his mother (or father, if he is the primary caregiver). Upon reaching two, he becomes aware that he is, in reality, separate. This presents the child with the task of establishing autonomy — separateness. The two words that best describe his new found selfhood, that he is in fact a separate person, are "No!" and "Mine!" Possession is a tool he uses to enforce that sense of a separate self.

Implications

Parents who have experienced their child's zealous work on this task of *selfness* without understanding it have no doubt at one time or another said, "He's reached the Terrible Twos." But the two-year-old is neither a selfish nor an obstinate child. He's looking for power and ways to assert it. Assisting this child's developing sense of self is a matter of allowing him power and ways to be (safely) assertive. This child needs to be given choices. For example, he can pick out which shoes he wants to wear or what toy he wants to play with. He can decide which book he wants to have read to him. In each instance, the child can be provided with two or three choices, all of which a parent can live with.

The autonomy the young child develops at this stage lays the foundation for being able to value himself. Through his "work" he learns that he can assert himself — the forerunner of independence. If the developmental tasks of being two have been met with a fair degree of success, at age three he will be quite independent.

AGE THREE: MASTERY

Having realized her separateness, the three-year-old goes on to master her environment. Mastery plays an important role in her perception of self: It influences her feeling of being capable (or not capable). Her need for *success* in her endeavors at this stage is crucial. She labors over each accomplishment. Because she is slow and methodical, it takes her forever to do each task! Needing feedback to know if she has been successful, she strives for *recognition* of these achievements. ("Watch me! Watch me!") That she has something to offer nurtures her sense of competence and proves her value — she is worthwhile.

The search for mastery stimulates curiosity. "Why? Why? Why?" she wants to know. Her *drive* for discovering (learning) is insatiable; her *capacity* for learning is unlimited. It's not uncommon for her to hum continuously or sing her thoughts — it helps her concentrate — because the mind is moving so fast. She has an incredible ease in learning languages and language-related skills. With vigor she explores her surroundings, observes people and examines how she fits into each relationship.

Implications

Parents need patience to answer this child's repeated questions. She is exploring her environment, examining everything closely. Her achievements should be recognized with much praise, and tangible signs such as putting her drawings up where they can be seen. Parents and daycare workers can show they have in fact listened to her by asking her to tell them about something she enjoys discussing, such as how or why she has drawn a certain picture, or why she has chosen to use certain colors in the picture.

AGE FIVE: SEPARATION ANXIETY

Parents are the name of the game for the five-year-old. At this age the mother or primary caregiver is the center of the child's world. He not only wants to please her, he wants to be near her, talk with her, play with her, go to work with her, help her around the house or go along on errands, and he would prefer to be with her than with friends. This does not mean that the father is left out of the picture. While the mother is the preference, the father is definitely important too.

The five-year-old's adoration of his parents is unquestionably heartwarming. The result is almost totally parent-pleasing behavior. The good news for the educator is that since children transfer their feelings of respect for their parents onto the teacher, teachers at this stage are adored and loved. (Ever notice how kindergarten teachers long to stay in their assignment for decades and rarely burn out?) The child's basic framework is, "I want to be good all the time. I want to not do any of the bad things. I'll do whatever you say." Not only does he want to be good, and mean to be good, but more often than not he succeeds in being good. In his determination to do everything just right, he'll ask permission for even the simplest thing, even when he needn't, and he will then beam with pleasure when you smile and give permission.

Implications

Most important in this period is helping the child recognize that he is a person in his own right, that "separate" feelings are all right. It is especially important to allow this child the feeling of being good, doing right and winning your approval. Because separation anxiety is very real to him, reassure him that you are safe.

AGE SIX: ME-NESS

"Self-centeredness" comes before "other-centeredness." At the preschool stage this child discovered she was separate from her parents, yet she still kept her parents at the center of her existence. At six she must shift her focus from her parents to herself. She now places herself at the center of her world instead of parents or others. Though she appears to be self-centered, this is an important milestone in her development. She is now ready to undertake the task of being receptive to her own interests as she attempts to understand them.

Implications

Allow this child reasonable room to make some of her own decisions. This doesn't mean you let her have everything she wants; it means that you show acceptance while simultaneously setting boundaries and healthy limits.

MEET YOUR ADOLESCENT

The timeline for a child's development is more regular (normative) than not. For example, most development in normal healthy babies occurs at or around the same time, with not much more than about a six- to ten-month variation in time. You can observe this when your baby cuts a tooth. In human development, the brain gives the directive, "It's time," and a particular growth is put in motion — for example, a tooth bud appears. Such is the functioning of the time clock for adolescent development. Like early childhood development, adolescent development is pretty much a phylogenetic imperative, that is, it's run by the biological time clock.

Because childhood is a series of transitions leaving behind one stage of development and embarking on another, the child often fluctuates between the two ages, acting like one age one moment, and the next age the next moment. Because a child is somewhat of a compilation of "two ages," I have combined a grouping of two ages in providing you with a profile of your child at specific stages.

You live with your child every day, and so you know him in a certain way. In the following sections you will get to meet your child in yet a different way, the way he unfolds as a person, in his intellectual, physical, psychological, social, moral and ethical development. Though at first this section may seem a bit clinical, the information is designed to provide you with practical information about your child's formal development. Such information can help you see what issues are involved at each stage of development, allowing you to stand back and observe your child objectively, yet closely. Knowing what each age and stage of childhood/teenhood is about can help you provide your children with the skills and support they need in order to traverse adolescence in a healthy and satisfying way.

A Profile Of The 12- And 13-Year-Old

Ask the average seventh-grader what is the most important feature of being that age, and she will tell you that there are a couple of huge issues in life: Lighting up and smoking one's very own cigarette, trying alcohol and having a very best friend who will be there for you no matter what you do or say.

Ask the average eighth-grader what is the most important feature of being that age, and he will tell you that to "give or get a *serious* kiss" is what it's all about.

Technically speaking, the 12-year-old doesn't qualify as a teenager. But just ask any parent about his sixth or seventh grader, and that parent will tell you there is a budding adolescent in the works. It's more than parental perception: Research shows that biological development now occurs *five years sooner* than adolescents of the last century — for example, the average age of menarche has dropped from 17 to 12 years of age.

The 12- and 13-year-old child is uniquely different than the 10- and 11-year-old, though we could reasonably argue that the *preadolescent stage* is setting in for the 11-year-old girl. The marked changes associated with preadolescence begin around the second semester of sixth grade for girls, and around the second semester of seventh grade for boys. During this time the rate of growth and development for boys and girls who are the same age is roughly one to one-and-a-half years — with girls developing first;

for same-age, same-sex children, a variation of about four to ten months is considered the norm.

This stage of development reflects a wide range of individual differences between boys and girls, and between same-sex children as well. There are very few similarities between the 13-year-old girl and the 13-year-old boy, but even fewer between the 12-year-old girl and the 12-year-old boy. During these two years, girls will be about one-and-one-half years further along in their development.

It's an incredible time of growth in many areas. All systems are *go!* The need to be physical, and the curiosity and ability to expand understanding of the intellectual, social and spiritual realms are remarkable. Everything is explored and examined; it's a time of enormous growth in every way.

Intellectual Development

This is neither a slow nor a dull stage. It's a time of *doing*. This is an intensely curious child, with a willingness to learn almost everything and anything.

These children have entered peak years of enormous intellectual capacity. Their rapidly developing mind makes the transition from the concrete-manipulatory stage to the capacity for abstract thought. This transition makes possible:

- propositional thought
- consideration of ideas contrary to fact
- reasoning with hypotheses involving two or more variables
- ability to project thought into the future, to anticipate
- insight into the motivations behind attitudes and behaviors

The 12- and 13-year-old child learns best under two conditions: (1) when the activity is experiential (active/doing) rather than passive (listening or reading); and (2) when she can interact with the same-sex peer during the learning experience.

Physical Development

This stage of development reflects a wide range of individual differences between boys and girls, and between same-sex children as well. For the next two years, girls will be about two or four inches taller than boys, and further along in their physical development. The differences in physical development between same-age, different-sex children and between same-age, same-sex children creates anxiety for both sexes. Girls are more likely to focus on physical changes that accompany sexual maturation; boys are more likely to feel anxious about receding chins, cowlicks, dimples and changes in tone of voice.

The 12- and 13-year-old child gains more weight, height, heart size, lung capacity and muscular strength than was true of the previous four years of development. Bone growth exceeds muscle development, generally resulting in poor coordination and being clumsy and awkward; bones may lack protection of covering muscles and supporting tendons. Both boys and girls begin a process of slow change, not only in height and weight gain, but in body contour — for example, an elongating and thickening of the nose, protruding ears, long arms.

In mid-adolescence the body is charged with readying itself for sexual reproduction. This stage of puberty produces some of the most dramatic sexual changes in the teen's life: the growth of pubic hair, development of breasts, the menarche, the ability to have erections and nocturnal emissions (wet dreams), and the discovery of arousal through manipulation (masturbation).

This is a time of same-age, same-sex peer groups. Boys pair up with boys and girls with girls. This is preparatory to moving into relationships with the same-age, opposite-sex. For now, they feel much more comfortable with friends of their own sex, even though they may be eager, although not quite ready, for heterosexual relationships. There is safety in numbers. When a boy goes calling on a girl, he takes the gang along. Standing on the corner, he whistles boldly at passing girls, backed up by his buddies. Girls cling together too. The girl hangs out with other girls in search of reinforcement of her own role. Helen will write a note to her love interest, Jimmy, and give the note to Suzie to give to Linda to give to Maureen to give to Janey to give to her brother, Jimmy! Being with other girls makes her feel more secure in (and confirms) her femininity. Even when making advances toward boys, the girls involve the same-age, same-sex peers.

The 12- and 13-year-old child experiences fluctuations in basal metabolism that can cause extreme restlessness and listlessness.

The child's taste buds begin to discriminate likes or dislikes in foods based on what the body's hormones are needing to sustain it in this period of rapid growth. Female children tend to desire starches, such as macaroni, while boys favor sugars and sweets.

Psychological Development

Whereas the behavior of the 11-year-old girl and that of the 12- and 13-year-old boy is generally stable and could be described as good-natured, this is not true for the 12- and 13-year-old girl. As hormones begin accelerating the 13-year-old's sexual development, her moods will fluctuate frequently. Inconsistent mood swings, tantrums and crying occur spontaneously "at the drop of a hat." She moves quickly between feeling jovial and being "down in the dumps."

The 12- and 13-year-old child is often introspective, easily offended and sensitive to criticism and desperately needs adults — especially parents and teachers — to show sensitivity.

The 12- and 13-year-old child tends to exaggerate simple occurrences and believes that personal problems and feelings are unique to self.

Social Development

The 12- and 13-year-old child is likely to have three or more media heroes and heroines.

The 12- and 13-year-old child depends on positive social relationships with members of the same sex, and experiences grave anxiety and disorientation when peer group ties are broken. This child is fiercely loyal to peer group values and often cruel or insensitive to those outside the peer group. The authority of the family is a critical factor in ultimate decisions.

The 12- and 13-year-old child is easily confused and frightened by settings that are large and impersonal, such as a new school.

The 12- and 13-year-old child is easily provoked. Humor, tears, aggression and shyness can all be experienced in a matter of moments.

The child is capable of sensing the thin edge between tolerance and rejection, and needs frequent affirmations from parents and peers about intrinsic worth.

Moral And Ethical Development

The 12- and 13-year-old child is essentially idealistic and has a strong sense of fairness in human relationships.

This child questions religious beliefs and is trying to decipher the nature and purpose of spiritual principles. This child is curious about the nature and habits of cults, customs, rituals and other seemingly mysterious or "different" ideologies. Exploring these subjects is often done unbeknownst to parents and teachers.

A PROFILE OF THE 14- AND 15-YEAR-OLD

Ask the average 14-year-old what is the most important feature of being that age, and she will tell you that having a best friend and being alike yet different from your same-sex peers is *very* important.

Ask the average 15-year-old what is the most important feature of being that age, and you will learn that it's to try those things considered to be passages to adulthood — drinking, drugs, sex and learning to drive.

This marks the end of preadolescence, and the beginning of adolescence. When viewing the scope of tasks that must be undertaken at this stage, it's no wonder that it's also a time of chaos. These are uncharted waters: All learning seems to be a process of trial and error. The awkwardness of physical growth is coupled with the psychic pain of feeling lonely and alone.

Intellectual Development

During this stage, roughly one-third of the brain is added on, once again expanding the adolescent capabilities and making possible:

- propositional thought
- consideration of ideas contrary to fact
- reasoning with hypotheses involving two or more variables
- mathematical logic expressed in symbols
- insight into the nuances of poetic metaphor and musical notation
- insight into attitudes, behaviors, values and moral and ethical decisions
- interpretation of larger concepts and generalizations of traditional wisdom expressed through sayings, axioms and aphorisms

The 14- and 15-year-old child shows a strong willingness to learn things he considers to be useful — that is, related to real-life problems.

The 14- and 15-year-old child is a curious learner, but considers academic goals secondary to personal-social concerns.

Physical Development

Physical maturation — internal and external — occurs at an amazing rate. Key hormones are at work now, moving this child from preadolescence to full-scale puberty. It's a time of enormous physical development in weight, height, heart size, lung capacity and muscular strength. Coping with the growing pains is traumatic. They are often tired and hungry. They can "feel" their bodies growing, and often complain about not wanting to go along for "Sunday drives" or long family excursions. Suggest that your child spend two hours in the car with you, and you'll have a debate on your hands. He will complain of joints aching, of headaches, of stomachaches and feeling carsick, all of which are possible.

Individual differences in physical development for boys and girls begin to slow. Girls tend to be taller than boys and are ordinarily more physically developed than boys, but it slowly begins to reverse itself.

This child's bone growth is still exceeding muscle development, resulting in poor coordination and awkwardness (especially for boys). Bones may lack the protection of covering muscles and supporting tendons.

Now adolescents move out of same-age, same-sex groups and into same-age, opposite-sex groups. If they experience rejection (unbearable teasing or ridicule, or repeated failure in social skills), they will turn their affection back again to adults, though not to parents. A coach, movie star or rock idol becomes the focus of affection. When teenagers feel secure again, they will venture back to the same-age, opposite-sex group.

The 14- and 15-year-old child desires to experience sex, but is largely unable to grasp the meaning of intimacy. Hormones moving the body toward sexual maturity are in motion, causing the child to *feel* sexual as well.

The 14- and 15-year-old child experiences fluctuations in basal metabolism that can cause extreme restlessness and equally extreme listlessness.

The child has a ravenous appetite and peculiar tastes; the child's taste buds discriminate likes or dislikes in foods based on what the body's hormones are needing to sustain it in this period of rapid growth. Proteins are favored by both males and females, though males also need and desire large amounts of starches.

Psychological Development

Building a solid sense of self and personal worth at this time is probably the toughest and most important task these children have ever faced.

Raging hormones cause fluctuating moods and erratic behavior; both boys and girls are prone to anxiety and fear contrasted with periods of bravado. Feelings shift between superiority and inferiority. It is not uncommon for this child to fluctuate between the behavior patterns characteristic of the previous stage of development (preadolescence) and this stage.

The 14- and 15-year-old child is easily offended and sensitive to criticism of personal shortcomings, yet exaggerates simple occurrences and believes that her personal problems, experiences and feelings are unique.

This child often feels self-conscious. Lowered self-esteem is normal as he attempts to search actively for his identity amid his own tempestuous and escalating state and rate of change. As he begins a serious search for a stable sense of self, "Who am I?" he turns to others for a sense of self and is vulnerable to their comments.

The 14- and 15-year-old child often has naive opinions and one-sided arguments. This child is egocentric; she likes to argue a point for the sheer sake of seeing if she can be convincing — *what* is being "debated" is beside the point!

The child has an emerging sense of humor based on increased intellectual ability to see abstract relationships, and can appreciate the double entendre.

The 14- and 15-year-old child is psychologically at risk. At no other point in human development is an individual likely to encounter so much diversity in relation to self and others.

Social Development

As the body moves closer to sexual maturity, sexual impulses are stronger. Adolescents' desires cause them to look at parents with renewed interest. This is a very frightening thing. They are impelled to move abruptly away from these threatening feelings by devaluing the parents, seeking shelter in anger, reaching out to substitute figures. One of the big tasks of adolescence is learning how to share love. With the advent of new feelings resulting from the natural sexual unfolding, teenagers need to figure out how they can love both the parents and a peer. Until now, the parents have received 100 percent. Obviously, teenagers will need to fetch some of it back from the parents in order to give it to a new boyfriend or girlfriend. Teenagers "in love" feel guilty about taking love away from what they owe or should be giving to their parents. This produces an unsettling feeling. Finding fault with parents helps teens justify the need to reduce the amount of love for one or the other. Being defensive then seems logical.

The 14- and 15-year-old child experiences traumatic conflicts due to conflicting loyalties to peer groups and family. This child may be rebellious toward parents but is still strongly dependent on parental values. He wants to make his own choices.

The 14- and 15-year-old child refers to peers as sources for standards and models of behavior. Media heroes and heroines are important in shaping both behavior and fashion.

The 14- and 15-year-old child becomes anxious and disoriented when peer group ties (friendships) are broken, is fiercely loyal to peer group values, and is sometimes cruel or insensitive to those outside the peer group.

The child acts out unusual or drastic behavior at times; and may be aggressive, daring, boisterous and argumentative all in the course of an hour.

The 14- and 15-year-old child does not trust adults who show a lack of sensitivity to her feelings and needs. She will challenge authority figures and will test the limits of set rules.

The 14- and 15-year-old child is socially at risk; adult values are largely shaped conceptually during adolescence; negative interactions with peers, parents and teachers may compromise ideals and commitments.

Moral And Ethical Development

The 14- and 15-year-old child is generally in awe of his or her expanding social and emotional awareness.

The 14- and 15-year-old child asks large questions about the meaning of life and is turned off by trivial adult responses.

The 14- and 15-year-old child is reflective, analytical and introspective about his or her thoughts and feelings.

The 14- and 15-year-old child confronts hard moral and ethical questions for which he or she is unprepared to cope.

The 14- and 15-year-old child is at risk in the development of moral and ethical choices and behaviors. Adolescents want to explore the moral and ethical issues they confront in the curriculum, in the media and in their daily interactions.

A Profile Of The 16- And 17-Year-Old

Ask the average 16-year-old what life is about and she will tell you that it is to experience or avoid sex and to have a car because it represents the freedom to exercise her newfound will.

Ask the average 17-year-old what life is about and he will tell you that it is total *stress*, hearing about the SAT college test and fearful about never making it to college or in life. Seventeen-year-olds begin to see themselves as either attending college or not. This "decision" influences their actions as a student.

Age 16 and 17 is a time of confusion and uncertainty, a time of duality. This physical and emotional jumble is hindered by the inability to look ahead and visualize the long-term effects of present behaviors. To tell this child who is skipping class that he might not be admitted to college or to tell the student who is not studying that she is cheating herself out of an education, is virtually meaningless. Today, this very moment, is what matters. Feelings of invulnerability and immortality lead youth to behave in reckless ways: The "It-can't-happen-to-me" attitude prevails as they drive too fast, have sexual experiences and experiment with alcohol and drugs. This is truly a time of identity crisis and an age of frustration.

Intellectual Development

This is not the most illuminating time of intellectual display. Seventeen-year-olds consider academic goals as secondary to the personal-social concerns that dominate their thoughts and activities. Learning about their world and how their friends are managing their lives takes priority over the school's curriculum. Learning is best motivated when it is considered to be useful. They enjoy using skills to solve real-life problems.

This child prefers active over passive learning experiences; and favors interaction with peers during learning activities.

The 16- and 17-year-old is able to experience the phenomenon of metacognition — the ability to know what one knows and does not know.

The 16- and 17-year-old is generally considered intellectually at risk because decisions have the potential to affect major academic values with lifelong consequences; yet it seems so difficult to get his attention — his awareness — in participating in these decisions and goals. He seems aloof and nonchalant.

Physical Development

Multiple hormones are responsible for mood swings, as well as changing general sexual feelings from ambivalent to specific. The goal is to experience intimacy; the self-esteem need is to belong. The task is to learn about oneself as a sexual being, (hers, femininity; his, masculinity) and how this is perceived by the opposite sex.

As a group the 16- and 17-year-olds generally have poorer physical health, lowered levels of endurance, strength and flexibility, and are heavier and unhealthier than the previous stage.

These teens experience fluctuations in basal metabolism which can cause extreme restlessness at times and equally extreme listlessness at other moments.

The 16- and 17-year-olds are physically at risk; major causes of death are homicide, suicide, accident and leukemia.

Psychological Development

It's not uncommon for these teens to experience feelings that range from invincible bravado to being confused, embarrassed, guilty, awkward, inferior, ugly and scared. They easily swing from childish and petulant behaviors to being sedate or acting rational or irrational, all in the same class hour; from intellectual to giddy, back and forth, as they try to figure out just who they are and what's going on. Often these swings come complete with easy tears and genuine sobs, great sensitivity, insights and sudden bursts of learning, flare-ups of anger or boisterous and unfounded giggles.

They see their parents as hopelessly old-fashioned and naive. This helps them complete the act of pulling away and establishes courage for asserting their independence — that is, toying with the idea that they could possibly manage life on their own. Most pronounced is tearing away from the same-sex parent — especially if the bond has been loving and close. To emotionally "leave" this loving parent, they'll have to make the parent wrong — how could they possibly want to leave someone wonderful? A great many 16-year-olds actually do leave home (or threaten to) for three or more days. This act is done out of frustration and is seen by teens as a way to coerce parents into providing them with more rope to be independent, to gain a bigger share of self-power in making more decisions on their own.

This adolescent desperately continues the search of individual uniqueness: "Who am I?"

Social Development

These teens need their friends, but will sabotage them if they appear to outdo them. Kristen roots for a friend out loud, but secretly wishes for her demise. Jack slaps his buddy on the back, but asks his buddy's girlfriend out at the same time.

They want total independence, yet are rarely capable of it. They don't really want to live without their parents, though they believe that their parents are a roadblock stifling their own life.

This teenager is fiercely loyal to peer group values.

Moral And Ethical Development

These adolescents ask in-depth and often unanswerable questions about the meaning of life; they expect absolute answers and are turned off by trivial adult responses.

These teens are reflective, analytical and introspective about thoughts and feelings. They want to explore the moral and ethical issues they confront in school, in the media and in the daily interactions they experience in their families and peer groups.

They are considered at risk in the development of moral and ethical choices and behaviors. Primary dependency on the influences of home and church for moral and ethical development seriously compromises adolescents for whom these resources are absent.

They want adults to understand their needs as budding adults rather than as children.

A Profile Of The 18-Year-Old

This age stands alone because there is really no other age like it. Ask the average 18-year-old what is important, and she will tell you that it is to be with friends, to be able to graduate from high school, and to learn how to be independent. This child is inwardly frightened and unsure. This stage of development is about establishing a sense of total independence, a desire to go from being dependent on others to being dependent on self, forcing the young person to confront some pretty big and frightening issues. The three tasks associated with this age are:

Determining vocation: "What am I going to do for work?" "Can I afford myself?" "What kind of lifestyle will I have?" Answering these questions gives meaning. Underlying this task is the self-esteem needed to be somebody — to experience positive feelings of strength, power and competence.

Establishing values: The goal is to sort out personal values, deciding which ones to keep and which ones to discard. Only in this way can the 18-year-old develop integrity. Perhaps most striking is his need to establish a workable and meaningful philosophy of life. Reevaluating his morality means searching for his own personal beliefs, complete with facing religious, ethical and value-laden ideologies. Developing personal convictions will be necessary, especially if there is conflict between what he believes, what he was raised with and what his friends find acceptable. Will he claim and stay committed to what is true for him? As he ponders the thought, he'll grasp and cling to sweeping idealisms, searching for what they must mean as he tries them on for size.

Establishing self-reliance: Accomplishing this task develops self-trust and confidence. The underlying need is to be oneself — looking at life through one's own lens and not through a role such as student, athlete, son or daughter and so on.

The 18-year-old faces the question of graduation from high school, and it can be especially jolting for two reasons: There is a sense of loss of friendships as classmates scatter across to college and training programs around the country; and second, there is the very real fear that the world is out there, and teachers, parents and others are expecting to pass on the baton to her and expecting her to take it and get going — on her own. It is a truly frightening time. What parents generally see one day is the cocky arrogance of the bold and confident 18-year-old, and the next day a mild-mannered, timid, shy child willing to carry in the groceries or join you for a leisurely walk. She is fearful and needs to step back for a moment as she once again gains her confidence to go forward in the outer world.

Intellectual Development

There are not necessarily any big breakthroughs here. The 18-year-old has learned to reason, analyze and question attitudes, assumptions and values, and he can transfer skills from one setting to the other. This is a stage of using his skills, not necessarily gaining new ones.

As in the other stages, the 18-year-old prefers active learning experiences and interaction with peers during these activities, especially as they relate to enjoy real-life problems.

The 18-year-old experiences the phenomenon of metacognition — the ability to know what one knows and does not know; it is at the heart of his worries — that he may not have spent enough time learning.

The 18-year-old faces decisions that affect major academic values with lifelong consequences.

Physical Development

The 18-year-old boy will grow about two or three inches and gain about ten pounds over the next two years. The 18-year-old girl will experience relatively little, if any, growth.

The 18-year-old now takes more personal responsibility for sexual behavior than in the past.

The 18-year-old, especially girls, experiences fluctuations in basal metabolism that can cause extreme restlessness at times and equally extreme listlessness at other times.

The 18-year-old is physically at risk. Major causes of death are homicide, suicide and car accidents.

Psychological Development

The 18-year-old is especially introspective as she continues her search for answers to questions about what she will do with her life.

The 18-year-old is psychologically at risk for feelings of alienation and loss of both adult and peer relationships.

Social Development

The 18-year-old experiences conflicts due to losing friends and knowing they must go (graduation). He also misses his parents, knowing that he will be leaving them.

The 18-year-old is less rebellious toward parents but still strongly dependent.

The 18-year-old is confused and frightened by the unknown future that lies ahead.

Moral And Ethical Development

These 18-year-olds confront hard moral and ethical questions, and now must act on moral and ethical choices and behaviors. They are reflective, analytical and introspective about thoughts and feelings. They greatly worry about their own emotional health; suicide among males and females of this age is high.

PART
FOUR

War And Peace: The Family

War And Peace:
The Family

 ### What Memories Will Your Teen Take From Your Family?

At its best, the family is the richest and most rewarding of social structures, fulfilling our deepest human needs for tenderness, sharing and love, and offering the greatest potential for human growth and nourishment. It can also create the most intense pain we feel, and can create emotional scars, from some of which we may never recover.

Many of us have wonderful memories of our own youth, memories of two-parent families whose members pulled together and supported one another. Some of us probably can remember the family gathered at the dinner table. We laughed together, made jokes and maybe even took votes on which television program to watch. Now the typical American home — should everyone even be home at the same time — is bristling with compact-disc players, multiple televisions, telephones, video machines, computers and personal cassette players. What we once watched, listened to and discussed together, we now do alone in separate rooms.

Imagine your teenager 20 years from now, recalling her teenage years in the bosom of her family. Will she see a loving, supporting family scene, or will the picture be one of pandemonium or hostility? Will she see a family unit sitting at a table having dinner together, or individual members microwaving a frozen dinner of their choice and then going their own ways? Most important, will she get the same warm, secure feeling you probably have from your own memories, or will her stomach tighten from feelings of anxiety? What kind of memories of her family are you building for your teenager?

As we learned from the 1992 presidential election, the family unit is multi-faceted, including a single-parent family, a two-mother family and so forth. In advertisements for a study *Newsweek* was conducting in search of the "happy family," the magazine stated, "The family is changing. Once upon a time families were all alike. Happy. But today even the happy family isn't the same . . . the family just isn't what it used to be. Today the family has become a barometer of the social, psychological and sexual upheaval that's shaking up our nation." If *Newsweek* is correct, this could explain why more and more families come in all shapes and sizes — married families, unmarried families, single-parent families, teenage-parent families, same-sex families, stepfamilies and midcareer-parent families.

If the Waltons were around now, would they be living in a condo, taking separate vacations and seeing a family therapist?

Today's family has been put to the test of surviving through new family dynamics, rapidly changing social mores and the ever-increasing availability of stimuli outside the home — many of which have rendered some former family interactions extinct. The high-tech information age we live in, for example, has allowed us to lead lives that are bigger, faster and more colorful, without necessarily bringing us closer together. No family is exempt from the influence of social change, and no doubt each will experience stress as it goes about "being a family."

A child often acts as a good barometer of what is taking place in the home. When family problems or stress occur, a child may act out or demonstrate how he is feeling through his behavior. For example, a 16-year-old boy who has not been helped to cope with his parents' divorce may vent that anger at school by getting into fights with other students. A 13-year-old who is feeling anxiety with a stepparent relationship might develop physical symptoms of that stress, such as stomachaches or headaches, or, if long-lasting, ulcers.

Sometimes we focus too narrowly on the behavior of the child and fail to identify its origin. A teenager who is continually getting into fights in school may inappropriately be seen as "going through a rebellious stage," while the real source of trouble may lie elsewhere. Generally, behavior is a symptom of something larger.

Assessing Family Stress

A child typically vents stress and pressure by misbehaving, withdrawing, suddenly doing poorly in school or developing psychosomatic problems. The following questions can be used as guidelines to determine the nature and intensity of stress being felt.

- Is the origin of the stressor from within the family system (mother goes back to work) or from outside the family (loss of a job)?
- Does the impact of the stressor extend directly to all family members (divorce) or to only some members (adolescent has argument with friend)?

- Is the onset of the stressor very sudden (illness) or does it emerge gradually (pregnancy)?
- Is the length of adjustment to the stressor short-term (child starts school) or long-term (terminal illness)?
- Can the stressor be expected (child becoming an adolescent) or does it occur unpredictably (an auto accident)?
- Does the family believe the stressor is one that can be solved (adjusting to a new home) or is it beyond control (inflation's effect on family finances)?

Asking yourself these questions will help you explore the changes and events that have occurred within your family in the recent past, and prevent emotional over-reacting or miscommunication between you and your child.

Three broad categories of stressors can cause problems for teenagers in families. These include the teenager's rapid growth and development, external factors (especially a parental separation, divorce or remarriage), and family dynamics (the way the teenager experiences the stressor). Let's look at these now.

GROWING PAINS

As children progress through the various developmental stages of infancy, childhood, adolescence and young adulthood, their behavior and emotions naturally change. These affect not only themselves but everyone else in the family as well. The last section examined some of the important developmental stages for adolescents, and the tasks and demands inherent in those stages. These are very natural and common events, such as identity crises in the adolescent, that can contribute to varying degrees of stress within the family. When parents and their children are aware of the changes and the likely types of behaviors to expect within each of these stages, the family is better equipped to cope effectively with the stress that arises.

Of course, it is not only the adolescent who shows the stress of proceeding through the life cycle. Parents also go through the stages of young, middle and older adulthood, as we saw in Chapter 4. The needs of family members may overlap and complement one another, or they may conflict or compete with one another. Parents may be going through one kind of crisis stage, while the adolescent works through another. Often parents are heard to say, "I wish I had been more settled in my career (or my marriage, or with myself) when my children were teenagers. They needed me more at that time than any other. I just wasn't able to give them what I am able to now that I'm more established (or more secure, or self-assured)." In recent years we have become more aware and more sensitive to the key emotional and social crises each of us experience throughout the stages of our lives.

Coping with the changes inherent over the normal life cycle, then, is a normal strain. Just as with all stress, it requires adjustment and adaptation by family members.

External Factors

A second major cause of anxiety and stress for teenagers is caused by events outside their control. For example:

- The family moves to a new city.
- A parent changes jobs.
- A parent loses a job.
- A previously nonworking parent acquires a job.
- The parents separate, divorce or remarry.

This final factor is a dominant stress for the teenager. Adolescents today have a good chance of living in a home in which parents separate, divorce or one or both remarry. These factors are wholly outside the teens' control. How the family deals with these kinds of situations determines the level of stress teenagers experience as a result of it.

SEPARATION AND DIVORCE

Only a few generations ago, divorce was considered tragic. No one talked about those who got divorced; family members who disgraced their relatives in this way were sometimes disowned. Now society accepts divorce almost casually. When I asked five-year-old Jared how his mother and Leo (her live-in lover of ten months) were, he replied, "Oh, they got a divorce." What Jared meant was, they were no longer living together. Unfortunately, it was less than a year-and-a-half ago that his parents divorced. Jared is accustomed to divorce — a veteran at knowing how briefly relationships can endure. Increasingly, children will be victims of their parents' divorce. The number of youngsters affected by divorce has more than doubled. Each year nearly 60 percent of the teenage population experiences the effects of their parents' separation and divorce.

Divorce is difficult for all children, but it is *devastating* to teenage children. Much of the stress an adolescent suffers in separation and divorce is a result of tearing apart the once-existing mother/father love relationship. Children and parents have been separated, either totally or partially, depending on the custody and visitation arrangements. Being separated from brothers and sisters is an additional stressor, as is being disconnected from a set of grandparents. Mourning these losses takes time for teenagers. A great deal of commitment is required on the part of adults in helping teenagers cope with fears and feelings, and to adjust to a new reality. The impact of separation and divorce on a teenager is compounded when:

- The adolescent has recently undergone other loss (for example, a recent move to a new city, enrollment in a new school, a best friend has moved away or any other traumatic experience requiring the child to make major transitions).
- The adolescent receives no professional help to work through the loss.

- Parents tell their teenager the severity of the marital problems only after one or the other parent moves out of the house.
- Parents don't allow the adolescent to express his feelings about the new circumstances of his life.

Young people feel torn apart by the parting of their parents. An adolescent facing this family crisis alone, or feeling alone, is particularly vulnerable because it comes at a time when he is evaluating the desirability of relationships for himself. He may be wary of marriage and of having children, and feel doubtful about subjecting children to what he himself has gone through. ("I would never want to put a child through this.") Sometimes an adolescent feels guilt — that he is responsible for the family's conflict.

THE SINGLE-PARENT FAMILY

By 1990, 11.1 million children — one out of every four — were living with only one parent. Single-parent families are most likely to be headed by separated or divorced women. The family life of teenagers in the single-parent family varies a great deal. The teenager may be abandoned (emotionally or physically) and left alone to work out her own crises. She may be treated by the parent as a friend, someone whom the adult can confide in. She may be expected to accept her parent's actions and to condone them without question. The single parent may somehow be impervious to what such adult laissez-faire behavior does to the teenager. "My dad and I check in every Monday morning," says 16-year-old Tony. "I don't ask about his life, and he doesn't ask about mine." "My mother and I double date," says 17-year-old Rebecca.

Some teenagers find living in a single parent household better than living in a two-parent home. As Brandon comments, "It's much easier to get one adult to make a decision than it is for two. When my parents were married, they would fight over making a decision. It got so bad that I quit asking because I was afraid I'd start an argument between them."

FAMILY DYNAMICS

The third category of family stressors includes the physical and emotional difficulties that may be experienced by a family member, either parent or child. The most prominent stressors in this category are sibling stress (especially where physical or emotional handicaps are involved), scapegoating, family violence, and drug and alcohol abuse. (The use of drugs and alcohol are discussed in Chapter 14.)

The way one family member copes with any stress greatly affects other family members as well. When adolescents develop formal operational thought, for example, each family member is forced to adapt to the adolescent's new demand to question everything about family functioning, much as family members have to adapt when an infant is teething. Siblings fear that the adolescent is "unhappy" or "insane," while other children in the family withdraw into their own worlds. Just as an adolescent's sullenness or moodiness may be felt by the other siblings and by parents, an argument between parents is felt by the adolescent as frightening. Similarly, the tensions experienced by a parent of a child who is under the influence of alcohol or drugs may be felt by other family members.

SIBLING STRESS

A teenager, while loyal to a brother or sister, is more concerned with how the sibling makes her feel than with how the sibling feels. A brother or sister who does something wrong or is somehow "different" can be a major source of stress for a teenager. A teenager may be embarrassed by the appearance of a sibling. "My sister wears so much makeup. She looks cheap. My friends look at her and then me and wonder. I wish she'd stop painting her face and fingernails in such wild colors."

A teenager may also be embarrassed by the actions of a sibling. Thomas and his brother were good friends. Because they were just one year apart in age, they had always shared many of the same friends. When his younger brother was hospitalized for drug addiction, Thomas showed enormous strain. He began doing poorly in school, stopped bringing friends home and started to become a recluse. His once outgoing and bubbly personality became sullen and introspective, and he began a pattern of over-eating. "I'm so embarrassed," said Thomas. "Now instead of the popular kids wanting to be my buddies, all the druggies hang around me. My brother has ruined my social life at school."

A sibling who drinks or does drugs can be a major source of stress for an adolescent on several fronts. First, the teenager is embarrassed by his sibling. He may be at a party and see his brother drunk and obnoxious, making a fool of himself. Second, he may resent having to be responsible for his brother. No 16-year-old likes to have to get out of bed and drive over to a party to pick up an older brother who is too drunk to drive. Third, he may worry that he too will take up drinking to excess or will take drugs he won't be able to stop using. Fourth, he may feel that he has let his parents down. Perhaps he is the older sibling and should have kept a better eye on the younger one. And fifth, he may feel that he is supposed to keep the sibling's problem a secret. Having to hide a sibling's problem from parents makes it even worse.

Even though children may be accepting of individual differences — including their own siblings — we underestimate their need and their ability to discuss how each is viewed and accepted by the other.

COPING WITH THE PHYSICAL OR EMOTIONAL ILLNESS OF A FAMILY MEMBER

"Riding the school bus with my ten-year-old retarded sister is the most humiliating experience I've ever known," said Jean. "Other kids make fun of her appearance. She stares blankly into space and chews on her tongue, rocking back and forth. I don't mind going to the same school with her, and I love her as my sister, but dealing with the comments of other kids is more than

I can handle." To make matters worse, she carries around the burden of guilt. It's one thing to avoid a sister who is just a normal pain in the neck, but quite another to avoid a sister who has a special problem. Feeling awkward themselves, most adolescents will be cruel and insensitive to differences; and worse, they will voice their insensitivity. This can be a major stressor for the teenager with a physically handicapped sibling.

SCAPEGOATING

Another problem is scapegoating. "He hit me first!" "I didn't do it. Barney did it!" "Yeah, it was Barney's fault!" "But Mom, Ellen made me do it!" "Well, everybody else did it!" At some stage in life, nearly every child goes through the "not me" phase, blaming her actions on someone or something else. This scapegoating can take place within a family.

Sometimes a family unconsciously scapegoats a teenager as the cause of its problems. The adolescent can develop increased feelings of rejection and alienation from other family members. The young person who either assumes the responsibility for family problems or who feels he is to blame has a tremendous burden to carry. All too often, our children tend to bear the brunt of our fears and our inabilities to accept responsibility for our actions. Our children become the scapegoats for these frustrations. As parents we must try to avoid these incidents and face up to the situations that we have created, or that have been dealt to us, without placing the blame on our teenagers.

Fifteen-year-old Janet, a cheerleader, spends most of her free time practicing for her school's games. Janet's mom has diabetes and, depending on her blood sugar level, she is either relaxed or extremely nervous and volatile. In addition, her mother is unhappily married and derives most of the joy in her life from her relationships with her daughters.

Last Thursday, Janet rushed home from school, grabbed a snack and was heading for her room. Her mother, feeling tired and forlorn, asked Janet about her plans for the evening. When Janet described her plans, her mother pointed her finger at her and began accusing her of being impertinent. Suddenly, she began gasping for her breath. "You're going to be the death of me. Can't you see I'm sick? Must you always do what you want to do?"

Clearly Janet had served as a scapegoat for her mother's loneliness and inability to deal with her own illness. Had the mother been in control of her emotions and had a handle on her condition, she would not have blamed Janet for her illness. What she really wanted was her daughter's time and attention. Instead, she tried to manipulate Janet by blaming her for her problems. Accusations like those made by Janet's mother can cause teenagers to shun parents rather than grow closer. Janet's case is not uncommon. Teenagers are often blamed for many of their parents' burdens.

Sixteen-year-old Patrick is an average student. In the evenings he works at a local hamburger shop. He is saving up for a car and for his college tuition. Patrick's dad has a drinking problem, and as a result, he is often dismissed from the various jobs he manages to be hired for. When the father isn't working, he focuses his negative attention on Patrick. No matter what Patrick does, it doesn't seem to be good enough for his father. "You look terrible!" "Get a haircut!" "This is the best grade you can get?" "No, you can't borrow the car! I'm not going to provide you and your buddies with a car to go off to some side street with a six-pack!" Patrick does not drink and rightly feels his father's accusations are unfair. He feels the impossibility of getting his father's affection. Patrick is clearly the scapegoat for his father's inability to confront his own alcoholism and accompanying feelings of failure.

Not all cases are as complex as these, but in many families the guilt syndrome is common. As parents we need to allow for our own bad days, our own fears and failures, and not blame them — directly or indirectly — on our children. Such blame would only further alienate our children from us. We would be teaching them how not to accept responsibility instead of helping them to admit their strengths and weaknesses so they can develop a stronger sense of self.

FAMILY VIOLENCE

A teenager in a family with a history of alcoholism, battering or sexual victimization faces duress that will last a lifetime. A young person in such a family is always in a bind: He can't go outside for help without betraying his own family and exposing family secrets. The young person is often afraid of retaliation, or at least of further rejection from other family members, and may grow up with a distorted view of what loving and caring mean. In such a family, whether the adolescent is a direct victim or not, the models of behavior are confusing and damaging.

There is a strong correlation between the adolescent's traumatic experiences and the gradual self-perception as a worthless and unlovable person. The escape from these feelings takes many routes, most notably that of alcohol and drug abuse, truancy, arson, fighting, stealing, cheating, thrill-seeking, sexual promiscuity, pregnancy or running away from home. These escape routes often lead the teenager into problems more overwhelming than any he was trying to escape. They are signals of a need for help. If there is no help and family support, the intensity of the emotional trauma the adolescent experiences is often repeated in his own family when he reaches adulthood. Research shows that children of violent families have a greater chance of victimizing their families as well.

THE CAPABLE FAMILY: RESISTING STRESS

Ah, for the illusions of the good old days of 1950's television, the days when every family had a mother who cooked in high heels and pearls and a kindly father who was all knowing. In just 30 minutes once a week, the "perfect parents" could solve their children's problems, no matter what they were. Today you and I are lucky to get our teenagers to listen to us for 30 minutes, let alone accept our advice!

Alas, families are not perfect. Families differ in the extent to which they promote the development of coping skills in children. We sometimes seem to create more problems than we solve, and give our children more stress than support.

Research has found that children who are good copers tend to have parents who are warm, loving, supportive, conscientious and good at communicating. They respect their child's independence, yet hold firm to their convictions about what is right, explaining their reasons to the child and insisting on proper behavior. This is an *authoritative* style of childrearing, in contrast to the authoritarian (controlling without warmth) and to the permissive (noncontrolling but warm) styles. The maximum of support with the maximum of challenge defines the authoritative style.

Families that produce effective, competent children often follow this principle, whether they are aware of it or not. They neither maintain strict control nor allow their children total freedom. They're always opening doors for their children — then encouraging them to move on and grow. This combination of support and challenge is essential if adolescents are to develop into capable young adults.

Along with teaching a child general coping techniques, you and your family can help in specific ways.

Supervision

The happiest teenagers are those who have supervision. Parents often make the mistake of thinking that teenagers are old enough to fend for themselves. While that may be true for short periods, it is not fair for your adolescent to be expected to "fend for himself." If your work schedule does not permit your child to be supervised, one solution is to change your schedule to build in greater flexibility or to provide other adult supervision. As do families with young children, families with teenagers will need to take into account job relocation, work shifts and work responsibilities. While that sounds unfair, we need to keep in mind that teenagers require some form of supervision, too.

Quality And Quantity Of Activities

Helping adolescents acquire a healthy and zestful life experience requires an approach to living that maximizes rational self-fulfillment and minimizes stress and burnout. This includes fostering and teaching adolescents enjoyment of the love and support of family and friends, enjoyment of constructive and productive work, the importance of spiritual fulfillment and the added self-fulfillment through meeting new and exciting growth challenges.

Effective Skills In Family Functioning

You may feel that your family needs to acquire skills that can allow it to become functional. Support groups for families provide a good outlet for teenagers to share their family experiences. The purpose of a group is to provide an opportunity to share feelings, frustrations and triumphs as well as strategies useful in coping with many kinds of stress. Although the family may, in some cases, need special therapeutic attention, just having the opportunity to share feelings with other families in discussion or therapy groups or to learn from informational materials is proving to be extremely helpful. Mutual support groups and courses for stepparents are emerging throughout the United States, and organizations are forming to act as support networks for families and to provide education for the community and professionals who work with families. You will find that a number of local organizations offer counseling and support for members of families. You may want to identify these and determine how they may be of use to your family.

RESILIENCE

One final bit of good news: What you always knew in your heart of hearts — that a loving family produces a loving and kind child — has been proven to be true by research. In a study spanning nearly 20 years, psychologist Emmy E. Werner attempted to identify some of the individual, familial and cultural factors that may increase or decrease a child's risk of developing serious problems in adolescence. Werner and a team of physicians, nurses, social workers and psychologists followed the development of more than 800 "high risk" youth (children of divorced parents and troubled parents) through young adulthood. Nearly one-third of the children in the study experienced a difficult and turbulent adolescence. Of those, one in five developed serious problems by age 17. By late adolescence, 15 percent had a record of serious or repeated delinquency.

But most of the children in the study did not get into trouble. The researchers were deeply impressed by the resiliency of the overwhelming majority of the youth. Even one-fourth of the high-risk youth, those whose records showed at least four risk factors by age ten, developed into stable, mature and competent young adults. What's more, they expressed a high degree of faith in the effectiveness of their own actions.

How did these resilient teenagers differ from their more troubled peers? Two characteristics emerged: They were from smaller families with fewer siblings to compete for attention, and they had caregiving responsibilities.

Basically, caregiving is lending emotional and physical help to someone who wants or needs it. Because of the adolescent's caregiving responsibilities (they were held responsible for helping other family members, it was looked on as a part of their duties), they were able to get the attention of other caregivers — grandparents, siblings, babysitters, parents and so forth. The emotional support of these caregivers was a major protective factor in the midst of chronic poverty or serious disruptions of the family. These adolescents reported a higher degree of satisfaction in helping others.

Other studies confirm similar results. A 40-year Harvard study, which started in the 1950s in an effort to understand juvenile delinquency, followed the lives of nearly 500 teenage children, many from impoverished or broken homes. When they were compared at middle age, one fact stood out: Regardless of intelligence, family income, ethnic background or amount of education, those who had responsibilities in shared home and work projects as children — even simple household chores — enjoyed happier and more productive lives than those who had not. When these individuals reached adulthood, they were better off than their childhood playmates who had been less industrious. They earned more money and had more job satisfaction. They had better marriages and closer relationships with their children. They were healthier and lived longer. Most of all, they were happier — much happier.

Feeling Lonely,
Being Alone

 One of the most emotionally wrenching scenes in any cartoon is the one where the mother bird, wiping a tear from her eye, kicks her baby birds out of the nest. Because the birds are old enough and strong enough, they can fly on their own. As parents, we have to face the same realities. We all know that one day our children will leave our nests and that their doing so is necessary and proper. Of course, we would never think of kicking them out before they are able to thrive on their own. Yet that is just what some parents do, by alienating them or actually making their children leave home.

"Increasingly, it is the parents who toss the children out," says Nick Clark, director of Alternative House, a runaway center in McLean, Virginia. He sees "throwaway children," whose parents drop them off at Alternative House, telling them, "I can't handle you. You're too much." While the public may have the idea that it is rebellious older teens who are kicked out by their parents, Clark notes that the average age of children coming to the center is 12.

According to data compiled by the House Select Committee of Children, Youth and Families, admissions of children under 18 to inpatient psychiatric services has more than doubled. In the '80s adolescent admissions to private psychiatric hospitals increased more than 350 percent. While many of those admitted were there for treatment of drug abuse and as a result of suicide attempts, others were confined for value afflictions such as "conduct disorder" and "adolescent adjustment disorder." According to committee testimony, most children were coerced into entering hospitals by their parents who were seeking relief from uncontrollable adolescents. Hospital officials say that up to 40 percent of the hospitalization cases were found to be "unnecessary."

Not to be wanted physically or emotionally is a terrible feeling.

There Are All Sorts Of Ways To Give Up On Your Children

Children who have been "divorced" by their parents have intense feelings of alienation, of being unwanted and unloved. Leslie, a 12-year-old second-time runaway and drug user for two years, says, "I really don't care about my parents anymore. Why should I? It only hurts. Why should I go home? Why bother them when they don't need me?" Many adolescents run away from home in their attempt to overcome or overthrow the feelings produced by alienation. According to the Senate Subcommittee on Juvenile Justice, more than one million children run away from home every year. Unable to take care of themselves, these runaways are almost certain to encounter severe problems.

John Rabun, manager of the Exploited Child unit in Louisville, Kentucky, said, "Adolescents abused or neglected at home become easy prey for adults who exploit them through pornography and prostitution, and many of them are murdered." Lois Lee, director of Children of the Night, a program that employs 20 counselors to help youths break out of prostitution, believes that many children are pushed out of their homes by uncaring parents and end up sleeping in parks or abandoned buildings. "These kids develop families on the street," she says. "They'll form groups and look out for each other."

"The children themselves recognize that they need help," says Ralph Alsopp, an Atlanta, Georgia, psychologist. "Teenagers feel helpless, not in control of their lives. Their parental support structures are falling away. They are lonely and they are alone."

These lonely children will reach out to whatever and whoever are available. The Runaway Hotline, established in 1973, fields over 600 calls each day from children who have left home.

Alienation is a pervasive, lingering feeling of being unwanted. These adolescents feel uncertain of their acceptance or status within groups that are important, such as family, friends and schoolmates. Youths who are alienated feel out of sync with others; their lives feel pointless. They don't see much chance that things will improve in the future.

Alienated adolescents are fatalistic in their understanding of circumstances; they see no hope for improvement. A jaded Michelle, age 16, related her feelings of despair this way: "I'll never know the good life. Many of the hopes and dreams of kids my age will never be realized simply because of the numbers of us. And besides, if you do manage to get into college, who can find a decent job? And then you'll probably die from job-related stress. So why bother?"

Even the support of family can seem dim: "My parents are so wrapped up in growing up themselves and working out their own problems that they don't have time for me. They are never around. I don't ever want to have kids. I would never put them through it. I don't even want to be an adult. They're so careless with people," said 16-year-old Dana.

This unending emotional isolation and loneliness can lead to problem behavior. Psychologists and child behavior specialists have linked eating disorders like anorexia nervosa and bulimia or obesity, promiscuity, drug and alcohol abuse, depression, and acts of theft and arson to adolescents feeling alienated within their families.

FEELINGS OF ALIENATION BEGIN IN THE HOME

Scientists who study human behavior and development found that the most causative factor in alienation is the home. We tend to see parents as being either good or bad without fully taking into account the circumstances in their lives. The circumstances surrounding the lives of today's families are different from those of a decade ago, making it less likely that significant time will be devoted exclusively to each youngster.

The physical or emotional absence of a parent can have a significant effect on the mental and emotional health of the child. Unfortunately, the number of such parents is increasing. There are five million "latchkey" children in the United States. According to Harold Hodgkinson, a Washington-based researcher who has been studying the problem for more than a decade, many of these children think of home as a "dangerous, frightening place, particularly if there are no other children in the home." They "check in" with parents by phone (or fax!), spend many hours watching TV, and have to make decisions about knocks on the door and phone calls from strangers. While some children may in fact benefit from having family responsibilities and time alone, many others suffer greatly from this unwanted experience.

Few parents are ogres who try to segregate their children emotionally, who intentionally set out to make their children feel isolated, unwanted, alone. Parents who accidentally cause these feelings in their children may be loving, caring people who are consumed by busy lives and problems of their own. Thus alienation can be considered a temporary marker, reflecting the increasing numbers of dual-career parents, single parents and stepparents, all of whom may be experiencing any number of crises on a regular basis.

The following vignettes illustrate the circumstances surrounding the lives of two adolescents. Pay attention to the important differences that make one home environment more prone to alienation than the other.

RUTH

Ruth is 13 and in the ninth grade. She has two older sisters, both away at college. Like her sisters, Ruth grew up coming home from school to "table talks," parent-daughter chats at the kitchen table. Ruth, her sisters and their parents always enjoyed the closeness of these few minutes, times when the day's happenings could be shared. Everyone felt close, accepted, loved.

Things have changed now. Ruth's parents have divorced. With two children in college, Ruth's mom has had to go back to work to help pay expenses. Because her mother frequently travels in her job, Ruth lives with her father and his new wife. Ruth's stepmother also works full-time. Ruth and her stepmother are not close; the stepmother doesn't feel it's her place to provide the parenting and has not formed a close bond with Ruth. Ruth's father works long hours and doesn't get home until well after seven-thirty. By that time Ruth has had dinner on her own and is buried in her room with her records or homework. Ruth is lonely even though she is not alone all the time. From her perspective, no one takes the time to listen or care anymore.

Ruth has become sullen and withdrawn. She is often rude and angry at her stepmother. Her father resents Ruth's behavior, thinking that Ruth should be a little more grown-up and accept the fact that his new wife needs his time too. Ruth spends every other weekend with her mother, who realizes that her daughter is lonely and feels guilty about it. She has given Ruth a number of things, such as her own phone, TV and stereo. Hasn't her working given Ruth a lot of nice things? Ruth and her mother know they are losing the closeness that they both value, but neither is certain what to do about it.

DAVID

David, also 13, is an only child. He is happy, easy going and spunky. David's parents are divorced, and he lives with his mother. Although David's mother works full-time, she has arranged her schedule so that she is home when her son returns from school. If she is unable to come home at the regular time, she arranges for a neighbor who is retired to look after David until she returns. David is very fond of the neighbor and considers it a treat when he is left in charge.

Even though it's just the two of them, David and his mother are fond of talking about themselves as a family. Their family evenings together have become a ritual. Homework is always done while dinner is being prepared. This also makes it easy for David's mom to assist him if he needs help. There is a family rule of no television during the weekdays; instead, special TV programs are taped and become a part of the weekend fun. David and his mother have dinner in the dining room. The dinner hour is a pleasant time during which the two exchange day-to-day happenings and discuss any concerns David or his mother may be experiencing. Afterwards, David helps with dishes and completes any undone homework. He is not an outstanding student, but he tries hard and is a favorite of his teachers.

David also helps with other household chores and works in the yard on weekends. Additionally, he spends three or four hours doing handy jobs for two neighbors. He is saving up for a special soccer camp he wants to attend at a local university this summer. His father said he would contribute half of the expenses. David is excited about the camp, and the goal of earning his share of the expenses is very motivating for him. Having these responsibilities has helped David understand how important it is to be dependable. This shows in his relationship with people; his friends know they can count on him.

David's favorite pastime is soccer. He plays for the school team, and is involved in a league as well. He receives a lot of encouragement from his mother and father, who often go to his games on the weekends. David's teachers describe him as an outgoing, well-liked, happy young man who is interested in his school and family.

How do these two scenarios differ?

WHAT'S THE DIFFERENCE?

All three of Ruth's parents are too busy to parent. Her mother is sensitive, but she feels paralyzed about acting. David's parents have found a way to successfully co-parent. They have made an extra effort to be sensitive to the needs of their teenager, and to create an environment that allows the family to function as a unit while still allowing each member to be an individual.

Today it's common for both parents to be working outside the home. Statistics show that 69 percent of all married women and 78 percent of all single parents work outside the home. These statistics bear on childrearing and thus become a family issue, not the "working woman's fault." The fact that so many families have both parents working has profound implications for the way families function, for better or worse. The determining factor is how well a given family can cope with pressures and demands.

As parents try to coordinate the disparate demands of family and jobs, family life can become more hectic and stressful. Tasks that were once taken for granted, such as meal preparation, shopping and cleaning can become major challenges. Dealing with these challenges may sometimes take precedence over the family's equally important childrearing, educational and nurturing roles.

The well-being of children is threatened when external havoc becomes internal, first for the parents and then for their children. The demands of a pressurized office may make the needs of a family seem secondary, though you don't need to be working away from home to make your child feel alienated. The stress and pressure that parents are under from their work often makes it very difficult for them to be sensitive to the changes a young-ster is experiencing or to deal with problems as part of a family unit. The guilt that a parent feels with the recognition that she is placing work before family can lead to increased stress, exacer-bating an already tense situation.

At the end of a stressful day, it is all too common for parents to react to adolescents in an abrasive and autocratic way ("You do as I tell you and don't hassle me!") simply because they are too tired to take the time to solve the problem democratically. The children feel inadequate, unloved, unwanted, and when they cannot get their needs for love and acceptance met in the family group, they will turn to their peer group for support and understanding.

A desire to belong to a peer group is natural and not in itself an indication of a problem. However, when an adolescent begins to rely on it for the emotional support and nurturing he normally would get from his parents, destructive behavior can result. Re-search shows that over-reliance on peers is a strong predictor of problem behavior in adolescents. Without constructive outlets for energy, such as family outings, play-time, athletics, projects, chores or hobbies, and in the absence of parental guidance, the youngster attempts desperately to be included in a group. This need for acceptance may cause the adolescent to do anything it takes to be "one of the gang."

ADOLESCENT SUICIDE: THE DARKER SIDE OF ALIENATION

Suicide is a topic most of us would prefer to avoid. But we cannot ignore the subject when statistics indicate that the number of teenage suicides represents a national epidemic and that the numbers of suicides continue to rise each year. Every 83 minutes in the United States, a teenager commits suicide. Each year 500,000 others attempt suicide (reported cases) and nearly 300,000 others contemplate it. Since 1965, the incidence of reported suicide has increased over 300 percent. (Note that while car crashes are the method used most often by older youths committing suicide, such suicides are not reflected in the preceding figures.) Suicide now ranks as the third major cause of death for adolescents, ahead of deaths due to alcohol, drug abuse and disease.

We must confront our fears and reach out to our children. It is imperative that we, and our adolescents, understand the dynamics of suicide, its causes, the complex emotions involved and ways to cope with suicidal feelings. Parents need to be aware of the many subtle ways teenagers can be made to feel unloved and unwanted. If and when death, divorce, alcohol or drug abuse, or suicide occur in the family, we must ease the hardship these may cause. Adolescents must be made aware of the importance of telling others if they suspect someone they know has become suicidal, or if they themselves are feeling despondent. The more we know, the better able we are to understand and therefore prevent suicide. If we can understand the causes of suicidal feelings and learn what to do in such an emergency, we may be able to help avert a tragedy.

Suicide is not an ordinary response to pressure. Attempted suicide is a scream for help, a desperate cry for needed change. Healthy, emotionally secure teenagers can deal with the stressors of daily frustrations and periodic trauma. Adolescents who are thinking about killing themselves, however, are beset by seemingly insoluble problems and are trying desperately to get away from feeling unbearable emotional pain. They feel helpless to change things and unable to identify those who could help them overcome the hopelessness and despair they feel. Adolescents who feel little control over their environment may experience their families as unavailable, rejecting or overprotective.

WHAT MAKES OUR CHILDREN SO DESPERATELY UNHAPPY?

What leads young people who "have everything to live for" want to give up everything? What makes some adolescents want to end their lives? Many adolescents are dealing with various levels of alienation and depression a great deal of the time. Often your child may have difficulty identifying the underlying causes of his depression. He only knows that he feels bad or lonely and doesn't know what to do about it. These feelings can give rise to suicidal behaviors. A young person may have had very negative personal experiences in reaching out to friends or adults, either in his family or in school. These experiences may account for his holding his feelings inside. In order to reach out for help, an adolescent may have to expose family secrets, such as alcoholism, violence or sexual victimization. He is often afraid of retaliation, or at least of further rejection by other family members.

Teenagers who feel little satisfaction or reward in life become depressed. How they deal with this depression is basic to their survival. Mounting frustrations can lead to an increasing and intense sense of helplessness to change the situation. In the midst of this agonizing complexity and without the experience to understand what is happening, a young person may begin to feel there is no way out. Suicide becomes one of the options. The child does not want to die, but cannot think of any other way to stop the pain.

As 16-year-old Kindra, who attempted suicide by drug overdose, said, "I thought everyone would be better off if I killed myself. You think that because you're miserable, you're making everyone else miserable. You think no one would care if you killed yourself."

Not everyone reacts to painful situations in the same way. Some adolescents are more resourceful than others. Some are more sensitive than others to emotional pain. Suicidal adolescents are not weaker or somehow less capable than others; for whatever reasons, some situations are harder to cope with for some people at certain times in their lives. This is why the incidence of suicide is prevalent in families of all types.

While it is true that suicidal feelings most often develop in a person who is deeply depressed, the fact that a child is depressed does not mean she will become suicidal. Any of us at a particular time may find the emotional pain we are experiencing absolutely intolerable. In that short period we might impulsively make a suicide attempt; if the suicide attempt is unsuccessful, we often later regret having made it. Taking drugs and alcohol in excess can exaggerate painful feelings, and a person who otherwise would not go that far might attempt suicide.

DISTRESS SIGNALS:
THE WARNING SIGNS OF SUICIDE

All too often, even the seemingly well-adjusted child becomes a victim. The greatest danger for any parent with regard to adolescent suicide is the belief that "my child would never do that." Most parents of teenagers who have successfully or unsuccessfully attempted suicide are initially surprised that their children have moved in this direction. On closer analysis, however, parents often realize that there were warning signs but they were unaware of the significance of those signs. Danger signals include:

- Preoccupation with themes of death; expression of suicidal thoughts.
- Giving away prized possessions; making a will or other "final arrangements."
- Changes in sleeping patterns (too much or too little).
- Sudden and extreme changes in eating habits; losing or gaining weight.
- Changes in school performance (lowered grades, cutting classes, dropping out of activities).
- Personality changes, such as nervousness, outbursts of anger or apathy about appearance and health.
- Use of drugs or alcohol.
- Recent suicide of friend, relative or admired public figure.
- Previous suicide attempt.
- Talk of owning guns, knives or other weapons.
- Beginning to show little interest in friends and peers.

- Verbal clues: "Soon no one will have to worry about me;" "Don't worry, I won't be a bother anymore;" "I won't be around to do that anymore;" "Maybe I should just kill myself;" "My family (or you) would be better off if I would just kill myself;" "You'll be sorry, just wait and see."

It is extremely difficult to be certain whether a troubled child will or will not commit suicide. The Los Angeles Suicide Prevention Center has devised the following indicator scale of a potential suicide to assess the probability that an adolescent might carry out a suicide threat:

Age and Sex. The probability is greater for males between the ages of 13 and 24, and females between 10 and 16.

Symptoms. The probability is greater if the child manifests such symptoms as depression, feelings of hopelessness or alienation, or a sense of powerlessness, or if he uses alcohol or drugs.

Stress. The probability is greater if the child is experiencing stress from the loss of a parent (through divorce, separation or death), from increased responsibilities as a result of serious illness or from other major stressors.

Acute versus Chronic Aspects. The immediate probability of suicide is greater if there is a sudden onslaught of specific symptoms. The long-term probability is greater if there is a recurrence of specific symptoms or a recent increase in long-standing tendency toward depression.

Suicidal Plan. The probability is greater in proportion to the lethal nature of the suicide method and the child's clarity about the plan (for instance, if the child is gathering knives, guns, pills, razor blades or other such items).

Resources. The probability is greater if the child has no family or friends, or if family and friends are unwilling to help.

Prior Suicidal Behavior. The probability is greater if the child has a history of prior attempts, a history of repeated suicide threats and depression, or if a close friend or sibling has been suicidal.

Medical Status. The probability is greater if the child suffers from a chronic, debilitating illness or has had many unsuccessful experiences with physicians.

Communication Aspects. The probability is greater if the child has no communication with family or friends, or if the child rejects the communication efforts of family and friends.

Reaction of Important Friends. The probability is greater if family members or friends whom the teenager considers important reject the teen and deny that he needs help.

Family Interaction. The probability is greater if there is an absence of a warm adult parental figure with whom to identify, or if a parent expresses a negative attitude toward the adolescent. Also it is greater if there is a family history of child abuse (sexual molestation or incest), emotional problems or alcoholism, or remarriage of a family member that has resulted in a sense of isolation, loss, guilt or conflict for the child.

PARENTING TO REDUCE FEELINGS OF LONELINESS, ALIENATION AND SUICIDE

Adolescence is a time when teenagers demand independence and freedom from parental supervision, yet need this supervision very badly. "The unhappiest kids in the world are those with the least parental supervision," asserts Bill Gregory, director of the Excelsior Youth Center in Denver, Colorado. "What adolescents want and need most from you is to have you take them seriously and to guide them toward a better understanding of themselves." The best way to ensure that your child is not suffering from feelings of being alone and feeling lonely is to keep the lines of communication open in your relationship with your child, take an active interest in your teenager's life and pay attention to how your child is doing in school. Here are some other things you should monitor.

Take Time To Appreciate Your Growing
And Changing Adolescent

Spend quality time with your child on a regular basis, even if it's only for a short time in the morning and an hour or two each evening. It's important to take an active interest. Find out what your adolescent is thinking, doing and learning. Become a part of her life.

Keep The Lines Of Communication Open

When your teenager comes to you with a request, evaluate it before responding. Parts of that request may be unacceptable to you, but don't reject the whole idea just because of the unacceptable parts. First, acknowledge that your teen's idea sounds like fun. This will let her know that you are on her side. Second, tell your teenager that there are parts of the plan that you must talk over with her. The important point is that you want your teen to know that you're considering the plan and that you're willing to negotiate something you both can live with. The key is to establish the groundwork for channels of communication so that you will not be shutting your teenager out or creating a situation in which your teen stops talking productively with you. For example, avoid saying, "Stop hanging out with Sue. All she does is hurt your feelings!" Instead you might say, "Janey, it seems that you often get your feelings hurt in your friendship with Sue. What does this tell you about the friendship?" Rather than saying, "Grow up!" ask, "What plans do you have to resolve the problem? Do you need some help?"

Have Fun With Your Teenager

You don't have to stop playing just because your child is older. Plan family play periods. Have regular family projects and games. Read together, share what you read, plan special activities. Just as you took your young child to the park to play and share time together, plan leisure and fun time with your adolescent.

Nourish A Sense Of Order

Guidance involves a combination of love and direction and is a determining factor in the behavior of teenagers. Be sure you are consistent with what you expect from your child.

Don't Ridicule Your Teenager's Friends

Criticizing your teenager's friends is not a good idea. This doesn't mean you have to keep quiet, but rather that you avoid attacking your child's friends. Remember, there is a fantastic loyalty among friends at this age. Chances are he *knows* when a friend is a negative influence, but he may not know how to disentangle himself from the relationship. If you shut out your child's friends, you will also cut off an important realm of your teenager's world. His response will be to alienate you from that part of his life.

Encourage Your Adolescent To Invite Friends Over When The Family Is At Home

Provide an environment your adolescent will want to bring friends into. During the adolescent stage, the adolescent's home becomes an important sanctuary. Adolescents will flock to the homes where parents are open and accessible to the teenager and her friends. Children from homes where parents allow other children to come and visit are candidates for being popular with their friends. A meeting place (to hang out) is one of the requirements of friendship. You may want to encourage your child to invite other children over, but only when you are there to supervise.

If your child doesn't want others to come over, it may be because he's embarrassed about something in the homeplace. "My sister throws her underwear in the laundry basket in the hallway where you enter the house. No way will I take the chance that my friends will see it," said 16-year-old Thomas.

Julie said, "When I was in high school, there was one particular boy I wanted to date. He was, as Bart Simpson would say, 'A real cool dude.' But I was always embarrassed about the way our screen door looked, tattered from six children opening and closing it over the years. You know what? I turned down every date that boy ever asked for! There was no way I was about to let such a guy see that door. And I was certain that if I had told my parents that the reason I was dateless for the prom was because of that screen door, they would have thought I was silly."

Ask your child about how he sees his home. There's a good possibility he has a few complaints — like the laundry basket in the wrong spot — that can be rectified.

Allow For Mistakes

Your teenager learns a great deal about life through exploring and experimenting; mistakes will be a part of the learning process. Give him privileges as he is able to handle them. When your teenager has been given a privilege and abuses it or "goofs," withdraw the privilege and then give him another chance later.

Consider A Support Group

Support groups can reduce the feeling of alienation among adolescents by providing a common forum in which they can share painful experiences. Support groups can also lessen the feelings of being alone and being lonely. It is important for teen-agers to have a place to go to share their problems. Support groups bring adolescents together and help them realize that they are not the only ones having difficulties, and they learn that many problems do have solutions. Peer support can be a powerful tool in preventing suicide. Adolescents who know more about what causes suicidal feelings, how to recognize when a friend is suicidal, and how to help and get help will be more likely to take their own feelings seriously. As a consequence they will be more effective as rescuers for others.

Support groups do work. For instance, Alcoholics Anonymous (AA) began with two members. Today, AA meetings are held all over the world. Spin-off groups such as Overeaters Anonymous, Cocaine Users Anonymous, Emotional Health Anonymous and

Gamblers Anonymous, to name only a few, have helped many people share common problems and lead happy and successful lives. If you are interested in forming such a group, visit one of the above-mentioned self-help groups just to see how the program is structured. These groups are listed in your telephone directory or you can call information for the group nearest you. The reference section at the end of this book provides others.

Be Sensitive To Your Teenager's Appearance

What you look like in the adolescent years does count. Children who do not dress like the other children — and that includes those who are overdressed in comparison with other children — feel *different* and have negative feelings about themselves. That's why so many private schools request that students wear a uniform and why some public schools have dress codes. Dressing alike puts students on an equal footing.

Just as you have an acceptable standard of dress at your place of work, so does your child. Are you familiar with it? You should ask these questions:

- How does my child's overall appearance compare with other classmates?
- How does my child look in relationship to her peers?
- Have I imposed restrictions that are unfair?
- Is my child overdressed?
- How does *my child* feel about his appearance?

Making sure your child looks like the other children doesn't have to mean a big emphasis on clothes, but rather seeing to it that your child is neat and clean and feels good about his appearance. After that, reassure your child that he doesn't need exciting packaging to be loved and accepted. You want to help him accept himself — to gain a greater sense of personhood in a realistic, self-assuring way, and not to have all of his self-perceptions come from his physical being.

Strengthen Home/School Relations

Your child's teachers are a good source of information about her welfare. Since teachers see your child nearly every day, they are likely to be aware of a problem or of changes in her behavior. Teachers can offer advice on how you can become more involved in your child's educational process. It is important for you to know what's going on in the classroom and what the teacher expects of the students so that you can be supportive of the program. If you are unhappy with the method of teaching, talk to the teacher and resolve it the best way you can. If necessary, you can supplement your child's classroom experience with other activities at home. Don't create a situation of conflict with the teacher, because this will be confusing to your youngster. When children sense that their parent is not supportive of the school, they learn not to value the school. If you aren't supportive of the teacher, your youngster won't be either. Fostering a negative attitude will result in poor performance. Interacting in a cooperative way with the teachers and the school staff members will serve to strengthen the school/home connection and will serve as a support system for your child. Remember that the goal is to help your child experience support and not feel alienated.

Help Your Teenager Set And Achieve Purposeful Goals

Help your teenager to feel that life is meaningful, purposeful and joyful. We all need to look forward to something that has scope and depth, and brings a sense of zest and zeal to our everydayness. Encourage your teen to think through the meaning he wants his life to take on. Help him identify important values and standards that guide actions and form behaviors. A goal is the tangible expression of the means to live out one's values. For example, if you strongly value education, your goal might be to finish college. If you value your health, your goal might be to avoid drugs and alcohol and other self-destructive behaviors. Does your child set and achieve goals? Help your teenager set goals that are meaningful enough to get him to want to carry them out.

There are nine key areas that give meaning to our lives. Help your child talk about his goal in each of these areas, why the goal is important, what his plan is for working at it, and then help him develop a plan to achieve it. You'll find that the time you spend communicating with your teen about these goals can be very meaningful. Each of these nine key areas has its place of importance and meaning in your child's life and helps him to have a balanced life, as well as helping him determine what is of purpose for and to him. Books like *Goal Setting Skills for Young Adults* and others can be helpful in this respect. This book and others are listed in the reference section at the back of this book.

1. *Goals for peace of mind:* The search for meaning and spiritual fulfillment.
2. *Personal relationships:* Goals in relationships (with parents, friends, teachers, others).
3. *Learning and education:* What would your child like to know more about?
4. *Status and respect:* To which groups does your child want to belong? From whom does your child want respect?
5. *Leisure time:* What activities (hobbies, sports, travels) would your child like to learn more about? To do more of?
6. *Fitness:* Goals for physical fitness and overall health.
7. *Money needs:* Goals for having enough money to do the things your child wants to do.
8. *Work goals:* What kind of job path is your child choosing? What are your child's goals for productive work and career success?
9. *Others:* Goals that may not fit into the previous categories.

We all need to feel purposeful. This need to feel purposeful is even stronger in children, who often believe they have little control over their lives. Feeling purposeful helps teenagers feel like vital, worthwhile contributors in themselves and then to others.

Don't Hide Your Own Pain

When you hide your own pain, your child learns to hold this as an ideal of what she should be like. When she can't seem to cope with her own painful feelings, she may feel like a failure. In contrast, when you as a parent admit to grief or anger and work through these painful feelings, your actions foster optimism in your teenager. The goal is to help your adolescent realize that it is all right for both teenagers and adults to be honest about how hard it is to cope with some of life's experiences, that we *can* work through difficult feelings, and that sharing the painful feelings with others is a sign of strength and not of weakness.

Take Your Teenager's Feelings Seriously

Not taking your teenager's feelings seriously results in defensiveness rather than openness. A teenager may be terribly upset over a friend's moving away, while that situation may seem rather trivial to an adult who has to deal with the loss of a spouse or job. The pain levels, however, can be equivalent. Sometimes a teenager will over-react to something minor, perceiving it to be larger than life. Again, it is important to remember that an adolescent does not have the backlog of experiences we do. To him, the problem *is* threatening. Your job is to help him identify the real problem behind his pain.

Sometimes we miss or choose to ignore warning signs from other people, or may feel it is not our place to intervene. That attitude can be dangerous. "People don't know how to approach you," said 16-year-old Dan. "A lot of times people won't be honest with you. Fortunately, I had friends who had the guts to tell me I needed to seek professional help. They told me I needed more help than they could give me. A lot of times it takes someone close to you to point out your crazy behavior. The best thing about depression — if there is a good thing about it — is that you find out who your real friends are because you put them through hell."

Acknowledge Your Role In Your Child's Pain

Don't put your head in the sand. There's no time to be defensive or embarrassed. Reach out immediately. A suicide attempt, though it is a personal cry of despair, can also echo a whole family's deep need for help. When parents are able to recognize their role in the child's difficulties and are motivated to do something about them, they may also demonstrate an ability to work together to diminish some of their own conflicts. The ability of parents to work together for the benefit of their child cannot be overly stressed. When you and your spouse present a united front, your child feels secure — part of a family.

Psychiatric Hospitalization

You may be unable to make immediate changes that will enhance your child's well-being. In this case an immediate alliance with a therapist can open pathways for productive communication. In severe cases psychiatric hospitalization for the child must be considered. Besides offering immediate protection, psychiatric hospitalization creates a defined radical change in the family system.

Communities can provide excellent assistance by establishing a suicide-prevention center, staffed with people who know how to spot and help troubled children. These centers can intervene during a time of crisis to ameliorate its intensity. Staff members who are receptive and who respect the principle of confidentiality can become important to a child. Dealing with the youngster's ambivalence is a most important concept in suicide intervention, and staff members can show the concern and empathy necessary to fight a child's ambivalence.

The Art Of Parenting: Are You Up To It?

Communication:
Getting Your
Teenager To Tune In

 We're not perfect; we don't always make the right decisions; we don't always say and do the right things. Revising, regrouping, adjusting and acknowledging our mistakes sets us up as human, not divine. Teenagers who have experienced their parents as open are more likely to feel that their parents are fair, to trust them and to seek their support and advice. Teenagers are more likely to respect parents who communicate effectively and to follow their guidance and direction.

Parents and teens working through issues together — it's a two-way street. Effective communication is the linking element in building and sustaining a positive parent-child relationship.

GOOD COMMUNICATION IS AN ATTITUDE

One of the biggest complaints that both parents and teens have of each other is not being listened to deeply. Teens and parents alike feel they are on different wavelengths, rarely *hearing* what the other has to say. How can we listen so our kids will talk and talk so our kids will listen? Much of it depends on our attitude. To communicate effectively with your teen, the following *attitudes* are important:

- Be willing to see your child as someone with his *own* beliefs and way of perceiving things.
- Want to *hear* what your child has to say.
- Be willing to take *time* to listen.
- Be *willing* to allow your child to express her feelings, even when you are upset.
- Be able to *accept* your child's feelings, whatever they are and however different they are from yours, as an expression of his momentary needs; and appreciate that for the teenager, feelings are often transitory and changeable.
- *Allow* your child to *participate* in working toward constructive solutions to her problems.
- *Help* your teenager sort out the consequences for his actions.

These attitudes show themselves in your willingness to understand and be influenced by your child's perception of what's going on. This does not mean that you are being permissive or that you have lowered your standards. For example, if cursing is unacceptable, it remains unacceptable, even though at the time you may ignore the cursing and respond to your child's feelings of anger and frustration. You can discuss the unacceptability of cursing later, when your child is not in the throes of his emotions — preferably when his feelings have been worked through and he is in a better position to listen to what you have to say and work toward a solution of the problem.

How To Listen So Your Teen Will Talk

Listening means attending fully to the words your teenager is saying and the feelings he is expressing. Real listening demonstrates empathy; the teen is able to tell his side of the story and express his feelings. Listening promotes trust in the relationship; it shows you are concerned and that you want to understand the situation and are intent on working toward resolution.

For example, Brian walked into the family study, where his mom was working on the computer. Brian muttered as he turned to leave, "Man, I can never get my homework done around here!"

"You sound upset," said his mom. "Are you frustrated, angry at me or just tired and hungry?"

Brian replied, "I'm stressed out because I have a big homework assignment tomorrow that I don't want to do, and I need to use the computer. I'm not angry at you; I'm sorry for dumping my stress on you, Mom. When will you be finished working on the computer?"

Active listening is a defusing device simply because one person acknowledges the other. In this case it conveyed that Brian is feeling frustrated rather than disrespectful of his mom. Active listening allows you to decide how to participate in problem resolution. The mother has an opportunity to show empathy toward Brian and alleviate some of her son's frustrations or decide not to participate in it at all. For example, if her own work is not quite as urgent, she could suggest he use the computer immediately. Or they could generate other alternatives. Mother and son have an opportunity to preserve their relationship.

A THREE-PART PROCESS

There are three parts to the communication process, whether verbal or nonverbal: the sender of the message, the receiver of the message, and the content of what is being said. An incomplete or inappropriately relayed message can result in stress and misunderstanding. If Brian says, "I can never get any work done around here!" his mother might say, "Well, I can't get my work done around here either, and it's because you wait until the last minute to do your homework and then feel frustrated and take it out on me!"

With active listening, the situation is placed in a more rational and reasonable perspective, both for the sender and for the receiver. Problem resolution is more likely to occur. If Mom is listening closely and with the intent of problem resolution, she might say something like, "You sound really upset!" to which Brian might respond, "I sure am. I have so much homework, and I had wanted to get it finished so that I could go to the class play at school tonight with my friends."

YOU'LL BE HEARING FROM ME

The teenager who wants to be heard will find a way to do so. This is especially true of adolescents who feel constantly frustrated in their efforts to have someone really hear what they are saying. For an adolescent, being heard might mean skipping class or purposely showing indifference toward classmates or parents, or refusing to value what parents say.

Two parents were told by the teacher of their ninth-grade boy that the child was becoming a distracting problem in school; mischievous attention-getting antics were an ever-increasing pattern of the child's behavior. The teacher had used all the customary ways of handling the situation, but with little success. The parents had scolded, punished and even worked out a system of rewards for good conduct of their teenager, but the poor behavior persisted. The couple then decided to get some help and were exposed to the benefits of active listening. It dawned on them they had not been providing the boy with much casual day-to-day listening time. They would come home from work and immediately become preoccupied with opening the mail, returning phone messages, preparing the evening meal and talking about the day's happenings. They had looked upon their son almost as an intrusion of their own time together. They changed all that.

The parents started focusing more on their son, sharing conversations about his activities and his friends. Slowly the behavior difficulties at school melted into the ordinary restless energies of a 14-year-old. It is, of course, unreasonable to suppose that listening is the solution to every adolescent's problem, but it certainly points out that there are positive results with good listening.

Communication is far more than just taking turns talking. Unfortunately, very little listening would be done at all if we didn't think it was our turn to talk next. And that's a problem, as was clear when public speaking was offered as an evening course in a local community education program. The course became so popular it was expanded into three different classes. At the same time over a four-year period, a listening course was offered. It was never once given: No one enrolled for it.

THE TEENAGERS' LISTENING QUIZ FOR PARENTS

Are you a good listener? How can you be certain you are hearing what your teen is saying, not just what you want to hear? The following quiz was designed for parents by teenagers. Read each statement and think about its implications in communicating with your teenager.

1. I listen to my teenager without refuting what he has to say or making him wrong.
2. I know my teen's boyfriends and girlfriends by name and can ask intelligent questions about them.
3. I show empathy when my teen talks to me about rejection; I don't simply offer bromides like, "That sort of thing happens to us all; it's just part of growing up" or "She wasn't good for you anyway, you have other friends."

4. I answer questions when they arise and don't try to postpone them.

5. I am not embarrassed to say, "I don't know," and am willing to help my teenager seek the information she needs in making an informed decision.

6. I give sympathy when due, and postpone constructive criticism until a time when my teen is calm and can be more receptive to what I am saying.

7. I paraphrase my child's remarks when he uses expressions or slang I don't understand, wanting to be certain I know what he is talking about.

8. I apologize to my teen when I am wrong, not always standing on my dignity as a parent, feeling that I must necessarily be right.

9. I give my teen my full attention when we are talking.

10. I don't interrupt my teen when she is talking, even when I am frustrated watching her struggle for the right word or annoyed at her for taking so long to make a relatively simple point.

11. I watch my child's body language as well as listen to the words he says.

12. I keep in mind that everyone is entitled to her own opinion, that on subjective matters there is no "right" and "wrong;" a teen's opinion is as real to her as mine is to me.

13. I actively seek my teen's opinion, both on family matters and on "grown-up topics," like world events.

14. I clarify when a comment of mine is a fact and when it is an opinion, and respect my teen's right to disagree with me.

15. I don't patronize or talk down to my teen.

How To Talk
So Your Teenager Will Listen

Peggy's 16-year-old son repeatedly left his dirty dishes and clothes all over their apartment. She would continue to pick them up, and he would invariably deposit more. Peggy justified not telling her son how she felt by saying to herself, "Well, we're never home together for very long, and I want that time together to be a happy time." The straw that broke the camel's back, however, came one evening after Peggy had spent a considerable amount of time the day before cleaning and shopping for a special dinner party that evening. She came home with just enough time to prepare the dinner and herself before the guests arrived. The apartment was a mess — dirty clothes, dishes and newspapers deposited everywhere — and no sign of her son. Feeling frustrated and angry at always having to pick up after him, she decided it was time to do something, yet she dreaded bringing it up for fear it would start a battle. She contemplated not discussing it at all.

Having to correct someone's unacceptable behavior is uncomfortable for most people, simply because of its negative nature. But negative feedback, if clear and concise, can be a positive step toward solving the problem at hand. The goal is to focus on the message being relayed rather than on the anticipated emotional consequences of the exchange. The following suggestions can help you clearly provide constructive criticism and send the message that you expect a change in the other person's behavior.

1. *Describe the situation clearly.* Be sure that you identify precisely the behavior that you would like to see changed. For example, your son does not pick up after himself, and you are left with the total responsibility of house care. The target behavior is shared participation. While you are describing the situation, focus on present not past behavior. Speak only about the issues relevant to the present situation. Avoid bombarding your teenager with all of the remotely related information you would like to offer. For example, we can imagine that what Peggy might like to offer goes something like this: "I clean the house, then my son leaves clothes and dishes and other articles about the house after using them. I end up spending more time cleaning up after him. He's old enough to participate. We had

agreed on responsibilities. He does this all the time. I'm just a maid around here." Such statements, however, will get in the way of clearly stating what is going on, will most definitely muddy the conversation and will not result in a resolution of the problem at hand.

2. *Clarify how the person's behavior is affecting you.* *Owning* your feelings will keep this exchange from becoming an emotional battle. Take responsibility for your emotions. For example, "I feel frustrated and angry when you don't pick up your things." When you use "I feel" messages, the other person does not feel accused of causing your response and has no need to react defensively. You are simply stating how you feel. You want to share how you are feeling about the event without allowing the feedback process to act as an emotional release.

3. *Specify the changes that you want to bring about.* Simply stating what you do not like does not guarantee that your teen will know what you want. Ask for a specific change in his behavior. Avoid being demanding as that indicates to your teenager that he has no choice; this will trigger a response of a defensive or attacking nature. Simply state what you would like to have occur, such as: "I would like to request that you pick up after yourself and share the responsibility of our home."

4. *State what you perceive to be the possible consequences of a change in your teen's behavior.* For example, "If you do your share of responsibilities in our home, I'll have some help and time to relax too." The consequences, or outcomes, are best stated in positive terms, avoiding, "You had better do it or else . . ." threats. Threatening may create temporary compliance, but generally doesn't create consistent cooperation.

Here's what the model looks like. Practice using it until it becomes second nature to you.

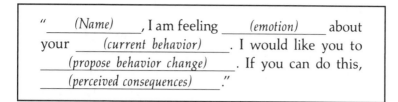

"_____(Name)_____, I am feeling _____(emotion)_____ about your _____(current behavior)_____. I would like you to _____(propose behavior change)_____. If you can do this, _____(perceived consequences)_____."

For practice, imagine that you are Peggy. How would you handle giving feedback to your son? Now recreate a scenario from a recent situation with your teen. Using the questions below as a guideline, decide how you should give feedback to your teenager.

- Exactly what is it that you want your teenager to change? Describe it, as well as possible, in objective and behavioral terms.
- Now what emotion do you feel when your teenager behaves this way?
- Next, what changes do you want? Describe them objectively and behaviorally.
- What positive consequences do you perceive as a result of the proposed change?

How Do You "Process" Information?

Studies have shown that a key factor that governs how we experience our environment and perceive others lies in our individual style of *processing* information. There are three basic modes of perception: visual, auditory and kinesthetic. Most people are visual — they *see* what you mean — and how they see things governs how they *feel* about them. Others are auditory — things *sound* or don't sound good to them. The third group are kinesthetic — they have a *feel* for things, or they go by their gut reactions.

Misunderstandings are most likely to occur when two people have different modes of processing information. For example, when a parent who is primarily auditory gives verbal instructions to a child who is mostly visual.

"DO YOU SEE WHAT I MEAN?"

Visual people tend to forget what has been said very quickly. Out of sight is literally out of mind — words seem to disappear into thin air. So if you're exasperated with your child because you keep asking her to do something and she hasn't, or she never remembers to do what she has been asked to do, try writing notes and leaving them where she'll be sure to see them — like on the door to her room or on the dashboard of the car if she is taking the car.

"TELL ME THAT YOU LOVE ME"

Auditory people love to talk; they describe things in great detail. They think in words, rather than images or feelings. They like to keep in frequent verbal contact, and they will remember what you said. To get your point across, talk to your verbal teen or make a tape for him.

"I KNOW HOW YOU FEEL"

A kinesthetic person would rather hold your hand and commune silently than explain verbally how much you mean to him. It's not that he doesn't care, but words don't mean as much to him as feelings. He's more apt to wash your car as a way of communicating that he cares. But if you're verbal, you might want to hear, "You are a great parent, and I love you." For the kinesthetic person, words have little meaning. His actions speak louder than his words. Touch the kinesthetic person's shoulder or arm, or hug him as you tell him that you need to hear, "I love you." This way, he'll *feel* what you mean.

Are you predominantly visual, auditory or kinesthetic? What about your child? The following checklist will help you determine your processing and communication style.

What Is Your Communication Style?

	Visual	Auditory	Kinesthetic
I need to *see* things to understand them.	_____	_____	_____
I like to get the big picture.	_____	_____	_____
I want people to *see* my point of view.	_____	_____	_____
For me, *seeing* is believing.	_____	_____	_____
Appearance is important to me.	_____	_____	_____
I remember *conversations.*	_____	_____	_____
I can *talk* and work at the same time.	_____	_____	_____
I don't have to look at someone to *talk* to him.	_____	_____	_____
I often *talk* to myself when I'm deciding something.	_____	_____	_____
I like to *tell* all the details when I *talk* about something.	_____	_____	_____
My *feelings* are easily hurt.	_____	_____	_____
I go by my gut *feelings.*	_____	_____	_____
It's easier for me to learn by *watching* someone *do* it.	_____	_____	_____
I *use my hands* when I talk.	_____	_____	_____
I can *commune* with someone close without talking.	_____	_____	_____

WHAT YOUR SCORE MEANS

If you answered "Yes" to the first five questions, you're primarily visual, and you perceive the world in a visual mode. You would rather see a picture than hear something described. The saying, "One picture is worth a thousand words" describes you. You're likely to want people to look at you while you're talking to them in order to feel that they're paying attention. It's probably easier for you to find your way to a strange place with a map, rather than by listening to directions. And if you don't have your shopping list, you might wonder, "Now what did I come here to buy?"

The next five questions are for auditory people. If you're auditory, you remember everything word for word. You can sit in a meeting or a class and never take notes. You can tell your child in detail what he said, or remember detailed instructions. You can converse with your child even if you're in another room. You carry on a lot of inner conversations. You're usually comfortable talking in front of large groups, and can "think on your feet" and field questions easily.

The last five questions describe people who are kinesthetic. Do you become tearful in sad movies, use your hands when you talk, find your stomach tightening when someone else is tense and learn better by actually doing? If you have these traits, you are kinesthetic. Things "feel" either right or wrong to you. When things don't "feel" right, it disturbs you. You go with your "hunches" or "gut reactions." You relate easily to other people's feelings, and especially want your partner to be aware of yours. You empathize readily — you can actually *feel* the other person's happiness or pain.

Most people have one dominant mode of processing information and a secondary mode. Those who can use two modes equally well are usually excellent communicators and, of course, people who can use all three with ease can talk the other person's language, whatever mode that might be.

Difficulties arise when you and your child (or spouse) start talking right past each other, because you are not communicating in the language mode that the other prefers. When the visual parent says, "Look at me when I'm talking to you," and the auditory child answers, "I can hear you" (while watching TV), a problem is at hand. The child doesn't realize that a visual parent needs him to look at her while she talks. She has to be able to *see* that he is paying attention and understands what she's saying. Otherwise, she feels that he just doesn't care or hasn't heard.

To find out your teenager's primary communication mode, go back to the checklist that you filled out for yourself, and this time ask your child to fill it out. Then when you are talking with your teenager, observe how he uses his predominant communication style. The next time you want to communicate something important, be sure to put it in his processing mode so that your message has maximum impact. For example, if you want to share more time together you could say:

- Visual: "I really enjoy *seeing* us do things together. It *seems* like we've become much closer."
- Auditory: "When I *listen* to you *talk*, I can *hear* how much closer we've become."
- Kinesthetic: "It *feels good*, like we're really *close*, when we spend time together."

As you become more skilled at talking in your teenager's preferred mode, you'll notice that your communication improves. Keep in mind that unless you literally speak in the way your teen processes information, he won't fully see, hear or feel what you're trying to convey. Ideally, each of you should learn about the other's preferred style, and when you do, you'll have a better chance of really "tuning in" to each other.

Principles Of Effective Communication

In addition to speaking to your adolescent in her preferred mode, there are a number of basic principles of good communication that lend themselves to being on the same wavelength. Familiarize yourself with them and practice using them until they become second nature. You'll find that communication between you and your teenager improves.

1. **Tell how you feel.** Use "I" statements, such as: "I want, I feel . . ." to let your child know what the impact of his behavior is on you.

   Example: "I want to spend more time together. When we don't, I feel disconnected." Or "When you make decisions without consulting me, I feel that my desires are unimportant to you."

2. **Clearly state what you want.** Directness goes with "I" statements. Instead of saying, "You never call when you say you will," which gets into blaming, state your wants directly.

   Example: "I want you to honor the curfew we agreed upon."

3. **Be brief.** Be brief when you talk to avoid overloading your child and having her tune out. State your wants in 25 words or less.

   Example: "I need your help on Saturday to watch Bruce while I take Joni to the dentist."

4. **Be specific.** Saying, "You never care about our relationship" doesn't let your child know what you want. State your desires as specific behaviors that you would like at certain times.

   Example: "I'd like us to share ten minutes together each evening to talk specifically about our day."

5. **Observe what your body language is saying.** Be aware of your body language. If your words say one thing, but your body posture and voice tone say something else, you're sending a mixed message. For instance, perhaps you have trouble expressing anger and therefore tend to cover up your feelings. At the same time that you try to express anger about a situation, you might smile nervously and speak in a soft voice, so that you're not taken seriously.

   If you feel discomfort when expressing yourself about a situation that you feel strongly about, rehearse first in front of a mirror. Practice taking a deep breath, and using your whole body when you speak, so that your voice tone is deeper and more assertive. Make sure that your body stance and facial expression fit in with the message you want to convey.

Example: Stand comfortably straight, with feet apart, look directly at your teenager and say in a firm voice tone, "I was really upset when you didn't let me know you were going to get a ride home from school with Miles. I left work early and waited for you outside your school for nearly 45 minutes. As a result, I missed an opportunity to attend a friend's office farewell party."

6. *Present alternatives.* Your teenager is more likely to respond positively to a situation when he has some control over the outcome. Providing options helps set the stage for mutual problem-solving.

Example: "You cannot go to the party on Saturday night, but you may have a friend over if you would like."

7. *Use active listening.* Let your child know she has your full attention. Lean forward, maintain eye contact and nod, or give verbal cues that show understanding or agreement. It also helps to restate what your child has said in your own words to make sure you understand.

Example: "It sounds like you really want to be with your friends more often."

8. *Give feedback.* Give your child feedback in a way that shows you understand a position, even if you don't agree with it. Be prepared for negotiation and change.

Example: "I understand that it's important for you to spend time with friends, but we never share time together. We had agreed that Thursday evening was our time together."

GETTING YOUR TEEN TO TUNE IN IS A MATTER OF COMMUNICATION

How do you communicate with your teenager? Do you give encouragement? Do you tell your children how important they are to you, and how much you not only love them but like and respect them as well? The messages you send your teenager, and the way you say it, helps her decide how valuable and worthwhile she is. It also helps her to adhere to your standards and want to behave herself — first, because it's what she wants to do, and second, because she doesn't want to let you down.

Even constructive feedback should be focused on the positive. For example, "You did a great job cleaning up your room. I like how you put everything neatly on the shelf; that looks very nice. Maybe next time you could dust the shelf first to make it look even better." Or "Thanks for taking the message from my boss, son. It was very important to me and I appreciate your taking it all down; I know it was long. Please let me know next time as soon as I come home, rather than telling me hours later. That way I can act on the information my boss needs and have time to be responsive."

Teach Your Children To Receive And Give Compliments

Every parent loves to hear how wonderful she is, how she is the best parent ever. Unfortunately, adolescents do not show their positive feelings as easily as they did when they were younger; we too rarely hear praise from them. When was the last time that your teenager took a moment to tell you that you are a good parent? If you are lucky and have a good solid relationship with your child, you may hear "I love you" occasionally, but you probably will not hear "You're a good parent" at all. Teenagers just don't think to tell us how we're doing at effective parenting.

Children are more likely to give compliments when they get them themselves. If you regularly praise your teen, if you let her know you are happy with her, proud of her, she feels good about herself and is willing to share that good feeling with others. The teenager who hears regularly how smart she is will be able to say to her friend, "Nice job on that spelling test; you got the hard one I missed." The child who is criticized is going to be envious and small-minded, begrudging her friends their successes.

Compliment Your Teenager

We often boast about our children to others; they need to hear the good news themselves. "Jack, I'm impressed with how you buckled down this semester and got your math grade up. And this extra-credit assignment you did is the icing on the cake. Good job!" "Sheila, I noticed how patient you were with your little sister when you were helping her clean up her room. You're a really good sister. Even though she may not say it or show it, I know she appreciates you as much as your father and I do."

Criticize The Action, Not The Child

You're not upset with your children; you're upset with what they've done. Make that clear in your criticism: "Chad, you didn't make your bed this morning. I want you to make it every morning without my having to tell you each time." How much kinder and more to the point this is than bellowing, "Chad! Get in here! How many times, how many, many times do I have to tell you to make your bed? Why don't you listen to me? When are you going to grow up and assume some responsibility?" With the critical comment, Chad doesn't hear the problem — the unmade bed — but only the disappointment that his parent has in him. He hears not that he has left an unmade bed, a small problem in the scheme of things, but that he is irresponsible and immature.

Teach Assertiveness Skills

Assertiveness skills enable your child to assert his rights without using intimidation or being intimidated. There are times when he'll want to tell others how he's feeling, what he thinks is important and what he is willing or is not willing to do. He'll need to be able to do this in a way that is accepted by others, and that gets his point across effectively. It doesn't do him any good to yell or to have people guess what his needs are. Besides, they'll most likely guess wrong, his needs will go unmet and he'll be disappointed because his expectations haven't met with success. It also doesn't do much good to hope that if he's nice to people, they'll somehow know what it is he needs and give it to him. Talk with him about this.

A good way to test your child's ability to stand his ground is to use the following questions, or other similar ones, in probing his skills. Select a time when the two of you are feeling especially close. Most parents find that the best time to do this is while they are in the car together, over a leisurely meal or when they are walking together not hurried, anxious or rushed. Ask questions such as: "What would you do if another student cut in front of you in a line?" "What would you do if a classmate asks to copy your answers to a test?" "What would you do if a kid calls you a name?" "If you didn't understand a problem that the teacher just explained, what would you say in asking for help?"

Guiding And Disciplining Your Teenager

Child psychologists and other childcare professionals often report that they have never met a parent who purposely reared a child to be unhappy and maladjusted, yet many such children exist. The parents of these children are simply *unaware* of how to develop appropriate and desirable behavior in their children.

All children must be guided in learning what constitutes appropriate behavior. Young children don't know that it is not okay to write on walls, and will learn to

165

express their artistic talents where it's appropriate *only* if their parents teach them where to do so. Likewise teenagers need guidance and direction in learning the code of conduct appropriate for young adults. The notion that teens need less guidance and direction is a myth.

As children go about growing and learning in each new phase of childhood, they must face the challenges along the way. Luckily, children are naturally curious. Trial and error is how they explore what works, what doesn't and why. All children need to know what is permissible and what is not as they venture forward. They must learn that established rules are for their benefit and safety, and that there are consequences for stepping outside the boundaries. Parents need to understand how important it is to provide guidance and direction, and feel confident in their actions, especially in the adolescent years. When the teenager slams a door to her room in frustration, or fails to straighten up her room, there's no need to take it personally. Like young children, teenagers rarely see their tantrums as a problem; they simply have not yet learned more appropriate or self-controlled ways to channel their frustrations and to vent their emotions. That's the tough stuff of parenting. *Parenting* and *parenthood* are two entirely separate matters.

DEVELOPING APPROPRIATE BEHAVIOR IN YOUR TEEN

We can give our children the opportunity to become capable and successful adults by reinforcing these values in our parenting actions. Think about how you discipline your teens and ask yourself the following questions:

- What am I trying to teach by my approach to discipline?
- Are my actions centered on the values I want to instill?
- Are consistent values being expressed and reinforced by my co-parent?
- What do I want my teen to assimilate (learn) by my actions (modeling)?

- Do I admire my style of guidance and direction (disciplining)?
- Would I like to be governed under this approach?
- How is my teenager faring under my guidance?
- Is my approach working? Am I getting the (positive) results I want?
- Is my style of guidance and direction consistent with my values?

The point of this exercise is to help you focus on *what you're trying to do*, rather than being driven by a momentary crisis.

No matter how many times you say, "That's different; I'm an adult," or "Do as I say, not as I do," your child is going to act from what she sees and hears. If you tell your child not to lie, but then have her lie on your behalf — "If that's Mrs. Peterson, tell her I'm not home now!" — you send out a contradiction. Our values always show up in our actions. Children learn what they live. Our children will do as we do.

When you clearly articulate your expectations for good behavior, your teenager comes to know what is expected; when you communicate the rules and spell out the consequences of their violation, your teenager learns to monitor his actions and become responsible for the behavior *he has chosen*. When you model the behavior you want your child to embrace, he is more likely to emulate it. In other words, your child learns appropriate and desirable behavior from you. By thinking about what you want your teenager to be, do and learn (as opposed to knowing only what behavior you won't tolerate), and by practicing what you want your child to be, do and learn, there's a better chance that your teenager will acquire and demonstrate it. Let's look at two examples.

1. My Mom, The Ogre

Twelve-year-old Peter and his nine-year-old brother, Michael, are wrestling in the family room. Their mother is trying to watch the news on TV, but is distracted and annoyed by the ever-increasing volume of noise the boys are making. After gritting her teeth for several minutes, the mother explodes into the family room, grabs the comic book lying on the floor and slaps both boys with it several times. Giving her sons a withering glare, the mother leaves the room and returns to her television news. All is quiet in the family room for a few minutes . . . then the noise returns as loud as before.

Poor Mom didn't get much satisfaction from her approach, did she? She gained only a brief respite from the noise.

2. My Mom, The Parent

The scenario is the same. This time, however, the mother enters the family room, smiles and asks the boys what they are doing. They reply that they are just play-wrestling. Still smiling, Mom says, "That sounds like fun, but you know, guys, I'm watching the news and I can't hear it that well, because it's too noisy in here." On their own, her sons acknowledge the validity of the problem and propose a solution. "Why don't Michael and I put the mat down in the garage. Our noise there won't bother you. Sorry, Mom."

It is obvious which approach had the best results. What is not so obvious is *why*. Why was the second approach so much more efficacious and satisfying than the first? The answer lies in two factors: *relationship* and *force*.

There is no right or wrong way to deal with children in every circumstance, but there are a number of effective and ineffective ways to interact. The goal is to maximize your effectiveness by using only the degree of force needed in the situation; how much force is needed is determined by the quality of the parent-child relationship. The better the relationship, the less force is needed.

The first guideline is to discipline only when an action warrants it. For example, two siblings arguing between themselves doesn't necessarily call for your intervention. Second, use only the amount of force appropriate to the situation; in other words, don't over-react. In the scenario above, a high degree of force was not called for. Sending the boys to their rooms or hitting them, for example, would be unnecessary force. In the first example, it was obvious that the mother's actions were based on her frustration. She demonstrated this to her sons first by being overly emotional, and second by swatting them with their comic book. Neither of these actions was effective, and no doubt will have very little effect other than leading the boys to disrespect their mother. In the second example, the mother was effective because she realized it did not call for force, and conducted herself accordingly. Always leverage your disciplinary actions. Some parents believe that they must resort to physical punishment to get their children to behave themselves. Other parents get the same results using their personal power — relying on the integrity of the personal relationship they have carefully and thoughtfully developed with their children. *Low-force methods rely on a relationship built on respect and integrity.*

The Effects Of Your Disciplinary Actions Depend On Love, Respect And Integrity

The effectiveness of your actions is determined to a great extent by the quality of the parent-child relationship. Judy and her 17-year-old daughter, Lynda, have cultivated a good relationship over the years. They respect each other's feelings and enjoy each other's company. One day Judy planned to hold an informal office staff meeting at her house. Two hours before her staff was to arrive, the house still needed a final once over. Judy said to Lynda, "I'm afraid I'm not going to be ready when my staff comes." Lynda immediately volunteered, "I'll do the vacuuming, Mom. Will that help?"

In contrast, Lana and her daughter, Mara, frequently argue and communicate in negative language by being sarcastic with each other. One afternoon Lana screeched, "Mara, I've asked you three times now to clean up the kitchen. How many times do I need to ask?" "I said I'm coming, Mom!" yelled Mara from her room. Twenty minutes later Mara still had not completed the task. Both mothers tried to get their daughters to help them. Judy got her daughter to help, Lana did not.

One of the best ways to build a quality relationship with your teen is to focus on the relationship.

RELATIONSHIP BUILDING: THE EMOTIONAL BANK ACCOUNT

With each relationship we have in our lives, we open an *emotional bank account.* Just as you can deposit or withdraw funds on your account at the bank, you have an emotional account with your child. What you do and say can be a deposit or a withdrawal in the emotional account. Deposits are made through the positive and considerate things we do and say — firm and fair rules, good parenting, kindness, keeping commitments. Withdrawals are made through discourtesy, disrespect, swearing, hitting, being emotionally or physically distant. Here's how it works:

When you tell your teenager that he can use the car to go to school, you mean just that. Rule or not, your teenager could get in the car, drive away but then skip school. It's out of your control and completely up to him. What would it take for your teenager to honor the agreement he has with you and not want to break that trust, regardless of what he wants to do? It will take a good relationship where mutual respect and honor abound. With a positive balance in the account, your teenager will not want to let you down and will want to value the academic commitment. If you have a negative balance in the account — if you are in the habit of making promises but not keeping them, for example, or treating him unfairly — then he may very well make a "withdrawal." He may skip school, do as he pleases and not care that his actions cause you worry and anguish.

When you make continual deposits in the joint emotional bank account, on the other hand, your reserves build up. You can even make an occasional mistake and be forgiven by him. If you keep making withdrawals, the emotional bank account becomes overdrawn. At that point you have little if any trust with your teenager.

Though fragile, emotional bank accounts are very resilient. If you were to have a large emotional bank account, say an imaginary sum of $1,000 of emotional reserve capacity with your teenager, you can make small withdrawals of $10 from time to time and he will understand and overlook it. For instance, you may need to make a very unpopular, authoritarian decision without even involving your teen.

Let's say your 13-year-old wants to spend the night with a friend whose parents drink heavily, and you are therefore uncomfortable with the quality of care or chaperoning she would receive. You may say, "No. I can't allow you to spend the night in this particular home." Your daughter may pout, throw a tantrum and storm off to her room. Your unpopular decision may cost you $100 in her eyes. But if you have a $1,000 bank account and make a $100 withdrawal, you would still have $900 left. It's unlikely that she will go to her room, pack up her overnight bag, climb out the window and go anyway. (Though that is always a possibility with a teenager!)

You might also try to lessen the amount of the withdrawal. For example, you could explain why you are taking such a stand, thus possibly redepositing some portion of the $100. You could work for ways to raise the cash to remove the negative withdrawal — perhaps you could suggest that instead she call up her friend and invite her over to spend the night in your home. You might offer to pay for movies (without asking her to use her own spending money), just to show your willingness to be compassionate about the fact that she isn't where she wants to be. Therefore, you may even get back 30 or 40 "emotional dollars" or some portion of the original withdrawal.

THREATS WORK WITH YOUNGER CHILDREN, RARELY WITH TEENS

To a large extent, your influence with children depends on the emotional bank balance. When withdrawals exceed deposits, the account is overdrawn. If parents threaten, yell, indulge their children or ignore, abandon and neglect them, relationships will deteriorate; discipline will be nonexistent or difficult. When children are young and susceptible to threats and manipulation, parents often get what they want in spite of their methods. With teenagers, however, a parent's threats no longer have the same immediate force to bring about desired results. Unless there is a high trust level and a lot of mutual respect, parents have little control over their teens. There are simply no reserve funds in the account. A lack of deposits leads to an overdrawn emotional bank account, a breakdown of the relationship and a lack of influence.

CORRECTING BEHAVIOR: THIS HURTS ME MORE THAN IT HURTS YOU

When your teenager needs to be corrected, do you react based on how you're feeling at the moment, or do you have fair and appropriate consequences for inappropriate behavior? Are you aware of your own tolerance for teaching your children appropriate ways to respond? Can you separate your child's actions from the behavior when you correct your children's behavioral faux pas? Calling a teenager lazy because he doesn't make his bed or pick up after himself will do little to get him to do these chores.

The best way to help your teenager learn to do what is expected of him is to concentrate on specific, constructive ways of changing behavior, such as explaining specifically what to do and how to do it, and then assisting him with those tasks until he understands the standards for them. Here are some basic guidelines:

1. *Decide on the specific behavior you would like to change.* Don't just nag and hope that because you call on your teenager to keep his books off the kitchen counter and his clothes off the couch that he will also keep his room neat. Be clear on the absolute rules you intend to enforce. For example, "Josh, all school books are to be put on your desk in your room, every day after school. Do not leave any articles of clothing in any room in the house other than in your room."

2. *Tell your child exactly what you want her to do and show her how to do it.* Don't just tell your teenager to be "neat;" explain what you want her to do (to do her math homework, to make her bed and hang up her clothes). Next, show her how to do it. Manually guiding your child through the desired action helps her understand exactly what you want her to do and what standards you are going to use in judging when it is accomplished. If you want her to make the bed in a certain way, for example, show her, step by step, then make a point of coming into her room for several days (or longer) to assist if she still doesn't have it right.

3. *Praise your child's doing of the behavior.* Don't praise the child, but rather praise what he is doing. Say, "It's great that you are picking up your room every day," rather than "You're terrific!"

4. *Continue the praise as long as the new behavior needs support.* Praising all the correct things that your teenager does reminds her of your expectations and continues to hold your own model of good behavior. Praise reinforces the correct way of doing things.

5. *Avoid power struggles.* Stay in your role as parent. Don't allow yourself to get baited in and act like a teenager yourself. Your teenager is more in need of a model than a critic. If your teenager starts to bait you in, say something like this: "Brenda, let's talk about this in an hour. I need time to think about what I'm willing to commit to, and that will

give you time to get clear on your feelings too. We'll make a better decision when we are calm."

6. *Supervise your teen.* Teenagers, like young children, need fairly constant supervision. If you stay abreast of the school's expectations for your child in his role of a student, you are more likely to influence his being responsible for homework and other related chores. If you're around while homework is being done, you can monitor study habits. If you run a check each morning on your teen's room, you are more likely to send the message that it is important for him to put away his things.

7. *Avoid being a historian.* Leave past bad behavior to history and don't keep bringing it up. If a child makes an error, constantly reminding him of his error will only lead to resentment and increase the likelihood of bad behavior. What is done is done.

8. *Sincerely apologize when you are wrong.* Children are very forgiving when you acknowledge that you have been unfair. When you can sincerely say, "I was wrong, and I'm sorry. What I said was unkind." If you embarrass your child in front of her friends, acknowledge it. Say, "Ramona, I'm sorry to have embarrassed you in front of your friends the way I did. That was unfair." Such recognition not only reduces the amount of the withdrawal, but becomes a deposit as well.

TEACH THAT ALL ACTIONS HAVE CONSEQUENCES

There's a consequence for everything. For example, the consequence of eating ice cream too fast is a headache. The consequence of doing a good deed is positive feelings. The consequence of staying up too late watching TV is being tired and sluggish the next day. It is important for children to learn that all actions have consequences. In Tyrone's home, the consequence for not getting school work done and turned in is to have television privileges taken away that evening. Susan has a rule that all items belonging to the children that are left around the house (other than in their rooms) get locked away for a week. Structuring consequences are a part of the leadership of parenting.

Consequences should be fair, in proportion to the offense and without recrimination. Children should always see the possibility and the necessity of making a fresh start. Decide on reasonable, clear rules and enforce them consistently. Make only those rules that you believe to be truly important, to which your child can adhere and that you intend to enforce. If your child breaks a rule, the consequences should be certain, prompt and related directly to the offense.

Seventeen-year-old Phil and his best friend left school at lunch. Lunch took longer than they had planned, and since they were late anyway, they decided they wouldn't go back to school. The school, alarmed at their absence, called their homes. When Phil came home, his mother did not threaten, name call, or become dramatic. Instead she said, "Do you know what your life would be like if you don't get your high school diploma?" Fitting the punishment to the crime, she said, "Phil, we agreed when you got the car that you would use it in a responsible manner. Driving off campus without permission and cutting classes and driving around all afternoon is not responsible. I'll take you to school and pick you up after school for the next week. At the end of the week, if you feel you can behave responsibly again, your driving privileges will be restored."

For the next week, Mrs. Burton drove Phil to school. You might argue that her response was a hardship on her too. That's often the case, but it pays off in the long run. Your children need to know that you are serious in your resolve to help them learn appropriate behavior. Phil didn't cut school again, ever. *Punishment has impact because of its* certainty, *not because of its severity.*

You must be consistent in enforcing consequences. If you said the keys would be taken away for breaking curfew, take them away each time. Teenagers, like young children, need continuity to be consistent. And finally, be sure the consequence comes close on the heels of the action. Teenagers do not learn the lessons you are trying to teach if they break the rules on Monday and are punished on Friday.

TEACH THAT YOUR TEENAGER, NOT YOU, IS RESPONSIBLE FOR HIS ACTIONS

Your adolescent needs to understand that he is responsible for his actions, not you. For example, it doesn't stand to reason that a child's teacher *gave* him an A or a C. The child earned it. The child is responsible for the consequence; in this case it is the amount of effort he put out in receiving the grade. A consequence is not something that you "do to him;" *it is the direct result of his actions.* Consequences are directed toward what he has done, not toward who he is. Show your child that while you are unhappy with his action, you still love him. "Eric, I know you like washing the car. I appreciate it when you do, but if you can follow the procedure we talked about and be more thorough, you'll do a better job. That way, I won't have to ask you to redo it, and we'll both feel better."

When the teenager experiences the consequences of his actions, he learns to be responsible. When the teenager sees a direct cause-and-effect relationship between his actions and the consequences (both positive and negative, acceptable and unacceptable), he realizes that he has obligations, to himself and to those around him. He learns to take credit as well as blame for the results of his actions, and to alter his actions if he wants a different consequence. Responsibility builds self-esteem because it gives him control. He is not attacked or berated, and he doesn't have to feel guilty; his relationship with you is not on the line. You still love him and care about him even though he made a mistake.

A classmate asked Diane to come over to her house after school. Diane called her mother to get permission to go. Her mother said no, reminding Diane that this was the evening Diane and her sister had chosen to go to the early showing of a movie the girls had wanted to see. Diane was to go home, start dinner and do her homework. Diane went to her friend's house anyway. Consequences followed.

"Diane, you will not be able to go out with your sister tonight. Your homework isn't done, and going to the movies was a special favor based on your being responsible for an early dinner and your homework being completed."

The mother pointed out the consequences of Diane's behavior. She didn't say, "Diane, you are an irresponsible kid!" Diane's mother avoided an argument or self-justification. She pointed out to Diane how Diane's actions led to an unwanted result. Diane's mother allowed her daughter to "own" the consequences of her behavior.

The following model is very helpful in getting adolescents to see how they choose a consequence:

1. What did I do to choose? (to stay home from the movies tonight)
2. What did I want to happen? What happened as a result?
3. What rule did I break? Did I make a problem for someone else?
4. Does _____ (staying home from the movie tonight) make me feel *sad, upset, pleased, glad?*
5. What I really want now is _____.
6. To get what I want I must (a) stop _____ (b) start _____.
7. I will make a plan to stop _____ (what action?) and start _____ (what action?).

Remember that good kids get into trouble too. Parents can't always control their children's behavior. Whether the teenager skips school or gets elected class president, he has a role in it. Teenagers make their own individual choices — whether right or wrong, good or bad.

GOOD ACTIONS HAVE CONSEQUENCES TOO

It's easy to get caught up in the responsibilities of disciplining for negative behaviors and forget to praise good actions. In a week of a hundred "What were you thinking when you . . .!" we tend to overlook the good behavior because it is expected. Teenagers need to see both sides of the results of their behavior. Just as ignoring rules and misbehaving have consequences, being good and behaving well have consequences. Just as you did with bad behavior, emphasize specifically what good behavior brought about the consequence. "Dan, you did a great job of cleaning out the garage." As you did with inappropriate behavior, make the stroking commensurate with the deed.

Rachel came home from school and excitedly shared with her mother the news that she had received a high score on a history exam. "That's terrific, Rachel!" said her mother. "You studied very hard and you earned that grade. You should be very proud of yourself." The mother has pointed out to Rachel the consequences of her behavior. She had worked very hard; she had produced the good grade. Therefore, she deserves to be very proud of herself. Her pride should lie in doing good work, not in making her mother proud.

SOLVING PROBLEMS, EVALUATING CONSEQUENCES

A number of skills can enable your child to make better choices and decisions and thus lessen the need for reprimands. One very valuable tool is to learn to solve problems effectively. Most adolescents act impulsively or make rash decisions from time to time; good problem-solving skills can help reduce the incidence of irrational resolutions. Solving problems effectively is achieved by clearly identifying the problem, brainstorming for solutions, committing to one of them and then evaluating the consequence of that solution. The four-step process shown below can help your teenager develop a more organized approach to problem solving:

1. What is the problem?
2. How can I solve it? What are my alternatives?
3. What is my plan?
4. How did I do?

To begin, recreate a scenario your child has recently encountered and go through this problem solving step by step. Here's a scenario for practice.

Sara and Jill have taken the local bus to the mall where they plan to meet a third friend, Kelly. All three girls are in the eighth grade. They have their parents' permission to see a movie; they are to be home by 10:00 P.M. Kelly, without telling the other girls, has arranged to meet her boyfriend at the movie. The boyfriend shows up with two other boys. The teenagers meet, talk and decide to go to the arcade games instead of the movie. Because her brother was in a fight last year at the arcade, Jill has been forbidden to go there.

What is Jill's problem and how can she solve it? Using the four-step process shown above, let's analyze Jill's problem.

First, *what is the problem?* Jill has been given permission to attend the movie with friends, and now her friends want to go to the arcade, even though Jill is forbidden to do so.

Second, *how can she solve it? What are the alternatives and their consequences?* Let's take a look.

Action: She could go along with the new plans against her parents' wishes.

Consequence: She will break the trust she and her parents have established.

Action: She could tell her friends the new plans sound fun, but she cannot accept since she only has permission to go to the movies.

Consequence: She runs the risk that her friends will mock her.

Action: She could tell Kelly that it was really stupid of her to put her in this predicament.

Consequence: It will put a strain on the friendship; Sara may feel dragged into the middle of their argument.

Action: She could leave a message for her parents with her sister, telling them of the change in plans and go off to the arcade.

Consequence: Jill's parents will most certainly feel taken advantage of and may not allow her independent trips in the future.

Third, *what is the plan?* Jill decides to tell Kelly and Sara that the new plans sound fun, but that she won't be able to go with them.

Finally, *how did I do?* Pretty good! Jill took the chance of being alienated by her friends, but then Kelly expressed her relief because she too felt that her parents would be upset if they learned what she did, so she also decided not to take the risk.

The next step would be to help your adolescent examine the likely outcome of proposed actions by asking questions like, "If you do that, what do you think would happen?" This question is often followed by, "And then what would happen?" If the adolescent proposes solutions that are not very realistic, guide her back to reality by asking, "What is the problem?" Encourage your adolescent to generate more alternatives to the problem and then to assess realistically the potential impact of each of these options. The goal here is to help your teenager learn that there is more than one way to handle a problem, that not all solutions work equally well and that thinking before you act can lead to a better outcome. Be realistic. Don't expect your teenager always to select the best choice. Your teenager learns by the decision she makes. Mistakes are important too. They show us what doesn't work and what is not appropriate. Be patient. When your teen does make an obvious mistake, avoid the "I told you" routine. Point out how a different alternative might have lead to a different outcome.

You can also help your teenager think about the choices of her actions through role playing (discussed in Chapter 13). For example, Jill may want to tell Kelly that she can't go to the arcade, but she may be intimidated by the fact that both of her friends are going, or she may lose her courage because she fears Sara and Kelly will be upset with her decision. Role playing can be a good way to rehearse strategies, allowing your teenager to try out acceptable and feasible solutions, and to determine what she will commit to.

DOS AND DON'TS IN DISCIPLINING THE ADOLESCENT

The guidance you provide for your teenager will depend on your willingness to help her learn appropriate ways to behave. Here are some things to keep in mind:

Don't Ignore Negative Behavior

A normal stage of growth and development doesn't negate the need for parental intervention and guidance. Adolescents do not possess the natural ability to raise themselves. Intervention, direction and loving guidance from responsible parents is a necessary part of every adolescent's life. Adolescents typically display bouts of rebellion, moodiness, a preoccupation with peer acceptance and often even alcohol or drug use. These negative behaviors *should not* be ignored by parents.

Though adolescence is a stage of development in which adolescents certainly do go through a time of independence, displaying some normal rebelliousness as part of the process of separating, you need to take a stand against those negative behaviors. It may be a very normal stage of development for a ten-month-old baby to stick things in his mouth, but it certainly doesn't mean his parent should not intervene if the object he is putting in his mouth can harm him. The same holds true in a parallel sense for parenting adolescents. Negative behaviors won't go away or resolve themselves. On the contrary, they can have permanent or damaging effects to the adolescent and on family members as well.

Believing the adolescent will "grow out of it," to simply hope, pray and be patient while he experiments in a dangerous vein — using alcohol or drugs, smoking, reckless driving, lying, stealing and ditching school — can foster and perpetuate problems that can lead to potentially severe and life-threatening problems.

Don't Get All Of Your Self-Esteem Strokes From Your Role Of Parent

While parents need to shoulder responsibility for teaching children to behave themselves, our self-esteem needs should not rest solely on our role as a parent. Parents who let their self-esteem be tied to their child's behavior will not be able to respond to destructive behavior effectively. They will come up against the crippling effects of guilt, fear, anger and frustration. Personalization of adolescent behavior is probably the major cause for what is referred to as "parental denial." Parents in denial are often unconsciously blind to the destructive or negative behavior their adolescent demonstrates and do little, if anything, to correct it.

Detach When Necessary

Teach your adolescent to accept responsibility for her behavior. Eventually, you have to hand the baton over to the child to accept responsibility for her own behavior. Parents who fail to teach their children and instead assume all the blame, breed irresponsibility in their children. To accept responsibility for their choices and develop a sense of responsibility as individuals, adolescents need to have parents who have attained a certain level of detachment in dealing with them.

Detachment is not rejection or insensitivity. In a psychological sense, detachment refers to the process of achieving emotional distance, objectivity and perspective in close, caring relationships. A necessary ingredient in loving parent-adolescent relationships, detachment allows adolescents to become independent and responsible. Parents who are too close to and involved with their adolescents on an emotional level tend to lose their objectivity and their ability to separate their needs from their adolescents' wants. Overly attached parents also have difficulty distinguishing between what is best for their adolescents and what feels comfortable to them as parents. Detachment is necessary for parents to effectively set and enforce limits, since making rules and applying consequences are particularly unpleasant, yet extremely important, tasks for parents.

Instill Values

Kids will do exactly what they choose to do. Granted, they will frequently choose to do what their parents tell them to do, but the choice is an active one. Their behavior is not directly controlled by parental statements. Healthy choices result in positive consequences; unhealthy choices result in negative consequences. Adolescents need to learn this; the earlier, the better. Your job is to impart values on which your child's choices will rely.

It's Okay For Children To Feel The Pain And Discomfort Associated With The Consequences Of Their Decisions

Children are in the process of learning, growing, changing — maturing. Children are constantly making choices. Making choices is a healthy, powerful, self-affirming process. Awareness of the ability to make choices is a key ingredient in self-esteem and self-confidence. Children won't always make the right choice; they learn what is right based on the consequence of their action. They will feel pain and discomfort. Kids need to learn that pain often comes not from the problem itself, but from the way they deal with it; their particular choices and approaches to problems can have an effect upon how pain is experienced. Too often adolescents identify their pain as stemming directly from their problems and want to escape the trouble or have parents remove the problem for them. Adolescents need to know that their parents are not responsible for removing all problems and negative feelings from their lives. In fact, it is parental discipline that sets the stage on which adolescents learn how to deal with pain in the form of frustration, disappointment and negative consequences.

Monitor The Health Of Your Parent-Child Relationship

Run a check on the goodwill and respect between you and your child. Your relationship with your child is in danger of being bankrupt when . . .

- You receive no messages of caring and affection from your child.
- You frequently experience negative emotions concerning your child's behavior.
- You always find yourself angry with your child.
- Minor problems become catastrophes.
- You use destructive patterns of communication, such as name calling, lecturing, sarcasm, shaming, blaming and threatening, which undermine the child's self-confidence and sense of worth.
- You frequently use high-force methods to obtain desired behavior from your child.

Other signs indicate that your relationship with your child is a healthy one. Positive signs include:

- Frequent verbal and nonverbal messages of caring and affection.
- Open expression of feelings (both positive and negative) between parent and child.
- An atmosphere in which both parent and child feel free to express themselves.
- Timely and orderly resolution of problems, along with a sincere desire for such a resolution.

When your teenager wants to maintain his good relationship with you, his actions will be influenced by knowing how you will respond to what he is doing. He'll strive to do those things that please you and avoid doing things he knows irritate or anger you. When your parent-child relationship is healthy, the child provides much of his own force, thus allowing you to use much less forceful methods than you would otherwise need.

You are probably nodding your head now, agreeing that a child who monitors himself is much easier for you to deal with. But what if your child gets out of control? In the next chapter we'll look at guidelines for the child who needs more than relationship building, more than the average method of monitoring good behavior.

12

If Your Teenager Is Out Of Control

 Is your teenager out of control? Let's look at three teens who are.

Tom, The Bully

Karen Williams took a deep breath as she walked up the steps to her son's second-floor bedroom. She held her hands over her ears, wincing as the volume from Tom's stereo became so loud as to be painful. The few lyrics she could make out were filthy. Just as she got to

185

the door, she heard her son and his best friend, Ron, singing or rather shouting along to the music.

She knew from previous experience that knocking on the door would do no good, so Karen opened it and walked in. Immediately, her son glared at her, and walked over to her. She said, "Honey, please turn down the volume! I can't hear myself think!"

Tom hovered over his mother, enjoying this display of defiance. She looked up at him, afraid of her own son, who had grown so sullen and so mean these past few months. She was ashamed of herself for being afraid of her own son. Tom grabbed his mother's arm. "I told you before," he yelled in her ear. "I *told* you! This is *my* room and you're off-limits. Get out!"

Karen's arm was beginning to hurt where her son held it. Tom yanked his mother's arm very hard, pushing it up behind her. The pain was intense, bringing tears to Karen's eyes. Her son continued yelling loudly, "Get out! Get out! Get out!" As she was being almost bodily dragged to the door and shoved out, Karen saw her son's face. It was red, flushed. The veins were throbbing. "He looks as if he could lose it completely and kill me!" Karen was terrified by her out-of-control son.

JESSICA, THE LIAR AND THIEF

"Jessica!" bellowed her father, George. "Come down here right now." Jessica slunk down the stairs and plopped onto the couch. "I just got a call from Mr. Nguyen, who says that you were over at his house yesterday with Van and now no one can find Mrs. Nguyen's earrings. Did you steal them?"

Jessica shook her head. She looked her father right in the eye, as she had so many times before, and said, "I don't know what you're talking about." She got up to leave. She was used to walking away from him.

"Where is your purse?" her father asked. "Is it in your room? You stay right there, I'm going to go get it."

Jessica shrugged and laughing she replied, "That stupid woman just can't remember where she put them."

A few moments later her father returned, purse in hand. He dumped it out on the couch, and immediately saw the earrings described by Mr. Nguyen. "Jessica! You did steal them! How could you do this? What is happening to you? Am I raising a thief? Do you want to become a criminal and spend your life in prison?"

Jessica gave her insolent shrug again. "Not much different than living here."

"You're grounded, young lady. You don't leave the house except to go to school. And you go right back and give these earrings to Mrs. Nguyen with an apology."

Jessica looked her father in the eye. "No." She stood there for a minute, then began to leave. Her father grabbed her arm, so angry he was shaking. "Did you hear me? I've grounded you!"

Jessica looked her father in the eye again. "You gotta do what you gotta do."

Her father was so angry that he was afraid he would strike and hurt his daughter. He let her go, staring after her and wondering whether he would ever be able to gain control of a daughter who could look him in the eye and lie to him, a daughter who could steal from her friends.

MARK, THE ALCOHOLIC

Sixteen-year-old Mark lay on his bed, snoring in an alcoholic haze, as his parents looked at him tearfully. They had begged him, punished him, bribed him, threatened him, loved him, done everything they could to get him to stop drinking. They had tried (without much success) to keep him away from his friends who were also heavy drinkers, and told their own friends not to leave alcohol out in their houses (Mark had several times been known to take full bottles and finish them at home). Now Mark was beginning to look terrible, shaky and pale, and to lose concentration and be unfocused all the time. His parents looked at him and knew that they had a child who was completely in thrall of alcohol and out-of-control.

Is Your Teenager Out Of Control?

Tom, Jessica and Mark: Three out-of-control teenagers. Their stories are tragic, but all too familiar. Tom is a big bully who has learned that he can physically intimidate his mother. Jessica has chosen to ignore anything she ever knew of right and wrong, consistently stealing and lying about doing so. Mark is in such an alcoholic fog that he doesn't care about anything but getting another drink. All three of these children come from good homes, from parents who care about their children. You may have the same situation in your own home. Does your teenager frighten you? Are you ashamed of your adolescent, and ashamed of being ashamed? Do you recognize that you have no control over your teenager, physically or emotionally?

If you don't lead in your household, your teenager will. Now is the time to make a stand. If your teenager is out of control, it's time to get in control and get your teenager back in control.

You're The Parent: Get In Control

First, move forward, not backwards. It's too late for lamenting: "If only I had done this . . ." or "I wish I hadn't been so. . . ." Self-flagellation is not going to do you any good now. Move ahead. Accept that your teenager has been completely out of control for a variety of reasons, some of which might be your doing, others of which were completely out of your hands. The reasons belong to the past. Right now just accept there is a major problem and work is needed to get the control back.

It's hard being "mean" to your children. Every fiber in your body yearns to give love, understanding and acceptance. Many of us think that if we can just love a little more, give a few more hugs, be there more, our children will lose their demons and turn back into the wonderful people they used to be. That's a comforting thought, but by the time you have a teenager like Tom who tells you to your face where to get off — when his respect for you is nonexistent — you are not going to get control back with a hug. You can't *talk* him back in control. You've probably given all the nurturing love you can. In fact, at this stage you probably actually dislike and maybe even think you can't love this child for all the grief and anguish he has caused you. It's not easy to live with the fact that your own child can hit you or threaten to, or yells or swears at you. We would never tolerate other people who do that to us. How can we accept this from our own children? We love our children and want them back in control. It's frightening to think that this child can be so irresponsible and so mean that he will be going into the world with those behaviors. We feel like bad parents, for sure.

How can we let our love get these children back? It takes an inner strength such as you have never had to use before. It takes raw courage, strength of character and incredible determination.

Step One: Do Whatever It Takes

Your first step is to resolve to do whatever it takes and that means *whatever*. Your children may even be angry with you, maybe even hate you for a while, so be prepared to accept that possibility. Your children will continue manipulating you (changing an argument into a digression on something else, following well-worn paths); after all, it worked in the past. Don't let it work now.

At this point you needn't fret about reasons children won't do what you say. You would do anything for your children, right? Now is the time to prove it, so that you can help them.

Step Two: Get Yourself In Control

Muster up your courage and resolve to take action. By now, you have probably cried more tears than you ever thought you had in you, had more fights with your children and perhaps even with your spouse than you ever wanted in a lifetime. Many times out-of-control children place a large strain on the marriage. However, before you begin taking back control, be certain you are in control of yourselves. Provide a joint front with the other parent, whether your spouse or an ex. Resolve that you are not going to

break down in front of your children. If you act as if you have
the power, you begin to empower yourself. Over the months or
even years that your children have grown out of your control,
you have been manipulated, tricked into thinking that they have
the power.

Step Three: Take Back The Power

You need to take charge, even if you feel afraid. You have
begun to feel helpless. Now is the time to change all that. Remember that you know more, you have more experience and you have
more power from a legal and financial standpoint than your teen.
And you are a lot more determined not to let your child waste his
life. You are the boss. You are in the leadership position. You are
the adult. You are regaining control and don't have to answer to
anyone. Don't defend yourself.

Step Four: Set Unambiguous Rules

Make absolutely certain your teenager knows what is expected
of him. That does not mean merely expressing your opinions. If
Tom's mother were to say, "I don't like it when you play your
stereo so loudly," all she is doing is giving Tom more ways to
annoy her. Tom will probably see her statement as just one more
example of the woes of having to live with "a parent." He then
will turn up the volume to "show her." She is not setting a rule
or making a demand. Setting a rule means saying, "You are to
play your stereo no louder than notch number three on the volume control." No ifs, ands or buts. Mrs. Williams made her rule
and gave the specifics of it. If your teenager is getting in late
because you say, "You have to be home early on school nights,"
you must say, "Tonight you are to be in the front door to stay by
11:00 P.M."

Be clear about what you want. Unambiguous rules are not
phrased as questions. A teenager who hears, "How do you expect
me to live in the same house as your blaring stereo?" doesn't hear
a demand to turn it down, but just another annoying parent

babbling away. The same is true when a rule is phrased as a favor. You may think your children are still your buddies and that they will want to do something for you, so you say, "Honey, for me, would you please turn down your stereo?" or "I'd really like you to turn down your stereo." The fact is that by this time your children don't really care what you want or what would make you happy. They see you as the enemy, the opponent in a battle they have every intention of winning.

One of the ineffective ways to make a rule is to phrase it as an observation, almost as an aside. "Your room is a mess again." Said in passing, that phrase means two different things to a teenager and to a parent. To the teen, it is just Dad griping again. To a parent, it is a request for action. Remember, children are not mind readers. Those teenagers who are truly out of control have built walls around them that require major efforts to breach. You have to make your rules loud and clear and your requests specific.

Unclear: "I don't like those friends you're hanging around with. It makes me feel funny when they are here in the house. I always feel they are going to take something and I won't be able to replace it."

Clear: "You are not to have Roger over to this house for any reason, at any time."

Unclear: "You are frightening your father and me, and your little brothers."

Clear: "You are not to raise a hand to anyone in this house. You are not to touch anyone in this house, unless someone hugs you and you hug back, gently. You are not to slap or hit or pinch or tickle anyone in this house. You are not to shove anyone in this house. There will be absolutely no nonloving physical contact between you and anyone in this house."

Leave No Room For Escape Clauses

For example, you leave an opening any devious child can get through when you say, "Roger can't come to the house if he isn't invited." Perhaps Roger will show up at your house by inviting himself there. If you make a rule, leave no escape clause.

State Time Frames Clearly

When the situation has become completely out of control, you obviously have already gone through the hysterics and dramatics. Your children have learned to ignore you, thinking you are just having a fit again. If you set a rule such as, "You are not to take telephone calls from your friends," they think they can ignore you because you couldn't possibly mean FOREVER, or could you? Give a specific time: "You are not allowed to take telephone calls between 5:00 and 9:00 P.M. Mondays through Fridays for the rest of this semester."

Step Five: Follow Through

Don't explain your rules. Don't spend hours letting your children manipulate you by arguing against the rules. When you set a rule, it is carved in stone. This is where the tough love, the determined caring, comes into effect. It was the tough stance, the clearly stated rules, and most of all the closely monitored follow through that helped the families we met at the beginning of this chapter get back together again.

TOM REVISITED

Karen informed Tom he was not to touch anyone in the house again, not to lay a finger on anyone. In order to back her rule up, she learned judo in case her son became violent. She also took a basic safety and self-defense class in which she learned how to protect herself from a mugger. The first time Tom grabbed his mother, she used her self-protection class trick of yanking his little finger back as hard as she could, stating, "I told you you are not to touch anyone in this house. That is the rule." He backed off, she turned the stereo down and left the room.

Tom bided his time for a few days, then began the loud stereo music again. When Karen went to his room, he was braced, obviously looking for a fight. Without letting herself be drawn into an argument, she told him to turn the music down and waited for him to do so. He did. And, Karen was glad to note, when he slipped past her through the doorway, he made especially certain not to let any part of him touch her body.

Note how much preparation Karen Williams did before she could in fact follow through effectively. She took judo and self-protection classes. If you are physically intimidated by your children, you may wish to do the same. This is true whether you are a male or a female. Fathers can use the help too. Teenage children are often bigger and stronger than their parents. Self-defense classes are available through many universities or police forces. Martial arts of all types are taught privately. If you are too shy to take a class, hire a private instructor. All you need to learn are a few basic moves; you don't need a black belt. If you sincerely feel that your child will hurt you physically, look for the community resources that help parents with out-of-control teens.

Are you wincing as you read this, thinking that confronting your child could lead to you or your child getting hurt? At this stage you have to be tough. You are not perpetuating violence. If you slug your child, you start a cycle in which he slugs you back and the violence increases. You are using self-defense tactics to protect yourself and to regain the upper hand. You just want to show your child that you are no longer frightened of him and will not tolerate his intimidation. The fact that you obviously do not hurt him when in fact you can, and when he knows in his heart that he has certainly given you plenty of reasons to lose your temper and do so, reassures him of your resolve to get him to respect you and himself. He feels secure in your authority and your love.

JESSICA REVISITED

Sometimes following through means constant surveillance. Jessica's father and mother took time off from work and followed their daughter night and day. She was never out of sight of one of her parents. One day they rode the bus to school with her. They sat in her classroom. They sat in her room at night when she was doing her homework. The first time Jessica's mom, Mary, saw her daughter take a pen that Jessica's friend Jennifer had left out on the lunch table, she spoke in a very loud voice. "Jennifer, my daughter just took your pen. You left it on the table. She took it when your back was turned and put it into her purse. You will find it there now. Please take it back." Everyone at the table was shocked, and Jessica was embarrassed beyond words. She tried to make a joke of it, saying that parents were so uncool.

Mary and Frank remained on watch and kept telling Jessica that they would stay with her constantly and continue to call attention to every theft. Within a few weeks, Jessica was no longer taking anything. Her parents kept up the surveillance, but it was not embarrassing Jessica anymore because since she was no longer stealing, they were not saying anything to humiliate or call attention to her.

Once again, the parents were prepared. It wasn't easy taking off work and rearranging schedules to be with Jessica every minute. It wasn't easy watching her, never taking their eyes off her. (Mary even went to the bathroom with Jessica and made Jessica accompany her. When Frank had to go, he had the teacher watch Jessica for the few minutes he was gone.) These parents were also incredibly determined. They constantly felt guilty and knew they were hurting their daughter's social life, but they were resolute.

MARK REVISITED

Mark's parents did a lot of preparation. They searched his room thoroughly, getting rid of all alcohol, all posters that showed alcohol being glorified, all magazines. Then they restricted Mark to his room for three days, bringing him his meals, not letting him talk to his friends on the telephone, just having him dry out. They took away all his money and made sure he couldn't get any more. They got rid of all the alcohol in the house, even cough syrup. They called all of Mark's friends and told them they would call the police on them if they gave Mark a drink. They talked to the parents of Mark's friends. Most of them were sympathetic and agreed to keep an eye on Mark, making sure he didn't have anything to drink. The few who thought Mark's parents were making too big of a deal about a "few drinks" were intimidated by threats of police action (serving alcohol to a minor) or lawsuits if they didn't help. (These parents weren't fooling around!) Mr. and Mrs. Reilley took careful note of which of Mark's friends drank or seemed to have parents who didn't feel as strongly about teen-age drinking as they did, and told Mark he was not to visit those friends again or have them over to the house. They even went to the local groceries, liquor stores and bars and explained the situation, showing a picture of Mark. He was not to be sold any liquor under any circumstances. Again there were warnings of the consequences of serving alcohol to a minor.

Mrs. Reilley arranged to keep Mark very busy. She hired a private tutor to come to the house two nights a week to work with Mark (as his schoolwork had suffered terribly from his drinking). She enrolled him in a swim team program, took him to practice and waited for him, and brought him home three nights a week. She or her husband drove Mark to school and brought him home every day. Mark was not allowed to drive at all. His comings and goings were always in the company of one parent. Mrs. Reilley asked the high school principal to see that Mark did not leave the high school campus all day, even for lunch. Two to three times a day, she dropped in unexpectedly on Mark to make sure he was, in fact, at school. After doing without alcohol for a month and not being around the other kids who thought alcohol was cool, Mark almost forgot about it. He stopped talking about drinking, and stopped plotting ways to outsmart his parents to get a drink. He got so involved in other activities that soon he was as "addicted" to them as he had been to alcohol. When he finally got his driving privileges back, Mark was too busy to stop at a bar for a drink even if he had wanted to.

If it had been necessary, Mrs. Reilley would have sent Mark to a 28-day alcohol treatment center and/or 90 days of AA meetings.

ADDRESSING YOUR FEARS

Being assertive with your teenager is tough and can be very trying. You may worry whether you are in fact ruining your children's lives with this strong love, as they keep insisting you are. The three questions below are commonly asked by parents.

1. Am I Abusing My Child?

No. You are being assertive, using tough love to help your child through what is probably the worst time of his life. You are being a role model to show your child that love is expressed in strength. You may be forced to be more physical than you like, but reassure yourself that it is temporary. Think about when your children were little. Didn't you bodily drag them away, sometimes screaming and kicking, when they got too close to the fire? Didn't you lock up the poisons and household cleaners to keep them away from small hands? Didn't you use a folding barrier to prevent your children from entering dangerous spaces, such as a balcony? You are responsible for your children. *You have the right*, the responsibility, to keep them safe. When your child reaches the stage of being out of control, you must use whatever measures are necessary.

2. Won't My Child Hate Me Forever?

Forever, no. Now, yes. You have to steel yourself to accept screaming, swearing, hitting and the most hurtful words you can imagine. A child who has gone so far and become out of control is already showing contempt for you by not heeding your rules; the hatred he feels at that point is for himself. He may transfer it to you temporarily, but when you are back in control, he will respect that. The affection and love may take a little longer. Right now you are not looking to be The Good Guy. If you want that, you are going to fail and your children will remain in control. What you want to be is The Boss. Your children may not like you, but they will respect you.

3. What If I Can't Go Through With It?

Get outside help. There are special schools for troubled children. Churches, synagogues, youth centers, counselors, therapists, psychologists and psychiatrists can all help. Don't hesitate to call the police. They are accustomed to dealing with problem children, and can refer you to clinics and centers designed to help out-of-control children and their parents. You have probably heard of programs like Scared Straight, in which teenagers visit a prison and have heart-to-heart talks with the prisoners, in the hope the children become so terrified of prison life that they change their behavior. There are also private programs, like Tough Love or Outward Bound. For the addicted teen, 12-Step programs, such as AA or NA, work miracles every day.

You may also get the chance to be the loving, nurturing parent you want to be. It may take a while, but things will turn around. You will be proud of yourself for having had the strength and tenacity to see things through. Your children will be proud of you, and perhaps even shocked that you were strong enough — and that you loved them enough — to go through all of this.

The reference section at the back of this book provides resources for dealing with the teenager who is out of control. Get information and get help in helping your teenager.

PART
SIX

Keeping Your Teenager Safe From The Dragons Of Life

Talking About Sex
With Your Teenager

13

 One of the biggest responsibilities parents come face-to-face with in the adolescent years is helping the teenager develop a healthy attitude toward intimacy, and acquiring the know-how to safeguard his sexual health. It's a real challenge because of the inherent duality: You want your teenager to learn a healthy sense of loving. But let's face it, most of us parents would like our children to do so in a "look but don't touch too much" style. A parent at a recent seminar of mine in Boston summed it up this way: "I'm trying to keep my

16-year-old daughter preoccupied with sports, grades, girlfriends and family activities. My goal is to buy her time to grow up a bit before she has to deal with the complexities of sex and getting involved in sexual activities. I'd like her to *postpone* the inevitable. Hopefully, other things will seem more important for a while." Like other parents of teenage children, this mother will be going up against hormones and peer pressure. Puberty triggers key hormones that set in motion sexual maturity. They can create emotional upheaval as well.

Unfolding sexual development is often perplexing for the teenager. Intense and erratic emotions, conflicting feelings and new and changing self — this time of incessant rearranging — often create anxiety and insecurity about what's going on and what it all means.

Just because we parents would like our teenagers to postpone sex until they are older, more emotionally mature and can handle the responsibility of all that it entails doesn't mean they will. Helping your child learn healthy ways to respond to increasingly urgent sexual impulses, to withstand peer pressure to have sex, to avoid premature pregnancy and to learn how to protect herself from contracting sexually transmitted diseases, all require *active* parenting.

Don't sidestep your responsibility to help your teenager. Don't *pass the buck*, believing it's the "other parent's job." Don't *assume* that your teenager already knows all he needs to know. Don't rely on what you *think* the school has taught. Don't *count* on the accuracy of the information your child gets from her friends. Question the *validity* of what your teenager is telling you.

THE DRAGONS OF THE SEXUAL WORLD ARE MORE DANGEROUS THAN EVER

Prompted in part by news of a Chicago high school where one-third of the female students were pregnant, *People* reported, "In America, one million teenagers become pregnant each year. Four out of five are unmarried. More than half get abortions. Babies having babies or killing them." Dismay has turned to deep fear with recognition of the combined possibilities of adolescent sexuality and AIDS. Much has changed since that report. The ante has been raised. Now our children's sexual involvement could mean more than pregnancy and venereal disease — it could mean death, as is evidenced by the alarming numbers of adolescent children who have been infected with the AIDS virus.

For all the information that abounds, many teens are frightfully unwilling to accept responsibility for their sexual well-being. The reasons for ignoring contraception won't seem new: The boy's insistence that a condom reduces spontaneity and pleasure, the girl's willingness to give in to boy's pressure despite her better judgment. Even when knowledge seems in place and protection is at hand, many teens fall victim to that age-old plague of youth, believing they are exempt from the law of averages — a feeling of immortality, "It can never happen to me," leaving them open to unwanted pregnancy and/or a shortened life with AIDS.

TEENS BELIEVE THAT PARENTS DO NOT TALK FRANKLY ABOUT SEX

"Most parents, mine included, think they talk about sex much more than they actually do," said Laura. "When I ask Mom a direct question, she beats around the bush with a 30-minute conversation, much of it totally unrelated to the question I asked."

"It's not that parents don't talk with their teenagers," said 17-year-old Stacey, "but that they delude themselves about how often they need to. Many parents approach the subject only if they suspect their kids are having sex. Sex is like the drug issue. By the time parents suspect it's going on, it has been for a long time. Then their talk is too little, too late."

"Many parents avoid talking about sex with their children because they find it an uncomfortable subject," said Barbara Jamel, a high school sex education teacher. "When I called the parents of a 14-year-old student and suggested they talk with their daughter about her overt sexual behavior, the father said, 'I'm just not good at these sorts of things. I leave that area up to my wife. When she gets back into town, I'll tell her you called.' He has two other children, a 17-year-old son and a 10-year-old daughter."

Even when parents feel they have been frank and informative, teenagers often perceive parents as timid, embarrassed and unwilling to hear the real facts about what their teens are up to. "Most parents believe they are getting straight answers when they ask their kids sexual questions," said 16-year-old Lynn. "But rarely, and I do mean rarely, do teens tell their parents the whole truth."

"I would never be totally honest with my mother or my father," said 15-year-old Courtney. "They are very conservative Catholics and believe that I should not and, therefore, will not have sex until I am married. If they found out I was having sex with my 16-year-old boyfriend, they would disown me. So I'm making sure they don't find out."

"I had an abortion six months ago," said 14-year-old Denise. "My mother would be furious if she found out I had an abortion, but she wouldn't have known what to do if I told her I was pregnant. Her being mad isn't going to resolve anything. I just did what I had to do."

Many parents have one set of standards for girls and another for boys. "It may not be openly talked about, but double standards show up in the standards and expectations deemed appropriate for the teenager's behavior — such as a curfew," said Dr. Bob Whitman, Adolescent Counseling Center in Oregon. "Whereas parents of teenage girls may hold to a curfew, too often teenage boys are allowed to come in when they please."

"Some parents really don't want to know about their teen's sex life," said 17-year-old Tanya. "If parents knew, for example, how often date rape happened to teenage girls, they would ban dating altogether. Parents just aren't all that useful when it comes to talking openly and honestly about the realities of teen sex."

"My dad said that he would 'kill the guy' if he found out I was having sex," says Lisa. "My dad is locked into a vision of my being his darling little daughter with a snow-white virginity. Yet he takes a 'boys will be boys' approach with my 15-year-old brother. My father teases my brother about getting sex and having sex with girls. Why should one set of rules be okay for my brother but not okay for me?"

Some teenagers believe that even when parents would accept their becoming sexually active, parents aren't necessarily a good source of information. "Most parents haven't a clue to what is going on," said 17-year-old Gena. "Many parents are unable to discuss current trends or the latest and safest methods of birth control. A lot of parents focus on AIDS as a scare tactic, rather than talking about how to protect oneself from getting AIDS from the many possible sources, not realizing that there are a lot of things teens need to know besides protecting themselves against AIDS."

"The average high school kid has received very little substantial information from their parents, and a tremendous amount of misinformation from their peers. For many, the best advice comes from the centers, such as planned parenthood," said Blaine Thomas, a high school psychology teacher. "Many parents think they owe that obligatory first talk, and when that's out of the way, kids will do what they're supposed to do."

Obviously, many parents find it difficult to talk about sex with their teens. If we parents are sending a message of embarrassment, misinformation and denial, our teens are reading it loud and clear. "Basically, you just tell parents what they want to hear. No more, no less," said 17-year-old Tony.

Though it's sometimes difficult to discuss sexual matters with our children, we must do it. We must confront our feelings about our adolescent becoming sexually curious. It can be both frightening and rewarding to see your child struggling to become independent, to make his own decisions, to "try on" his newfound sexuality when he still seems too young to experience sex at an age when it is doubtful he can accept the responsibility for all that it entails. This is another reason why we cannot sidestep our responsibility. We must realize that sexual curiosity and sexual contact during adolescence — whether it be kissing, hand-holding, caressing or intercourse — is an inevitable and normal part of human development. Don't disconnect. You need to talk to your adolescent openly and honestly about all issues of human sexuality, including romantic or sexual rejection, the decision to have sex for the first time, having intercourse, the risks of pregnancy and sexually transmitted diseases including AIDS, homosexuality, sexual molestation and more.

What your teenager wants and needs most is for you to be approachable for information, guidance and reassurance. Your teenager also needs your help in making important decisions should she become pregnant, contract a venereal disease or deal with sexual harassment. And remember, talking about sex means helping your sons become sexually responsible, too.

HELPING YOUR TEENAGER DEAL WITH REJECTION

Even if your teenager is voted the smartest, most popular, most attractive and wittiest kid at school, she will probably experience rejection in one form or another. Rejection is a part of exploring relationships, ending unsatisfactory ones and establishing new ones. Being rejected and rejecting others can be a very traumatic experience for the teenager.

Be sensitive to your teenager's feelings, even if you are feeling a bit pleased about the boy or girl who has broken off the relationship with your child. A parent can sometimes make the mistake of saying something unhelpful or unkind just when the teenager is feeling intense hurt when a special friendship falls apart. Saying something like, "Don't take it so hard, she wasn't good for you anyway," or, "You always got into trouble when you hung out with him. Good riddance!" is likely to be more damaging than soothing.

Be a good listener. Focus on your child's feelings and help him with them. Reassure your teenager that the hurt he feels will go away eventually. Teach him *how* he can deal with the special pain he is feeling, and how beneficial and healing it is to be especially kind to himself while he's coming to terms with the hurt. Encourage him to get involved in physical activities or to focus on hobbies, or to spend time alone or with good friends as a way of coping. Explain how doing so is therapeutic and can help him channel his feelings in an appropriate and constructive way. Such actions can go a long way in helping your teenager feel validated in his worth as a person and secure that he will make it through this and be okay. You might then share a story of your own, one that parallels what he is going through. "I came home in tears because the love of my life said I was no longer his type," said Anna. "My dad listened patiently to my sob story then shared a similar harrowing experience. It made me feel that I would survive this and, as Dad pointed out, it probably wouldn't be the last time it would happen to me. He said that no matter what, I could always count on his love. It was comforting to know that my dad's love for me was stable."

TEACHING YOUR TEEN ABOUT REJECTING OTHERS

Just as being rejected can be a difficult experience for the teenager, saying "no" — learning how to reject others — can be stressful, too. You want your teenager to treat others with consideration, but not back down in respecting her own needs. Your teenager needs to know how to assert her rights. Help her understand that she has a right to say no, but that she must do so courteously. An effective way to do this is to use a role-playing technique. Role playing allows your teenager to try on potential stressful interactions and rehearse how she could handle the situation. It can also help you assess your teen's skills in implementing her decisions under pressure. Role playing can help your teenager learn the skills to interact with others in a positive way.

Here's an example of how role-playing might work:

Sixteen-year-old Tara has been asked by Josh to go to the movies on Friday. She agrees to go out with him, but when Nate asks her out, she decides that she would rather go out with Nate than Josh. Lacking the courage to tell Josh she wants to call the date off, she decides to stand him up — to not be at home when he comes to her house to pick her up on Friday.

You want to convince her that this is not an appropriate way to handle it. You also want her to learn how to confront others — in this case, Josh — face-to-face, and to do so with courage and consideration.

Here's how your role playing might go:

Test Run 1:

(Your teen represents herself; you represent Josh.)

> **Teen** (Pretending to phone Josh): "Hello, Josh?"
> **Parent:** "Hi, Tara!"
> **Teen:** "I'm calling about our date tomorrow night."
> **Parent:** "Oh, I know! I can hardly wait! My big brother is letting me borrow his car, so we don't have to use my old wreck. We're going to this great new place for dinner before the movie starts, and oh, I bought this really great new shirt in your favorite color! We're going to have so much fun. I still plan on picking you up at 6:30."
> **Teen** (Unprepared for Josh's enthusiasm and afraid to disappoint him): "Oh, um, well, okay." (Disappointed in herself, she hangs up the phone.)

To this your teenager may well say, "No way, Mom, I don't care if he is excited, I'm not going. I'd rather go out with Nate. You know I've been dying to go out with Nate." To this you might add, "Well, okay, let's try it again!"

Test Run 2:

(Your teen represents herself; you represent Josh.)

> **Teen:** "Hello, Josh?"
>
> **Parent:** "Hi, Tara, I'm glad you called. I hate to have to tell you this, but I've got the flu. I just know I won't be well enough for our date tomorrow night. I'm really sorry. Listen, I feel lousy, can we talk later — like at school on Monday?"
>
> **Teen:** "Sure. Oh, Josh, I'm sorry you're not feeling well." Surprised, Tara hangs up the phone.

She might say something like this to you, "Boy, am I glad I listened and didn't just blurt out that I wasn't going. This really lets me off the hook!" To this you might add, "Okay, but let's try once more!"

Test Run 3:

(Your teen represents herself; you represent Josh.)

> **Teen:** "Hello, Josh?"
>
> **Parent:** "Hello, Tara. What's up? Why are you calling?"
>
> **Teen** (Feeling put on the spot): "I'm calling about tomorrow night. I know it's very late to back out, but I really have to. I hope you'll have time to make other plans."
>
> **Parent:** "Well, I'm sorry to hear that, Tara. I was really looking forward to going. Why are you backing out?"
>
> **Tara** (Again feeling put on the spot): "I've made a decision to go with someone else. I'm sure you know Nate Williams. Well, I have really wanted to go out with him, and it just happens that he asked me out. I really want to go, and I hope that I haven't hurt your feelings. You're a really nice guy, and I don't want you to be offended."
>
> **Parent:** "Are you sure I can't change your mind?"
>
> **Tara:** "Yes, I'm sure, Josh. I'm sorry. Thank you for not being too upset with me."
>
> **Parent:** "Oh, c'mon, Tara. Don't say no. Besides, Nate is a nerd. Please say you'll change your mind. Besides, I won't be able to get another date by tomorrow — I'll be stuck with nothing to do!"
>
> **Teen:** "I'm sorry, Josh."

> **Parent** (Still sounding disappointed but accepting it): "All right. Bye, Tara. Oh, if you change your mind, please call me back. OK? Bye."

Of course, there are many other likely responses that could have come from the scenes above. You may even want to go through a scenario where Tara must call Nate and tell him no. The point is that this kind of rehearsing can help your child build her confidence in handling situations that have potentially stressful outcomes.

This role-playing scene actually took place between a parent and daughter in one of my workshops. When the exercise was over, Tara commented, "This exercise really helped me to practice how to handle the situation, because I really didn't know how to tell Josh that I'd changed my mind about going out with him. To tell the truth, before I role-played this with my mom, I just wasn't going to be home when he came to pick me up. Standing him up would have made him feel really awful — like you said, rejected and humiliated. Role playing gave me the confidence to go through with the conversation I should have had in the first place."

The next step would be for Tara and her parent to reverse roles, with Tara playing the part of Josh, and the parent representing Tara. By exchanging roles, your child gets to put the shoe on the other foot — to put herself in the other person's place.

ROLE PLAYING: HELPING YOUR TEEN BUILD COURAGE IN CONFRONTING OTHERS

Being rejected can be a very traumatic experience for the teenager, especially when the other person does it in an insensitive way. Teenagers are often rude and insensitive with one another, particularly when they are unsure of how to get out of a situation they want to change. Learning interpersonal skills in treating others fairly and with consideration — communicating effectively — is an important skill to help your teenager acquire.

Once again, you can use role playing to help your teenager try on potential stressful interactions and rehearse how he could handle the situation. It can help you assess your teenager's skills in implementing his decisions under stress. It can also help your adolescent face the possibility of rejection without losing his confidence in himself. Here's an example of how role playing might work:

Seventeen-year-old Luke wants to ask Kerry to the school prom. He has not dated her before, but has wanted to ask her out for some time. He fears she may say no, doesn't want to face the possibility or worse, feel silly for asking her out. He decides not to ask her and thinks about staying home from the prom altogether, since he would rather be with her than anyone else.

You want to convince him that asking is worth the risk and, even if Kerry declines, not to feel diminished. You would like to help him develop more confidence in dealing with rejection.

Here's how that role playing might go:

Test Run 1:

(Your child represents himself; you represent the other teen.)

Teen (Pretending to phone Kerry): "Hello, Kerry? This is Luke."
Parent: "Oh hi, Luke!"
Teen: "I'm calling about the prom next week."
Parent: "Oh, I know! I'm so excited about it! Jason asked me to go with him, and my mom is buying me a new a dress. Who are you going with?"
Teen (Unprepared for Kerry's news): "Um . . . I don't know yet, I haven't really given it much thought." (Feeling devastated that she already has another date.) "Kerry, my dad has to use the phone, so I have to hang up now."

At this point he might say to you, "That does it. I'm not going to run the risk of sounding stupid. And I'll bet she does have another date." To this you might add, "Maybe. Let's try again!"

Test Run 2:

(Your child represents himself; you represent the other teen.)

> **Teen:** "Hello, Kerry?"
> **Parent:** "Oh hi, Luke."
> **Teen:** "I'm calling about the prom next week."
> **Parent:** "Oh, that's right. Gosh, I had forgotten all about it. Are you going?"
> **Teen:** "Yes. I was wondering if you would like to go with me? We could have dinner first."
> **Parent:** "I'd really like to, Luke, but my father won't let me go out on dates until my sixteenth birthday. It's only a few months from now, in March, and I can't wait."
> **Teen** (Certain it is just an excuse): "Oh."
> **Parent:** "I could always meet you at the prom. My parents said I could go. I'm really excited. My mom is buying me a really great dress. Would you like to meet there?"
> **Teen:** "That would be great, Kerry. Would you like to eat lunch together at school tomorrow?"
> **Parent:** "Yeah, see you tomorrow."

To this your teen might say, "That works!" And you might add, "Yes, but let's try it one more time!"

Test Run 3:

(Your child represents himself; you represent the other teen.)

> **Teen:** "Hello, Kerry?"
> **Parent:** "Yes?"
> **Teen:** "This is Luke."
> **Parent:** "Luke, the Luke in my math class?"
> **Teen:** "Yes, Luke Masters."
> **Parent:** "Oh hi, Luke."
> **Teen:** "I'm calling about the prom next week. I was wondering if you would like to go to it with me."
> **Parent:** "I'm sorry, Luke, I've already made other plans just yesterday, but I would like to see you. Would you like to go to a movie sometime?"
> **Teen:** "Yes. Would you like to go out this Friday?"
> **Parent:** "That sounds great."

Of course, there could be many other possible responses. Once again, this kind of rehearsing can help your teenager build his confidence in handling situations that have potentially stressful outcomes, and give him the courage to face potential rejection. It can also teach him to expect the best!

SEXUAL READINESS

Sexual intercourse, when engaged in carelessly, promiscuously or selfishly, can be an emotionally scarring and damaging experience. It's another reason we would like our children to postpone their involvement with sex. You may want your child to wait until he is out of high school before getting involved in sexual activity. You may wish that your child abstain from sex until she is married. As a parent in Ohio told me, "Sure we want our daughter to develop a healthy attitude toward sex, but we want her to wait to have sex until she finds a lifemate." You may want to help your son or daughter avoid making the same mistake you made, particularly if you married because of a pregnancy. Perhaps you want your child to remain "innocent" longer, to enjoy her activities and friends and to acquire an education before she must cope with the complexities and demands of relationships. Not all adolescents will postpone sexual activity. Parents must face the fact that sexual activity is likely to be a part of the adolescent years.

"BUT IF I DON'T HAVE SEX WITH HIM, HE WON'T GO OUT WITH ME AGAIN"

Aside from hormones reminding adolescents that their bodies are developing sexual maturity, their peers are also likely to remind them. The teenager often faces enormous peer pressure. One friend may brag, "I have sex after the third date." Another may warn, "If you don't have sex with your date, he will never go out with you again." A girl or boy may surrender to intercourse without ever learning what true intimacy is about. Ultimately your adolescent is the one making the decision about whom to have sex with and when.

As a parent you may wonder and worry about whether your teenager is sexually active, but today the question of when sexual intercourse starts is no longer the biggest concern. Adolescents are making their own choices, and the real issue facing many parents is whether their son or daughter is using a protective condom. As issues of sexuality are openly discussed, you can guide your adolescent toward the right attitude for responsible sex. You can serve your adolescent by helping him gain an understanding of what love and sex mean — and the responsibilities involved.

TEENAGERS NEED TO KNOW HOW TO SAY "NO" TO SEX

Teens want to "be adults," and they see sex as a passage to adulthood. Teenagers need to know that it's okay to say no to sexual intercourse, but they need to know how to assert their rights. One girl said, "At school, I'm always asked if I'm a virgin. If I say yes, I'm considered a prude. If I say no, I'm considered loose. What am I supposed to say?"

Assure your teenager that there is nothing wrong with being a virgin and that it's appropriate to tell friends it's none of their business if they ask. Help your teenager feel confident about asserting her own rights — in this case, to privacy. Discourage your adolescent from equating sex with social gain or reward. A girl should not feel that she has to "repay" her date with intercourse, nor should a boy think he has to "perform" in order to prove he is masculine.

Many adolescents confess to having sex out of fear of being ridiculed or rejected. Teach your adolescent that he needs to learn to control his sexual impulses. He must respect the rights of others. For example, when a girl says, "No," the boy should not pressure her into changing her decision, nor should he make her feel guilty for saying no to sexual activity. Help your adolescent understand that sexual activity is a responsibility with consequences.

CHILDREN HAVING CHILDREN:
TEENAGE PREGNANCY

One consequence of increased sexual activity among teenagers is a comparable increase in teenage pregnancy. One out of every five children in the United States is born to teenagers. Every day in America, 40 teenage girls give birth to their third child. Although young women are able to conceive, the pelvic girdle does not attain its full size until the adolescent reaches the age of 17 or 18. This puts the teenage mother and her infant at physical risk. Teenage mothers tend to give birth to children who are premature. Prematurity leads to an increased chance of major health problems, resulting from an insufficiently developed immune system. The death rate for infants of teenagers is 2.4 times that of infants born to mothers 17 and older, and the maternal death rate of children under 15 is 2.5 times that among mothers age 20 and older.

Pregnancy flings the teenager into premature parenthood. Being a teenager with a baby is a displacing experience that seriously impairs the efforts of both the teenage mother and father to develop a healthy sense of personal identity. As David Elkind reminds us, "To be in the place of a parent while still being in many respects a child, to be in the place of nurturing when one's own needs for nurture are still strong makes for the formation of a consistent, whole and meaningful definition of self, difficult, if not impossible to attain." Teenagers are rarely prepared to cope with parenthood.

The notion that the boy and girl will get married and live "happily ever after" almost never happens. Understandably most young mothers and fathers are unprepared for the time, money, patience and commitment a baby requires. Many feel trapped, and they are.

"If only we knew how emotionally taxing and physically fatiguing this would be, we wouldn't have let this happen," says

Bobby, an 18-year-old father. "I love Carrie and our baby, and I want them to have more. We are living with my parents and trying to finish school, but it's hard. Carrie is often up late at night with the baby and goes to school tired and drained. I'm sometimes tired and irritable from holding down a job and completing high school. Sometimes I find myself drawing two columns listing the pros and cons of decisions to quit school so as to work full-time to support the three of us, or to quit my job so as to have the time to study and improve my grades to get into college in order to earn more.

"My life has changed and not for the better. It has become so complex. My high school friends talk mostly about upcoming football and soccer games, but I no longer have the luxury of playing sports. The time once devoted to practice now belongs to financial security for Carrie and the baby. Where I once worried about money for having a good time on the weekends, I now worry about how I will ever afford a place of our own.

"I spend a considerable amount of time trying to repair the relationship with Carrie's parents. They feel we were irresponsible and blame me for 'ruining' Carrie's life. It's been five months since the birth of our baby and they still aren't talking to me. Carrie is 16 and they wanted her to have an abortion so that she could continue their plans for her. We love our baby, but it has changed us, too. If I had known how much and how fast our lives would change, I wouldn't have let this happen."

Bobby's story illustrates the inherent stresses of teenage pregnancy. The teenager is thrust into responsibility for an infant at a time when she is still learning to be responsible for herself. She is set apart from peers and friends, unable to join in many of the activities enjoyed by teens. She cannot afford to do things she used to enjoy. She eventually comes to resent others, sometimes even the baby. She faces parental disappointment. Sometimes the new parent isn't even old enough to qualify for a driver's license!

Bobby and Carrie were fortunate, to a degree. They were able to remain together, to get married, have their baby and have a tolerable living situation. Bobby is secure in his love for his wife and child and is a loving, supportive part of their lives. Not all teenage fathers or mothers are so lucky.

TEENAGE BOYS BECOME
PARENTS AS WELL

For the most part, pregnancy is still viewed from the girl's perspective, but it quickly becomes a painful issue for the teenage father as well. Decisions about the mother and child are generally made without regard for the teenage father — that is, the teenage father is not allowed by angry parents to see the mother or child again. This special problem carries problems of its own, producing feelings of loss, rejection and alienation for young fathers. The perspective that teenage boys are interested only in sexual gratification and have fleeting casual relationships with their girlfriends is always the case.

Boys usually know their girlfriends for a year or more, are emotionally bonded by feelings of affection and love, and have been having sexual intercourse for ten months or longer. More than three-fourths of the fathers continue seeing their baby's mother for two or more years after the baby is born.

Contrary to the myth that young fathers prefer to leave after learning that the girl is pregnant, many young fathers do not want to abandon their babies. The pregnancy, then, can cause overwhelming stress for teenage fathers as well.

"Elaine and I had been together for a year when her parents learned she was pregnant," said 16-year-old Gary. "They said they would kill me if I ever showed up at their house again. After a month of trying to call and get through, I became so depressed that I contemplated suicide."

The feelings of young fathers have been routinely neglected by parents. Many teenage fathers report that the girl's parents don't accept them, don't approve of them or worse, refuse to speak to them. They are generally excluded, primarily by the girl's parents, from decisions made about their babies. Often the teenage father is not told if and when the baby has been born, whether the child has been adopted or turned over to foster care or if the pregnancy has been terminated by abortion.

"A BABY GAVE ME SOMEONE TO LOVE"

Many explanations have been offered for teenage pregnancy. Among these is lack of information about pregnancy and being sexually active without the benefit of birth control. "I had no idea I could father a child at age 13," said Matt, "so we didn't bother with contraceptives." Another explanation involves the teenager's desire to have someone of her own to love, and to be loved and wanted in return — "I just need someone of my own," said 14-year-old Kathy. "My mother and new stepdad have each other, and my dad lives out of state. Who is there for me? I was always so lonely. My baby will need me and I won't be alone. Somebody will finally care." Finally, there is the need to be regarded as an adult. "My mother treats me like I'm a child, but I'll have her know that I can be an adult, too. When my baby is born, she will have to deal with me like an adult," said 16-year-old Tracy.

You must not be passive in teaching your teenager about the consequences of sexual intercourse. All adolescents must know the answers to these questions:

- How does pregnancy occur?
- How can I prevent pregnancy?
- How can I avoid contracting a sexually transmitted disease, such as AIDS?
- What should be done if a girl becomes pregnant?
- What should be done if you are fearful you have a venereal disease or AIDS?

You must communicate with your adolescent. Start now. A 12-year-old child is not too young to learn, and a 17-year-old child is not too old to review. Assure your child she can turn to you for information and for help when needed. Don't feel that you have to know all the answers. Get help if you need more information. Contact your child's pediatrician, your family doctor, a school nurse or a family crisis center for help and referral services. The section at the end of this book provides additional resource information.

TEENAGE ABORTIONS

The dramatic increase in teenage pregnancy has also resulted in an increase in abortions among teenagers. Nearly all states report an increase in teenage abortions. Abortion for U.S. teenagers under 15 has risen 220% in recent years. Abortion has become a viable alternative for young people. Yet abortion, for whatever the reasons, is always sad and often emotionally damaging. Preventing children from having to face abortion is a powerful reason for parents to teach children about responsible sex.

Because the emotional trauma of abortion can cause life-long trauma, parents want to eliminate its possibility from their teenager's experiences. Your teenager needs to understand exactly what abortion entails and should not view it simply as a way to resolve a pregnancy. "We figured if anything happened, she could always get an abortion" is not a healthy attitude for teenage couples to have. Abortion should not be something that serves as a backup for teens, but rather should be fully understood, with all of its ramifications. Teens must know this before they become sexually active. We can aid this understanding in many ways. If you feel you need assistance in helping your teen, obtain professional counseling. Healthcare centers can help you. Learn as much as possible about abortion on your own, then be prepared to stimulate and answer your teenager's questions. Purchase materials or photocopy articles on abortion and make them available for your child to read, and discuss them. And remember, your son needs this information just as much as your daughter does.

SEXUALLY TRANSMITTED DISEASES

Part of being responsible in sex is being informed about all of the consequences of sexual relations. Aside from the risk of pregnancy, young people need to be informed about sexually transmitted diseases. We need to talk openly, honestly and intelligently about things such as syphilis, gonorrhea, herpes and AIDS.

Educate your teenager to be aware of the signs and symptoms and how to lessen the risk of contracting a disease. You may not know all the answers and may need to turn elsewhere for help. The reference section at the end of this book lists books that provide the hard facts you need to have a credible discussion with your child. Pediatricians, gynecologists and school counselors as well may be able to provide information or refer you to someone else who can help. It is important not to turn away from difficult questions or from those you are unsure of.

THE SHAME THAT BINDS: INCEST AND RAPE

Incest is a criminal offense and is considered an illegal act in every state in the United States. This kind of relationship is banned by almost all religions and societies; it is often called the "universal taboo." Incest is a particularly frightening problem because it involves intercourse between an adult and a child in the same family. At least half of the one million youngsters sexually abused each year have had an incestuous relationship. Incest is a sexual relationship between close family members: brother and sister, father and daughter, mother and son, grandparent and grandchild. With the increasing number of stepfamilies there is a proportionate increase in incestuous relationships involving a step-father and teenage daughter.

It's not easy for youngsters to expose sexual victimization. The young person is often afraid of retaliation or at least of further rejection. The child involved in incest is usually so young she doesn't know what is happening. Sometimes the child thinks that all children are expected to agree to an adult's sexual demands. By the time the child understands that this is not true, she is too ashamed or frightened to tell anyone. The adult usually continues to molest the child, threatening to hurt the child or send her away if she does not agree to the relationship.

Incest often causes the young person to grow up with a distorted view of what loving and caring mean. For most young people, gradually breaking away from parents and finding new love relations is a painful yet necessary step in the process of self definition. In some cases this process of breaking away and self-definition is made more difficult and extraordinarily stressful when the teenager has been the object of sexual advances by another family member.

Studies strongly suggest that incest does have lifelong repercussions. The most commonly reported outcome of incestuous experiences is sexual acting out and promiscuity. Other young people who have had incestuous experiences may engage in homosexual activity as an expression of their extreme emotional pain and confusion. In addition, if and when incest is discovered, the teenager must suffer the guilt of being responsible for the adult's punishment and for the disruption of the family. Some teenagers leave home rather than face this possibility. Teenagers involved in incestuous relationships account for a large number of runaways each year.

Incest is a terrifying experience for the teenager. It is not something teenagers want to share with their friends, or for that matter, with anyone else. Incest is a barrier to discovering the self, for it embeds in the person a sense of being vulnerable, of not really being in charge of her own body.

A child who is involved in an incestuous relationship and cannot find anyone close enough to talk to should look in the phone book under Social Service Organizations or Mental Health Services (or call information) for an organization that can help. Many listings will have the terms "child abuse" or "family counseling" in their descriptions. The resource section at the end of this book provides additional information.

RAPE - BY A STRANGER

Rape is a way of expressing hate and inflicting pain. It is an act of violence, punishable by law. Teach your adolescent that some instances of rape can be avoided by self-protection. Review safety rules with your child, such as not hitchhiking and not going out alone at night. Without using scare tactics, alert your child to the high incidence of danger involved when these commonsense rules are neglected. Again, be sure your child knows she can turn to you for help. Additionally, crisis lines and crisis centers have been established in each state and most cities. Review with your child the information he might need and the steps to take if your child or a friend should ever need emergency help. Teenagers who have a knowledge of safety rules will be more likely to protect themselves and be of help to others.

DATE RAPE

Not all rape occurs with a stranger. The sad truth is that a big percentage of rapes occurs with someone the girl knows. As Tanya said earlier, date rape for adolescent girls happens more frequently than parents would like to think it does. Again, teach your adolescent that she does not have to have sex because she is pressured to do so, either emotionally or physically. The reality is it is possible that she could be physically forced or bullied into having sex with a first-time date, or even with a boy she has been dating for some time. Aside from reassuring her that she does not have to succumb to sex through pressure and against her wishes, you can help her back up her choice of "no" by arming her with a self-defense course and other measures of personal protection.

You should also talk about where she can turn for help should she become a victim of date rape; there is always the possibility of pregnancy if she is not using birth control. And even though she knows her assailant, she will need help to deal with her feelings of violation. Help her become familiar with these resources, such as the family doctor, women's center and so on. Most important, if your teenager has been involved in date rape (boys can be manipulated into having sex against their wishes also), it is important that you take a stance of support and help; avoid blaming and accusing — your goal here is to help your teen recover and move forward in a healthy way. As always, *talk* about it. An open conversation may not prevent your teenager from becoming a date-rape victim, but it can help her sharpen her instincts and possibly avoid or avert this hurtful experience.

VERY SECRET SUBJECTS

Masturbation and sexual fantasies are two other sexual subjects that parents and their adolescents find embarrassing and difficult to discuss with each other. The word *masturbation* means handling or massaging one's genitals for sexual pleasure and to reach orgasm. For hundreds of years, masturbation was considered a sin, and myths arose and circulated about its dangers. People were led to believe that if a male ejaculated as a result of masturbation, he would be weak and listless, would not have enough sperm left for reproduction, or would slowly go insane. The tales were so numerous and widespread that people were filled with guilt and fear about masturbation.

Today we know that masturbation by both males and females is a very important and natural part of growing up. Masturbation is one of the ways children learn about their own bodies and it is considered a harmless outlet for sexual tension.

Some young people, usually during adolescence, find that they become overly-involved with masturbation to the point that it interferes with other activities. Your adolescent may masturbate more when upset or disturbed about something, instead of trying to determine the source of his unhappiness and do something about it. Often a little counseling with an adult the teenager trusts can help him understand why this is happening. Your child needs to know that masturbating will not hurt him or anyone else.

Your teenager may also be concerned about the unusual kinds of daydreams he is having. He gazes off into space and imagines he is kissing or loving someone he knows or wants to know. The daydreams involve all sorts of people and all kinds of situations. Another word for daydreaming is *fantasizing*. Sexual fantasies are a normal part of being a sexual human being. Most people have sexual fantasies throughout their lives and accept them as an enjoyable aspect of sex.

HELPING YOUR TEENAGER:
WHAT YOU CAN DO

You can help your adolescent understand his unfolding sexuality. In addition to what has already been discussed in this chapter, you can do the following:

Strengthen Gender Identification

During early adolescence, physical maturation is a particularly sensitive matter. Many of the dramatic changes his body is going through are frightening to him. Assure your adolescent that these physical changes bring him closer to maturity. Help him understand *what* is going on as well.

Recognize Self-Involved Behavior For What It Is

Many of the changes produced by unfolding sexuality cause more self-involved behavior because the body is transforming very rapidly. These body changes tend to produce some strong but ambivalent feelings within the adolescent, particularly with respect to the need for peer approval. For example, it is reassuring for a 15-year-old boy to observe his facial hair in the mirror, but embarrassing for him to be teased about it by other adolescents. A 13-year-old boy may be concerned about his own development when he observes that 12-year-old girls are more developed than he is.

Inform Your Adolescent

In addition to understanding her sexuality, it is also important that your adolescent be fully informed regarding these changes and how the sexes and individuals differ in growth characteristics. Your teen needs to know *why* each change is occurring. The meaning and normalcy of such events as nocturnal emission and menstruation are major examples. Your teenager feels anxious about the many physical and emotional changes now taking place. Changes such as wet dreams, menstruation and feelings associated with masturbation, may evoke feelings of fear, joy, embarrassment or relief. Your child will vacillate between feeling unique and alone to feeling a need for peer comparisons as she accepts this new identity. The child who feels awkward and unattractive will want assurance from you that he is loved, accepted, and most of all, normal. Expect too that your child will seek approval from peers as to how these new changes fit into their social environments.

Don't Withdraw Affection

Uncertain as to how to relate, you may alter your response to your adolescent at a time when she needs you most. You may become less physically affectionate, withholding kisses and hugs. You may become more cautious in touching your adolescent for fear that these actions will cause her to develop sexual desires toward you or contribute to promiscuity or homosexuality. You may view the impulsivity and emotions of your teenager as frightening (and they may look frightening to the teenager as well). Your caution may be due to memories of your own adolescence or to your feelings of being unsure how best to help your teenager. Communications may be less open at a time when it is vital for you and your child to relate to one another. A parent of a 13-year-old boy said to me, "I stopped kissing my son as often as I used to. I thought he was getting too old for that type of thing. I didn't realize that my sudden withdrawal made my son feel that he had done something wrong. One day he asked me if I was mad at him!" Because your actions are closely monitored by your teenager, rejections are felt more acutely.

Listen, Care, Communicate

To cope with the monumental changes during the adolescent years, you will need to talk with your teenager about human sexuality and the responsibilities of being a sexual individual. Remember that his peers often provide erroneous information, so most kids are taken by surprise.

Modeling

Children learn by what they see. Your adolescent acquires a good many of her attitudes by what she sees at home. Perhaps this is a good time for you to re-examine your own relationship and to analyze the ups and downs, the good times and the struggles. Your adolescent has a natural curiosity about love and love relationships. She is busy forming an ideal of what she wants a relationship to be. Be aware of the messages she receives from you when she observes your own relationship.

Get More Information For Your Adolescent

In early adolescence there are hormonal changes that may be so intense that the adolescent feels his body is out of control. Attending a sex education class or reading current literature on the subject can be a useful means of gathering additional information.

Get Help

Sometimes it is easier for parents and teenagers to disentangle themselves from their anxieties and difficulties about these issues if they seek help from a professional. Often the task of the therapist is to help the family talk with one another about sex. Counseling may be one way for some families to overcome their own fears and resolve their difficulties.

If you don't talk to your teenager about sex, he will look for answers to his questions elsewhere. You can't help and guide your youngster if you don't know his feelings and confusions. If you work them out together, you can be assured that your adolescent is progressing to sexual maturity. Only then can you feel confident that you have prepared your teenager to take on the responsibilities involved.

How Do You Talk About Sex With Your Teen?

Where do you begin talking with your teenager? Young adults are just waiting for someone to take an interest in their lives, especially someone who loves them and has experienced much of what they are going through. Don't worry that talking about sexual intercourse will encourage sexual experimentation. Information usually discourages rather than encourages adolescents to become sexually active. Remember, too, that they are encouraged and pressured by their peers. It's up to you to provide the knowledge and the balance they will otherwise lack.

We all want our children to experience mature love. Part of attaining that goal is in their knowledge of what is involved in a caring, loving, responsible relationship. Your teenager will not know what a mature relationship is unless you share with him what you know that to be. Liken it to your own relationship, if this is appropriate. This is always a special conversation because you can reveal what you learned in your early love relationships when you were an adolescent. Share how you learned mature love and how you knew when you had finally discovered it.

Teenagers are eager to learn all they can about human sexuality. They want and deserve realistic and personal answers. When offered an opportunity to discuss sex seriously, teenagers talk freely and sensibly. They look for standards and meaning. They want to come to terms with their sexuality. You can help your child to integrate sexuality into his life as a meaningful dimension. Look for opportunities to have meaningful discussions — for example, when your adolescent discusses the boasting of one of his classmates or talks about the "hot and heavy" couple at school. Today more teenagers have cars and more freedom. There is maximum temptation and minimum supervision, and parents must therefore be realistic.

Chances are your child may disagree with or challenge much of what you say. This is natural and to be expected. Even if your opinions differ, share with your adolescent your experiences and wisdom. Doing so will provide him with alternatives.

Sarah, 17, was furious with her parents for disapproving of her new boyfriend, Mike, 24. Her parents warned her that she probably was not ready for the type of relationship Mike might want. They urged her not to date Mike exclusively. Sarah felt her parents were over-reacting and making unfair judgments about Mike. Later, when she was pressured into a sexual relationship, she realized her parents were right. If Sarah's parents had forbidden Sarah to continue to see Mike, she might not have learned to trust her parents. Though her parents offered firm counsel, they left the decision to Sarah. A short while later, Sarah stopped seeing Mike on her own accord and felt secure about her decision. Her actions might have been different had her parents demanded that she stop seeing Mike, without allowing her to participate in the decision.

Your teenager is gaining maturity and is trying to discover what everything means. After you share your values with your teenager, she will make her own choices. You can't shield her from the world forever. She may still mistake sexual intimacy for mature love, and that too is what learning is about. Sexual intimacy is a powerful, exciting feeling. But sexual maturity is gained from understanding the issues and the consequences of love relationships through experience. It is not a textbook education. By being open and accessible, and by providing your child with the necessary information she needs, you can better prepare your adolescent for maturity in a healthy way.

Will Your Teen Say No To Alcohol And Drugs?

 One of the most difficult tasks parents face is getting their children through childhood unharmed by alcohol and drugs. Substance and chemical abuse can alter our children's lives forever. Keeping the adolescent drug and alcohol free is no easy task today when "huffing" gasoline, freon or Scotchguard is their cheap-and-easy (and also brain-damaging) drug of choice.

Today's young people are more likely to use drugs and alcohol than any age group before them and to do so at a far younger age. Even if they have never smoked marijuana, taken pills that were not prescribed for them or used cocaine or crack themselves, most young people know someone who has. Drug use is all around them, from the adult who takes tranquilizers to cope with daily stress to older youngsters who sell crack or pot at school, to movie idols who glamorize drug use on and off screen. The result has been the increased acceptability of drug use over the last decade, making it a rite of passage, the difference between being part of the crowd and an outsider. Like an adult who has a drink "just to be sociable," a child will share a paint-soaked rag and a plastic bag with a friend; others use chemicals and drugs to escape from what they consider intolerable lives. Still others use them "because they're there." It's estimated that over one-third of all U.S. adolescents are using alcohol and illegal drugs.

GETTING STARTED

The progression of drug use often moves through what is generally referred to as "gateway drugs" — first the legal ones, alcohol and tobacco, then on to marijuana and other more harmful and addictive drugs. Multidrug addiction is common; its common denominator is alcohol. If a teen begins to drink, there is a greater possibility that he will also use one or more drugs. Once drug or alcohol involvement begins, it can accelerate from occasional indulgence to dependence. Teens, even more than adults, are susceptible to this snowball effect. Here's one teenager's story:

I began drinking in eighth grade because a lot of my friends did. It made me feel important when I would tell my friends how I got drunk over the weekend. My parents drink occasionally, and I would raid their liquor cabinet. They never noticed.

I started with pot because all the kids had it in eighth grade, and besides, by now I was buying cigarettes from ninth-grade boys. One cigarette seemed no worse than another. One day a good friend asked whether she could copy a homework assignment, and when I said in fun, "It'll cost you," she offered to pay up with a joint. I couldn't just say I hadn't done marijuana, with me being the big guy who was getting drunk and smoking and all, so I said okay to her offer.

At first drugs seemed to help me. They made me feel good about myself, like I was important, and I seemed to function better. Using drugs is a funny thing: You're sure that you have everything under control, that you don't really "need" them. But gradually you get pulled in. At the beginning of ninth grade, I started to get high when I arrived at school every morning, and some days I'd just never make it to classes.

Soon I decided my old friends were boring, so I switched to older kids who were more exciting. Besides, the older guys had cars. Since I always had money and shared it for beer and grass, they were happy to have me along. They introduced me to wild parties and good times. But it was a bad move. The new friends I was hanging out with weren't real friends — they were just convenient. I used them and they used me. I would steal drugs or money from them, and they'd do the same from me. There was no one I trusted. Then I really started losing it. I no longer cared how I dressed, whether I was clean or how I talked in front of people.

It was a vicious cycle. I would do drugs to feel better about myself, but I'd end up feeling worse, so I'd do more drugs. Getting high was no longer a thing I did to feel happy and have fun. It was a part of my life. I had to get high just to feel normal, to be able to cope and not feel drained and burned out. The drugs had flattened everything out.

When I finally got in trouble with the law and my parents were called to pick me up from the police station for disturbing the peace, I know it sounds crazy, but I was so relieved. I had been rescued. I would no longer need to keep hustling to keep afloat. I could get real help from my parents.

YOUR TEEN IS AT RISK TOO: DETECTION

You can't afford to be naive about substance and chemical abuse. You may be caring, emotionally and physically accessible, not drink or use drugs, yet your children may encounter and abuse drugs just the same. Every teenager needs to learn the effects of alcohol and drug use on his health. Teens also need to learn ways to withstand the extraordinary peer pressures for using them. Those who do not are at risk. Anything that accentuates the self-doubt that teens harbor about themselves or their abilities may subtly lead to alcohol or drug use.

Factors that make a teen vulnerable to the influence of alcohol and drugs include:

- divorce, separation or remarriage of parents
- death of a parent, sibling or friend
- home or school relocation
- loss of a long-standing friendship or love relationship
- major tests or exams
- poor self-image
- family discord
- sexual or physical abuse
- lack of emotional and physical affection by parents
- disharmony in the child-parent relationship
- parents who smoke, drink, use illegal drugs or abuse prescription drugs.

IS YOUR TEEN USING? HOW CAN YOU TELL?

Parents often see many clues that they ignore, hoping they will go away. Don't. No one knows the intricate habits and patterns of your child quite like you do. No one can detect changes as you can. Watch for abrupt changes in:

Peer group: The child suddenly starts hanging out with a new group of usually older kids. He may begin to spend a lot of time with new friends he does not want you to meet. He no longer brings friends home and is secretive about who they are.

Personality: Your child may suddenly have extreme bouts of hostility, or avoidance of family contact, moodiness or wild elation. She may become depressed or demonstrate a "get off my back — leave me alone" attitude toward you or other family members. You may notice unusually violent behavior.

School performance: Do not overlook or dismiss a sudden decline in grades, tardiness or the onset of absenteeism.

Neglect of responsibilities: Noticeable and persistent neglect of chores or routine responsibilities, or work done carelessly, can be a sign of drug use.

Physical changes: Look for physical manifestations, especially a sudden change in physical characteristics, such as reddened or bloodshot eyes, dark glasses worn indoors, persistent use of eye drops, persistent cough, vomiting, frequent listlessness, drowsy behavior, staggering, morning headaches, weight loss or loss of appetite, peculiar odor on breath and clothes.

Be aware of unusual smells, such as burning incense to mask orders.

Watch for signs indicating . . .

— disappearance of prescription pills from the medicine chest

— tablets and capsules among his possessions

— repeated requests to borrow money

— unexplained disappearance of cash, cameras, televisions, VCRs, computers, radios and jewelry or other valuable possessions, or any other signs that money is needed to pay for drugs

— large supplies of model cement, paint remover, correction fluid, aerosol sprays, paint, gasoline, freon, Scotchguard and glue or glue-stained plastic bags

— bottles of cough medicine containing narcotics

— bent spoons, syringes, eye droppers and cotton balls

— a persistent sweet or gasoline odor on clothing.

ARE YOU AFRAID YOUR TEEN IS DRINKING? HOW TO KNOW FOR SURE

Listed below are clues that specifically apply to alcohol use:

Is the liquor supply dwindling? If your child is abusing alcohol, your stock might evaporate mysteriously or turn into colored water. Unless you keep an inventory of your liquor, such practices may go undetected for months.

Do you hear consistently from neighbors, friends or others about your child's drinking or questionable behaviors? An alcoholic youngster's reputation suffers. Listen to these reports.

Is your child in trouble with the police? Even one arrest for an alcohol-related offense is a red flag that may well signal alcoholism.

Does your youngster "turn off" to talks about alcohol or strongly defend his right to use it?

ARE YOU AFRAID YOUR TEEN IS SMOKING? HOW TO KNOW FOR SURE

Most teens know about the danger of smoking cigarettes. They know their parents do not want them to smoke. Apparently this makes no difference because it is reported that 67% of all junior and high school age youngsters smoke two to three cigarettes every day. Research concludes that virtually all sixth- and seventh-grade kids try smoking at least once. Half will lose interest without going beyond the experimental stage. It's estimated that of the 50% left, more than half will become serious smokers (smoking one or more packs a day) by the time they are in ninth grade. Experts warn that the most vulnerable period for addiction is in mid-adolescence.

Specific clues can alert you that your teens are smoking:

Are your children buying and using a lot of room deodorizer (to get rid of the scent of cigarettes), breath mints and breath spray (to get the scent off their breath)?

Are you missing a few cigarettes here and there out of your own packs, or missing a pack every now and then from a carton?

Do most of your children's friends smoke? Although it's not a definite sign that your children smoke, peer pressure is a very strong persuader. If your child's boyfriend smokes, it is even more likely that your child will smoke.

Have your children become belligerent when you talk to them about smoking, calling you a hypocrite for continuing to lecture them about how bad smoking is while you go through a pack or two a day?

Do your children have heroes, such as rock stars or actors, who smoke?

HOW CAN YOU GET YOUR TEEN TO JUST SAY "NO"?

To discover that your teen is using drugs or alcohol is a shattering experience. After your first response of shock and outrage, you may be tempted to react with pity or with rejection, even physical punishment. Don't. These responses will not be helpful to you or your child. Parents are still the first and best line of defense. "Parents have to take primary responsibility for their family's education about drugs and what drugs do to their kids," says Joyce Nalepka, former president of the National Federation of Parents for Drug-Free Youth. It's not enough merely to tell your kids to just say "No." You have to explain the dangers and give your teens mental ammunition to combat the pressures to use drugs. *You* can help your child *want* to avoid substance and chemical use.

1. *Be a (positive) role model.* Treat a nondrinking guest with respect, and don't pressure anyone to have another. Don't create the impression that the only way to socialize is with a drink. Don't intimate that alcohol or pills are to be used to relax, alleviate anxiety or counteract depression, melancholy or tiredness.

2. **Don't glamorize drinking or taking drugs.** Don't praise someone else's tolerance for alcohol or stories about the guest who "drank everyone under the table" or used drugs as a way to relax. Explain that while alcohol is enjoyed socially to accentuate a good meal or celebrate a special event, it is not a prerequisite.

3. **Communicate.** Provide the honest facts about alcohol and drugs. Scare tactics or hysterical exaggerations should not be used. Share your values and point out what is and isn't legal. And what is and isn't safe.

4. **Get to know your child's friends and their parents.** Provide responsible supervision at your house when your child has friends over. When your child is spending the evening at a friend's house, check with the parents to see that an adult will be supervising.

5. **Be aware of the early signs of drug and alcohol abuse so you can get help for the family as well as the child.** Speak with your community pharmacist, who is an expert on drugs and their effects on humans. A number of resources are listed in the reference section of this book. You can check with your public library for additional resources.

6. **Encourage your children to get involved in activities that can give them a natural "high."** Sports, recreational, spiritual support and volunteer activities can help channel the need for risk and fun and can be real substitutes for drugs.

7. **Participate.** Form groups with other concerned parents. Join your PTA. Invite drug counselors to meetings. Talk with school superintendents, principals, coaches, physicians, church personnel and local politicians to make sure that everyone is not only aware of drug problems, but that they are responsive to them and concerned about prevention as well as intervention tactics in your community.

8. **Commend business establishments that enforce no smoking on their premises.** We need all the help we can get in sending

the message of being responsible about alcohol and chemical use. Applaud those who do.

WHAT TO DO WHEN YOU KNOW YOUR TEEN IS ABUSING DRUGS

Denial can be fatal. You must be honest with your teen and yourself. If you look the other way, the problem will only get worse. Confront your teen. Honest dialogue is absolutely essential. Help your teen see the necessity of licking the habit early on. It won't go away. It will only get worse. Here are the ground rules:

The first rule is not to discuss the matter when the child is high on drugs or alcohol. Whatever you say, it will not get through.

When your teen gets back to normal and you can talk calmly, show your concern and ask questions. What is happening? Why?

Listen — without interrupting. I repeat: *Listen without interrupting.*

Examine your own attitudes about drugs and alcohol. Is it possible you are sending conflicting messages?

Confront the problem. When you see your child has signs of a problem, don't look the other way, or worse yet, pity him. At this stage, he needs your help, not your tolerance and acceptance of his "weakness." Real parental love may best be demonstrated by helping your child help himself. Teach him to develop his own strength, to find other constructive ways of dealing with his problems and feelings. If you find your child's problem is too much for you to handle, seek help. There are many programs that you and your adolescent can attend together, such as Alcoholics Anonymous. Information about AA as well as other excellent programs are given in the resource section of this book.

The best ammunition parents have to safeguard children against the ravages of alcohol and drugs is the attitudes and skills we help our children acquire.

The transition from childhood to adulthood in contemporary society calls for an ever-increasing ability to endure anxiety, tolerate tension, overcome doubt, resolve conflicts, reduce frustrations and manage stress. A teen who uses drugs and alcohol is less likely to succeed at these necessary challenges.

Alcohol and drug use among our adolescent children is so prevalent that no parent can afford to be complacent. Some of the most unsuspecting youngsters become dependent on alcohol and/ or chemicals. When this happens most parents react with shock and disbelief that a problem of such serious nature could have afflicted their child. Other parents feel that drug or alcohol use is just a phase in which all adolescents will experiment but will get over if they don't interfere. Some parents may even look the other way. This is particularly the case with alcohol: In comparison with drug use, drinking seems less frightening to many parents. This kind of passivity can be dangerous. The consequences of alcohol and drug abuse can be lethal.

Many adolescents depend on a wide variety of methods to squeeze more "productivity" and "up-and-on" time from each day. They listen to tapes while sleeping, review lecture notes while eating, have a study date with a girlfriend, or simply operate on less than adequate sleep and nutrition. Some take drugs. Among the most popular drugs are those that provide a quick fix for an added edge of stamina, stimulation, energy or creativity. Many teens believe they provide a boost for confidence, mood elevation, relaxation and overall coping with the demands of their multifaceted lives. Unfortunately, many of our teenagers have been led to believe that drugs and alcohol provide relief and solutions. Many adolescents are unaware of the damage to their well-being. These substances not only delay the adolescent's ability to recognize that he is in distress, but also work against his ability to detect the underlying problem and gain mastery over it.

Drugs do not frighten many youngsters. Drugs and alcohol are not only on the six o'clock news, but companies that sell them often sponsor the news. Not only do ads claim drugs will "fix" what ails you: Drugs and alcohol are offered to improve the very quality of life! Television ads convince us not to put up with any discomfort. You feel tense, take a tranquilizer. You feel like eating, take an appetite suppressant. You feel pain, take an aspirin. The medicine cabinet is the answer.

Young people have been led to believe that there are "soft" drugs, "hard" drugs and "dangerous" drugs. They think that hard drugs like heroin or crack are dangerous, but soft drugs do little or no harm; they do not cause dependence of any kind and can be used with impunity. These beliefs have created a situation in which young people associate soft drugs with soft drinks. Through their friends and families, in the magazines they read and the movies they watch, at parties, at home and in school, teenagers have come to regard illicit drugs as commonplace. By making drugs seem "cozy," we remove the awe and fear a child should feel about them. The result has been the increased acceptability of drug use over the last decade, making it a rite of passage for many adolescents, the difference between being part of the crowd and an outsider.

As parents you cannot afford to remain naive about the issue of substance and chemical use. Just as there is no specific addictive personality and no one set of parents who make it inevitable that a child will succumb, neither is there a set who can guarantee that their child won't abuse alcohol or drugs. You may be parents who are child-centered, caring, emotionally and physically accessible, and don't drink or use drugs, yet your kids may encounter and abuse drugs just the same. Every adolescent needs to learn the possible effects of alcohol and drug use on his personality, conduct and overall health, and acquire skills that will enable him to withstand the extraordinary pressures during the teen years. Those who do not are at risk. Teenagers often introduce drugs or alcohol to their friends, show them how to use it and convince them it will enhance their ability to "feel good." This outside influence and encouragement by their peers gets kids started on drugs and sets the stage for a repeat experience. The period following the initial introduction to alcohol and drugs is very deceptive. The adolescent may be able to use alcohol and drugs without becoming chemically dependent or even feeling endangered for a short while. In fact, during this period he often has the illusion that he can control his drug or alcohol intake; that the substances are not addictive.

Adolescence is a time of intense feelings and wide mood swings, and distinguishing their effects from those of drugs may not always be easy. This is another powerful reason why remaining close and accessible to your son or daughter during the adolescent years is so important. No one knows the intricate habits and patterns of your child quite like you do; no one can detect changes as readily as you can.

15

Getting Your Teenager To Value Physical And Emotional Well-Being

 Sometimes we think of fitness as meaning the shape our body is in. Physical fitness is certainly an important component of our well-being. But if you are not healthy emotionally and spiritually, you're not *totally* fit. Physical, emotional, spiritual, intellectual stimulation — all of these dimensions work together to make up our overall well-being. We must teach our teenagers that caring for themselves in these ways is a habit to cultivate for life.

SELF-ESTEEM: HELPING YOUR TEENAGER BUILD A HEALTHY AND DURABLE SENSE OF SELF

We all want our children to be healthy, happy, well-adjusted and secure in our love. One of the joys of parenting is seeing our children become confident, emotionally secure and self-accepting individuals. Sometimes it's difficult to gauge our children's true sense of emotional wellness, rather than see what our loving and hopeful eyes want to see. Your child's self-esteem contributes to his happiness and emotional well-being. It's a powerful determinant of the level of joy, satisfaction, energy and commitment she brings to living her life. The level of your child's self-esteem will contribute to how she experiences the events in her life.

Self-esteem is self-regard. It's a self-picture, the reputation you have within yourself from being and doing as you do. The picture your child has of herself is a key to her self-esteem.

The health of your adolescent's self-esteem can determine how well she will do in school, the goals she sets and achieves, and how much of her potential she will develop. Your child's inner picture is that important. Whether this picture is accurate or inaccurate, healthy or dysfunctional, her actions flow from this inner picture of self-worth. This is why a child who sees herself in a positive light acts positively; a child who sees herself as a problem child is usually in trouble. A student's perceptions of her capabilities become the baseline (standard) for her performance in school.

HOW DO YOU GET A HIGH SELF-ESTEEM?

You don't just wake up one day with bad self-esteem or good self-esteem, with high self-esteem or low self-esteem. It's developed over time. You *earn* your self-esteem. Healthy self-esteem is best achieved by actively participating in your life in a meaningful way. My work and research throughout the years have shown me that there are six vital ingredients that make up your child's view of himself. How your teenager is faring in each of the following categories contributes to his overall picture of self. When the experiences in these areas are positive, self-esteem is enhanced. If the experiences are negative or hurtful, self-esteem is undermined and eroded. These six vital areas are:

1. Physical Safety

The teenager who feels physically safe isn't fearful of being harmed or hurt. He feels safe in his home, school and neighborhood. Because he feels safe and knows how to be safe, he learns to be open and to trust others. He freely exercises a curious nature (this will contribute to learning). He moves about with a sense of healthy assuredness. His body posture displays confidence. His tone of voice is hearty and he maintains eye contact when he's talking with you.

2. Emotional Security

A child develops a high level of emotional security when she knows she won't be put down or made to feel less worthy, or be beat up emotionally with sarcasm or hurtful words. Because she feels emotionally secure, she learns to be caring and compassionate with herself and others. She becomes trustworthy. She feels secure in sharing her opinions and ideas. She is respectful and considerate. She is outgoing and friendly. She'll come to you for hugs of affection on her own. She'll reach out to touch you; she'll enjoy being close to you.

3. Identity

The adolescent with self-knowledge develops a healthy sense of individuality. He knows himself. He's friends with the face in the mirror. He's able to "knock, and find somebody (himself) home." He believes in his worth as a human being. He believes he is worthy of praise, and feels secure in praising and complimenting others. Feeling secure with himself, he is open and caring toward others. He takes responsibility for his actions and will own up to them.

4. Belonging

The teenager who feels accepted by and connected to others feels liked, appreciated and respected. He learns to seek out and maintain friendships. He is able to cooperate and share. While maintaining a sense of independence, he learns *inter*dependence — a healthy inter-relatedness. The most important and most powerful sense of belonging comes from the family, the messages that the family sends about acceptance and support.

5. Competence

When a young person feels that she is good at some things, she's willing to learn how to do other things. Because she feels capable, she is willing to persevere rather than give up when things become difficult. She is not only aware of her strengths, but is able to accept the areas where she's less able and can do so without developing "victim" behavior. Because she tries, she experiences the successes that encourage her to try new things. She is self-empowered through realistic and achievable goals, and therefore has initiative.

6. Purpose

The teenager with a sense of mission feels purposeful. Life has meaning. Because he has a sense of direction, he not only sets goals, but follows through on achieving them. He has identified his values and lives accordingly. His values are reflected in his behaviors; his actions are a reflection of his values. He has an inner knowledge, an inner peace. He is intuitive. He laughs easily. He is joyful.

A healthy self-esteem gives your child a realistic awareness of himself and of his abilities and needs. With an all-encompassing respect for himself, this child is unwilling to allow others to devalue his worth, nor will he let them deprive him of his needs. He is less likely to squander his talents and aptitudes, through procrastination, substance abuse or other means. He'll care about himself.

Your child's inner sense of self is mirrored back externally. His self-regard is reflected in our behavior. The way your child communicates — his choice of words, how well he listens, the style of relating to (treating) others, even your child's choice of friends are just a few of the many telltale signs of how he values himself.

Have you ever wondered why some children radiate happiness and seem to be more self-confident than others? One reason for these differences is the *value these children assign to their being,* their personhood, their lives. *All* children need a positive sense of self-worth and a feeling of being okay. The benefits speak for themselves.

CHARACTERISTICS OF HIGH SELF-ESTEEM TEENS

They are better able to cope with the ups and downs of life.

They are likely to attract others who have high self-esteem. Teens with low self-esteem seek other low self-esteem kids who think poorly of themselves. We are naturally drawn to others with a similar sense of self-regard.

They think about what they want out of life, they go after it, and it is likely that they will achieve it.

They are more secure in confronting obstacles, fears and interpersonal conflicts rather than avoiding them, and they try to solve problems instead of worrying over them. Low-esteem teens see problems as grounds for quitting and often say to themselves, "I give up." Instead of comparing their achievements with their own goals and potential, they compare themselves with others, and wait for others to create their "successes."

They are more secure, decisive, friendly, trusting, cheerful, optimistic and purposeful. Look closely and you'll also discover that they are motivated, or empowered. That's because they recognize their own worth and achievements without a constant need for approval from the outside.

They are better able to recognize their own worth and achievement without the constant need for approval from others.

They take more responsibility and control over many of their actions. This is very important, not only because children who monitor their own actions are responsible, but because these children are more willing to accept challenges *because* they have experienced previous successes. Recognition of personal strengths and capabilities serves as a powerful coping and buffer strategy for overcoming obstacles and helps compensate for weaknesses and setbacks.

They are more resilient to problems and defeats.

They are more content and self-fulfilled.

Sometimes your child's inner picture needs only minor repair. At times it needs to be fine tuned or refocused, and sometimes it needs to be replaced by an entirely new picture. You can help your child construct a healthy identity or repair a bruised one. Ensuring that your adolescent's self-esteem is sound and healthy has to do with the six vital ingredients. There are a number of resources found in the reference section of this book that can help you learn how best to strengthen your child's self-esteem. The book *The 6 Vital Ingredients Of Self-Esteem And How To Develop Them In Your Child* offers a good many suggestions for developing self-esteem. They include:

Keep your children physically safe.

Be cautious not to tear your children down. Avoid using sarcasm, don't swear, and don't always focus on what your children aren't doing well. Instead, catch your children doing things right, and when they do, acknowledge them.

Let your children know you are supportive of them, that you are in their camp and that your love is unconditional.

While you may not always support certain actions, you believe in their basic and inherent goodness.

Provide your children with a sense of self-knowledge. Help them puzzle out their place in the world and discuss the importance of living life in an aware fashion, and that we must each be personally and socially responsible.

Help your children feel capable. Help them to learn how to be capable, to set and achieve goals, to value achievement and to recognize their own innate interests and talents.

Help your children internalize their value and see life as something to be cherished and lived to the fullest in a responsible fashion.

Developing a positive sense of self-regard is an important facet in helping your child maintain good mental health, keep safe and secure emotionally — making it more likely that your child will fit into the overall scheme of things vis-a-vis their families, their neighborhoods, their schools.

Helping Your Teenager Value Physical Health

Have you taught your teenager the importance of safeguarding his body? Have you instilled the value of wellness and taking personal responsibility for one's health? Has your teenager internalized the importance of caring for her body's health via proper diet and good nutrition, adequate exercise and relaxation, and by effectively managing her response to stress?

TEACHING YOUR TEEN THE IMPORTANCE OF DIET AND NUTRITION

Your teenager's nutrition not only fuels his body and energy level for the day, but contributes to his overall health and wellness. To a great extent, as health experts say, "We are what we eat." Good health depends on a balanced diet. A deficiency of certain vitamins, minerals, and nutrients can upset body chemistry. An unbalanced diet, or any diet that emphasizes one type of food (proteins, vegetables, carbohydrates) to the exclusion of other foods may be very harmful to the body, especially when stress, illness and injury are superimposed upon it. When the body is depleted of basic nourishment resulting in deficient balance of essential nutrients, it is even less capable of withstanding the ravages of stress and strains of life, making it even more susceptible to major health breakdowns.

EATING DISORDERS: BULIMIA AND ANOREXIA

Bulimia, which literally means "appetite of an ox," affects 3 percent of all U.S. females between the ages of 14 and 40. Only 15 percent of the diagnosed bulimics are men. Bulimia is an eating disorder in which victims go on uncontrollable eating binges to relieve anxiety and hunger, and then induce vomiting, use laxatives or exercise excessively to counteract weight gain.

Anorexia is a disorder in which young women start dieting, then lose control and become dangerously underweight. With bulimia, young women don't lose a significant amount of weight. The key difference is that bulimics stay close to their normal weight, while anorexics lose a great deal of weight. Many anorexia victims also suffer from bulimia.

Bulimics suffer from anxiety and depression. Young women who have bulimia get relief from stress by binging on foods that taste good to them. When they eat a large amount of food, their blood sugar levels go up, making them feel tired and relaxed.

Binging and purging can be harmful. Severe purging can change the electrolyte balance in the blood which will lower potassium levels and make the victim susceptible to cardiac arrhythmia and cardiac arrest. Bulimia also decreases bone density, putting the woman at risk for osteoporosis.

HOW TO TELL IF YOUR TEEN IS BULIMIC

Binge eating or compulsive eating with no purging is easiest to recognize because of its inevitable outcome — being overweight.

But the very active adolescent who eats in binges may show no signs of obesity until early adulthood. However, binging itself is a danger sign that could signal any of the eating disorders. Frequent binges lead to trouble because the young person is learning to eat in a manner that gives more and more control to food, taking enormous control over the person.

Do not ignore the signs that indicate your child is not eating in a healthy manner. When our children are small, it's easy to know about their eating habits because we control them. It's more difficult when our children are teens. You'll need to observe your child closely. A teen who eats practically nothing at mealtimes yet maintains a normal weight may be binging privately. Because weight may be normal for the age and development stage, body shape may not provide any helpful signs for identifying the disorder.

Here are some signs of food abuse to look for:

- Large amounts of food disappearing quickly from the refrigerator
- Solitary eating or reluctance to sit down and eat with others
- Trips to the bathroom after eating
- Statements that express a displeasure with body shape or particular areas of the body
- Drastic mood swings
- Drastic changes in your child's grades
- A new group of friends or the dropping of her normal group of friends
- Frequently asking to be excused early from the table
- Consistently hiding under particularly baggy clothing.

WHAT SHOULD YOU DO?

1. Talk With Your Child

Approach this conversation in a nonaccusing and gentle manner. Ask your teen if she is having difficulties with eating. Unlike anorexics, many bulimics want help and are relieved when their parents intervene.

2. Get Help

Make an appointment to see your family doctor and get a referral to an eating disorder clinic. Counselors and therapists who specialize in eating disorders should network with counselors at school. Become aware of the mental health resources available in your community.

3. Build Your Teen's Self-Esteem

An important facet in treating your adolescent is to strengthen her self-esteem. Often the young woman has feelings of worthlessness and misconceptions of her body shape and weight. One of the most important things you can do is to give your child a strong sense of her individual worth. When your teenager feels confident about herself, she has a more realistic sense of her body and its needs, and is less preoccupied with her body's image. Aside from the measures you take to build your teenager's self-esteem, you may wish to supplement it by getting her involved in a teen support group or individual therapy.

4. Help Your Teenager Learn To Deal Effectively With Stress

The bulimic adolescent will need to learn better ways of dealing with the stresses and strains of life. Books like *A Stress Management Guide For Young People* and others listed in the reference section in this book can contribute greatly to her ability to manage her response to stress effectively.

5. Help Your Adolescent Learn About Her Disease

The bulimic teenager must learn to confront her disease and overcome it. She must first understand it. Often the bulimic is asked to keep a journal of her eating habits, when she binges and under what circumstances. She then learns to substitute other behavior for the binge-and-purge cycle. She must learn about nutrition and about the medical effects of bulimia. Antidepressants are sometimes effective in reducing the urge to binge.

HELPING YOUR TEENAGER TAKE NUTRITION SERIOUSLY

Teaching the importance of good nutrition starts in the early years, but making sure that it carries over into the teenage years is especially important. All adolescents, and especially those engaged in strenuous physical activities, need foods rich in protein, minerals and vitamins. When a child's body lacks essential nutrients, it simply cannot function properly. School performance is naturally affected, and makes the teenager tired and less able to cope. It's not always easy to improve our children's dietary habits, but the following suggestions can help.

1. Breakfast Is Essential

Breakfast should never be skipped (by adults or children). It should consist of fruits and grains which steadily release glucose during the day to fuel the body. Teenagers tend to rush off to school without breakfast. Planning the night before can help to make breakfast time a little easier. If the breakfast table is set with all of the bowls, plates, silverware and glasses so that a teen only needs to pour juice in a glass and pop the bread in the toaster, she will be more likely to eat something nutritious. If breakfast is ready on the table, most likely your teen will eat. It takes some planning for you to get everything ready the night before, but it's worth it.

2. Family Mealtime Should Be A Cooperative Effort

Good nutrition needn't be just your responsibility. Teenagers can take turns planning and preparing meals. Meal preparation can be a cooperative effort. Menu planning could be done on the weekend so that all the needed food items will be on hand for the meal. You can even go so far as to write a weekly menu, allowing each family member to plan favorite meals. Or one adult and one child can jointly share the responsibility and plan special meals. However your family decides to do it, meal planning and preparation can be fun when family members are all involved. This can make healthy eating a learned habit.

3. Conflict At Mealtime Should Be Avoided

It's difficult to digest food when the stomach is churning with anger. Pleasant conversation can make mealtimes a part of the day to which each member looks forward, a time to share the positive events of the day and exchange feelings of goodwill. This is not a time to resolve family conflicts. Don't allow arguments at mealtimes. Have fun, laughter, peace and tranquility at the dining table.

4. Watch Out For Your Teen's "Dieting"

Your "body-building" teen may have special needs beyond a balanced diet. For instance, if he is on the school boxing team, he may be trying to drop weight (to compete in a lower weight class). He may go on a binge-and-purge diet. Wrestlers, for example, eat little or nothing for three or four days before a match, then right after the match go on a food binge to make up for days of near starvation. Get expert medical advice before allowing your teenager to go on any diet that is not completely balanced. Calling on medical experts to give advice can often persuade your athlete to eat sensibly.

When teenage girls diet, they are trying to lose weight for appearance reasons. Because of their growing and changing bodies, many teenage girls are very self-conscious about being overweight. The incidence of eating disorders, such as anorexia and bulimia, is highest in adolescent girls, as is the use of diet pills. If you notice any drastic change in your daughter's eating habits, from excessive consumption to merely picking at her food, don't let it go unnoticed. Talk about it to see if she can tell you what's going on. Causes can range from a simple episode of stress she needs help in resolving, to a medical problem that needs professional help. If an eating problem lasts longer than a few days, take action. Ask your family doctor to assess your daughter's health and suggest the best way to meet her nutritional needs, especially when dieting.

5. Don't Encourage Overeating

Just as dieting can be harmful if not done carefully, being obese poses problems too. You can (unknowingly) be contributing to weight problems and poor eating habits in your teenager. Do you use food, especially sweets, as a reward? Are you serving too many easy dishes containing mostly starches? Is your teen using food for self-gratification, or does he eat as an outlet for depression? Look for patterns in eating. When does he snack? What are his favorite fattening foods? Does he overeat when he is depressed or bored or is slumped in front of the television? If you feel your meals are nutritious but your child is overweight, you may wish to consult with your family physician, school nurse or nutritionist for ways to help your child deal with a weight problem.

TEACHING YOUR TEENAGER THE IMPORTANCE OF FITNESS AND EXERCISE

We may be assuming that our teen is getting sufficient physical activity, yet this may not be true. Even in the schools, teenagers are getting fewer opportunities to get and stay fit. For example, in some school districts enrollment in physical education classes — which used to be mandatory throughout high school — is now elective in a student's final years. In some school districts, because of budget cuts, physical education as well as team sports has been cut altogether. Usual recommendations are that compulsory school physical education programs be instituted for 50 minutes each week. Too often this 50 minutes is scheduled into one class period once a week, usually the last period of the day, so that the school doesn't have to deal with teenagers taking showers, towel service expenses and water use.

"The inescapable conclusion," warns Ash Hayes, executive director of the President's Council on Physical Fitness and Sports, "is that millions of Americans in every age group are unfit. One important solution to this shocking national problem is for parents to accept responsibility for their own physical fitness and for that of their teenager. Working together in family activities in a spirit of fun and cooperation is one of the very best hopes we have of getting ourselves in shape."

HELPING YOUR TEENAGER GET PHYSICALLY FIT

Making sure that your teenagers are fit and healthy has to do with how much exercise they are getting. There are a number of benefits derived from exercise. Exercise can . . .

- strengthen muscles, bones and ligaments
- increase blood circulation
- contribute to a healthy heart
- increase resistance to disease
- add oxygen to the body
- sharpen mental acuity
- relax nerves and balance emotions
- reduce fatigue
- improve figure and complexion
- aid digestion.

You can take an active part in helping your children get the exercise they need.

1. Be A Good Role Model

We need to set a positive example for our youngsters. If you smoke a pack of cigarettes a day and slump in front of the TV munching potato chips when you get home from work, your teen will not learn how to become physically fit. You need to have credibility with your teen, so get involved yourself in some type of fitness program. If you aren't fit, work toward it; if you are fit, stay fit. Your teen needs to see the importance of fitness to overall health. Your child is setting patterns now that he will take with him into adult life. Remember, you are modeling what that will be.

2. Promote Individual Activities

Your teenager needs to be involved in activities where she can channel her need for risk, adventure and challenge in a positive way. Don't depend on her school to do this or assume that it is the school's responsibility to keep her fit. Encourage sports such as swimming, skiing, bicycling, surfing, horseback riding or other activities that combine a high degree of physical and mental coordination.

3. Support Team Sports

Have you ever watched your child during football practice? He will get as much exercise horsing around with his friends as he will from the formal practice. The same is true during baseball practice, soccer games and other team sport activities. Interacting with others allows a child to do a lot of shouting and laughing, releasing some of his aggression and lessening stress. Your child won't jog alone, yelling at the top of his lungs, but doing so during team practice is encouraged and a great way to blow off steam.

4. Encourage Family Activities

You probably loved going on family outings when your children were small, taking walks to the park, swimming at the lake. As they grew into teenagers, they may have pulled away from family outings, preferring to spend more time on their own. If you feel that your teen needs to work on her fitness, perhaps it's time for you to start up the family activities again. Saturdays and Sundays are a good time for family outings. Going to the beach, hiking, camping and bicycling are enjoyed by all. They can be a regular part of your family's time together. Family activities should include physical fitness routines. *The Reader's Digest Special Guide to Family Fitness* suggests four specific ways to get your family involved in physical fitness:

Sign contracts. Have each family member write down one fitness goal for the month. For example, "I want to be able to run one mile nonstop." Sign and date the contract and have it co-signed by a family member.

Exercise as a family. Agree to exercise one half-hour before watching TV or before dinner. If schedules are too complicated during the week, set a time on Saturday and Sunday. Then everyone can exercise individually during the week.

Record scores. Post a chart on the refrigerator for the scores of each family member. Update the chart each time you retake the test and record each workout.

Reward achievements. When you reach a goal, give yourself a prize (fitness clothing or sports equipment — not food). When all family members reach certain goals, reward everyone with an activity you all enjoy — and participate as a family. For example, you might take a fitness vacation (such as backpacking) together.

5. Start Your Fitness Plan Slowly And Regularly

The effective health program needs to be aerobic (one in which you have to breathe heavily but not consume oxygen faster than your heart and lungs can supply it). Experts recommend three 20- to 30-minute sessions of vigorous activity weekly. These can include walking, swimming, bicycling, aerobics, jazzercise and so on. If your teen is not in shape, start him (and yourself) slowly. Again, consult your physician before starting an exercise regime if your child is overweight or afflicted with any health problems.

6. Teens Should Have Regular Checkups

Immunizations, eyesight checkups and periodic medical and dental examinations can ensure that your teen is growing and developing normally. Most parents are cognizant of braces in the mouths of teenagers, but adolescence is also a time when many children will cut their wisdom teeth. Often these can become painful for the teenager, causing headaches and general jaw irritation.

Teach your teenager that good health isn't an accident: Keeping the body fit and healthy is a deliberate and responsible action.

TEACHING YOUR TEEN
THE IMPORTANCE OF RELAXATION

We tend not to realize just how stressful a child's life can be. But what about the 12-year-old girl who is seated this year next to a boy who is still in his "I'd rather eat worms than sit next to a girl" stage? What about the captain of the football team, already nervous about his performance in tomorrow's game? What about the teenager who believes the whole world will see he is a nerd because his parents are ogres and won't give him a car when all his friends have vehicles? Like adults, teenagers experience stress and need to learn to relax.

As adults, we all have our own ways of relaxing. One person might play a round of golf, while a second likes to take a hot bath. What works for one person may not be considered relaxation by another.

The same thing is true for teenagers. Teach your child the importance of relaxation to the body's wellness, and then help him learn some basic skills so that he can use them.

Fourteen-year-old Lenny sometimes gets excruciating headaches. When this happens at home, he goes to his room, puts on relaxing music and lies down. He pictures himself flying a plane (his goal is to be a pilot someday) over the ocean. The sound of the engines is a soothing drone, and Lenny hums along. He pictures the ocean as a vivid blue in some parts, an aqua in others and almost green in yet others. He rolls back and forth on his bed, imitating the gentle rocking motion of the plane as he takes it across the Pacific, seeing small islands below him. He is in control. No one is in the plane but him. He can go wherever he wants. After 15 minutes Lenny has "flown" halfway around the world. More important, he has relaxed physically and mentally. Sometimes he even falls asleep for a few minutes, and wakes refreshed and ready to go.

The are a number of ways to teach your children how to relax, ranging from mental imagery, to exercise, stretching, deep muscle relaxation and so on.

There are many excellent books on this subject, a number of which are listed for you in the resource section of this book. You may also want to ask your child's school librarian or the local public librarian for additional resource suggestions.

TEACHING YOUR TEEN TO DIFFERENTIATE BETWEEN "MUSIC" AND "NOISE"

Music has a profound influence on all of us. You can prove it to yourself: Just try reciting your ABCs without singing them! To a teenager, music represents many things: peer group acceptance (knowing all the lyrics to the same songs as your friends); rebellion ("Anything Mom and Dad can't stand can't be all bad!") and uniqueness ("No one but me can understand these lyrics, really; they describe my life to a T!") Music to a teen is not just the noise it may be to you; it is a way of life.

Studies show that teenagers listen to more than 10,500 hours of rock music between the seventh and twelfth grades alone — that's just about the same amount of time they spend in school over the period of twelve years.

Some psychologists believe that excessive exposure to the harsh sound of porn rock and heavy metal groups and to crude lyrics creates a "mean-world" syndrome — a perception that life is cruel and dangerous and that teens have a right to react with cruelty and violence. Many professionals worry that the messages found in today's music videos may be threatening the teenager's ability and willingness to trust and care about other human beings, including their own parents.

Dr. Thomas Radecki, a psychiatrist and director of research for the National Coalition on Television Violence, contends that there is a subculture of hatred and violence that is becoming a fast-growing element of rock entertainment for the young. School and health professionals believe that such music is reaching younger children, creating a false sense of puberty among children as young as fourth, fifth and sixth grades.

It may be that parents and their teenagers will always disagree about selection of music. What, then, can we do?

1. Use Your Support Base

Today's music emphasizes violence and explicit sexual descriptions. The messages purveyed to the young today through video are so provocative that parents and psychologists are warning of dire consequences. Many local governments and businesses are taking action.

Dallas, for example, has imposed a three-tier film-rating system, ranging up to a "not suitable" classification for 16-year-old moviegoers.

Cleveland's city council has passed a resolution urging radio stations not to play songs with blatantly sexual or obscene lyrics. Other radio and television stations are beginning to screen lyrics and refusing to broadcast certain materials.

On the national level, Parents Music Resource Center (PMRC), along with the national Parents Teacher Association (PTA), have been successful in getting recordings with explicit lyrics referring to sex, violence or substance abuse to carry a warning label. The purpose of this labeling is to increase a parent's awareness of what our children are hearing. The PMRC has developed a set of guidelines to help parents and their adolescents.

Monitor your local radio and TV broadcasts carefully. If you have complaints about the programming excesses on cable television, specifically MTV or music videos, write to: Executive Director, National Cable Television Association, 1724 Massachusetts Avenue, N.W., Washington, D.C. 20036, or President, MTV, 1133 Avenue of the Americas, New York, NY 10036.

If you wish to protest a record album, its contents or jacket, write to the representative of 85 percent of the recording industry at: President, Recording Industry Association of America, 888 Seventh Avenue, 9th Floor, New York, NY 10106.

Mail copies of your correspondence to the Federal Communications Commission and National Association of Broadcasters, and to your elected representatives at both the state and national level: Chief of Complaints, Federal Communications Commission, 1919 M Street, N.W., Washington, D.C. 20554, and President and Chief Executive Officer, National Association of Broadcasters, 1771 N. Street, N.W., Washington, D.C. 20036. Networks: CBS-TV, Entertainment Division, 51 W. 52nd Street, New York, NY 10019; ABC TV, Audience Information, 1330 Sixth Avenue, New York, NY 10019; NBC-TV, Audience Services, 30 Rockefeller Plaza, New York, NY 10020.

Send a copy of your letter to the PMRC at 300 Metropolitan Square, 655 Fifteenth Street, N.W., Washington, D.C. 20005.

2. Talk About Music Selection

Accompany your teenager to the local music store to inform yourself about the material he has to choose from. Review your teenager's collection with him, discuss the contents, give him appropriate guidelines and explain why it's "good."

3. Teach By Modeling

No doubt you have music playing throughout the house, probably it's relaxing and soothing in nature. Create a library of tapes, some of which are acceptable and popular with your teenager, too. Periodically, let your teen be in charge of putting on "family time" music. Teach your teenager how different music selections can enhance and/or distract from the task at hand.

For example, perhaps you turn down the volume even on soothing music when having dinner. Washing your car perhaps gets the Top Ten station. Music to accompany relaxation tapes is necessarily soothing and mystical. Just before bedtime, soothing music is played; the goal is to bring the body and mind to total relaxation and prepare it for deep sleep. You can appreciate his music, and he can appreciate your music. Together, you can have "your" music. The goal is to teach music appreciation.

4. Show Your Child How To Relax With Music

The National Music Association (NMA) has compiled a catalogue listing highly relaxing and meditative soothing music to bring about body and muscular relaxation. This list can be found in most major music stores. Teach your teen how she can use music to relax. Discuss how the mind and body react to different kinds of music. Your teenager will not be adverse to learning how to use sound in a positive, health-promoting way.

It is not a good idea, for example, for the teenager to wake up to harsh sound early in the morning or play it last thing at night. Help her note the difference in how she feels — tense and strained versus up, positive and sunny. When your child is just up and preparing for the day, suggest that she put on a tape that enhances and sets the tone for a positive and upbeat mood.

WE LIVE IN AN OCEAN OF SOUND

We live in an ocean of sound and, whether we are aware of it or not, these sounds exert a powerful influence over our physiological and psychological well-being. Of all modes of sensory perception, sound is the most penetrating. The work of numerous researchers has proven that whether you hear a sound consciously or unconsciously, your body hears the vibration and responds to it at all levels of sound especially at the cellular level. While some sounds can keep us well and "in tune" with ourselves, others can literally make us ill.

Radionics is the study of vibrations and their relationship to the health and vigor of the body, particularly the muscles and organs. Musical rhythms affect both our hearts and our brains. Heavy metal music produces physiological and psychological tension. Our responses to musical tempo are linked to our body's own rhythms. Human hearts normally function at a rhythm of about 70 to 80 beats a minute. Most music is paced at this tempo, which we perceive as moderate. Slow music slows down heart rate and pulse, and conversely, fast music speeds up the heart rate and pulse. Insistent rhythms arouse a range of agitated feelings, while sedate rhythms convey a range of soothing feelings.

TEACHING YOUR TEEN
THE IMPORTANCE OF MANAGING STRESS

You may feel that a teenager has little to be worried or anxious about, apart from the trauma of pimples, sweaty palms and overactive hormones. After all, she doesn't need to provide shelter, food, clothing or security for herself — you do all that. But teenagers are particularly vulnerable to stress. Teens lead multidimensional lives with fast-paced lifestyles. They spend great portions of energy quickly and become prime targets for fatigue, moodiness, psychosomatic illness, migraines and other diseases of maladaptation, including burnout.

Children are no more immune to stress-related illness than adults. In fact, they may be even more vulnerable because they have little control over their own lives and may not be able to articulate or may be afraid to say what's troubling them. Three months after 14-year-old Moyra began having severe headaches for no apparent reason, her parents remembered that her best friend of five years had moved 1,300 miles away. Her parents had restricted long-distance phone calls, and in spite of the barrage of letters the girls sent back and forth, the miles between them seemed like an insurmountable obstacle. Certainly no one had asked for Moyra's opinion about the move, nor until now had they noticed how she pined over the absence of her best friend. No one had prepared her for the trauma she was about to experience. Moyra's illness was a cue — a signal — that she wasn't adjusting well (she described the move as "loss"). Moyra needed emotional support to help her bridge the loss she felt, and she needed guidance in generating alternatives to help the girls preserve their cherished friendship.

Fortunately, Moyra's parents recognized that their daughter's illness was caused by stress. They were able to sit down with her, listen to her fears about losing her friend and give her a shoulder to cry on. They explained to her how separation doesn't necessarily mean the end of friendship, ways she could preserve the friendship and how she would have new friends soon. Through her parents' love and guidance, Moyra learned to accept the changed situation. Her headaches stopped, but her friendship didn't.

LIKE ADULTS, TEENAGERS SUFFER FROM BURNOUT

Prolonged stress can lead to burnout and eventually to a child's dropping out. When a child drops out of school, quite often we think, "The lazy kid isn't giving it his best." This is usually untrue and unfair.

After two years in high school, Vickie became a casualty of burnout and a runaway. Says Vickie:

Mom wanted me to have all the advantages, good grades, piano lessons, foreign languages, ballet, tennis lessons and pets to care for. What's more, I was to be good, really good, at all of it. At first it was fun, I just ran by the schedule. But one day I forgot my "to-do" list at home and I couldn't even function! After two semesters the days blurred into weeks, and the weeks into months. I don't even remember the past four months. I just got so tired. Soon it became more work than fun. I felt I just couldn't go on. I no longer wanted to be a National Merit Scholar finalist, first chair clarinet and an editor for the school newspaper.

I tried all the remedies my friends suggested — from the diet and caffeine pills to just coffee to help tackle the agenda. I even found myself stealing diet pills from the grocery store when my allowance wouldn't cover them. After a while even those didn't work. I would be really wound up for the first few hours and then experience this incredible tiredness by noon. I resigned from student government, began skipping a class here and there and began to copy homework assignments from friends. I felt so ashamed and so down on myself. I felt like I had really let everyone down, especially my parents. One day I went to my locker, threw the books in and left school with a friend — for four days. I just didn't care any more.

STRESS HAS AN UNDERLYING CAUSE

Vickie's case may seem almost melodramatic to you, but it's not uncommon. Don't take your teenager's fears lightly. Often there are causes beneath the fears we don't know about until an issue has been resolved.

Some years ago I took my daughter, then 11, to the doctor. A blood test from a lab was recommended. My daughter cried, pleaded with me and kicked the walls on the way to the lab, and screamed and refused to enter the lab door. She then proceeded to faint. After I cared for her immediate needs and removed her from the environment, I sat with her on the lawn outside the medical complex.

Nearly 30 minutes later I learned the source of her fear. It seems that in cartoons, shots are given out of spite and with very long needles. My daughter proceeded to describe a foot-long needle that she imagined would start at the base of her wrist and extend to her elbow. Under no circumstance was she about to be a victim to that! After debunking the myth and explaining the correct procedure, I got her consent. She insisted that she be allowed to watch blood being drawn. (In the bargaining process, I made the slip of saying I would "go first.") She then was able to proceed in a relaxed manner through the moment of a relatively painless (though scary) procedure.

Though both she and I remember the details of the incident to this day, what is most poignant is that through that incident, we both came to understand just how important trust is between parent and child. I had to trust that her fear was real and that it was painful, and she had to trust that my control over ensuing matters would take into account her sensitivity to fear and pain. She had to believe that the decisions I made valued her sensitivities, and that her concerns were equal to my insistence that the lab procedure occur ("No, we can't come back tomorrow. This must be cared for as soon as possible"); or for the convenience of the doctor (He had said, "I'll be leaving town tomorrow for three weeks so we should get this in the lab this morning.")

Don't miss the cues that indicate your teen is experiencing stress. If your teen is having trouble at school, instead of saying, "Oh, don't worry about that," or "Everything will be okay," say something like, "Would you like to tell me about it?" Over the years I have found that by asking a very simple question, "If you could make three wishes, what would you wish for?" proves to be very revealing of what is behind children's stress. The answers are sometimes painfully touching, but always revealing.

You can't and shouldn't protect your child completely from stress. I like the idea of what's known as psychological immunization. Children psychologically become more capable of dealing with the larger stressors in life by first learning how to deal effectively with the smaller more manageable ones, such as thwarted desires, the move of a friend, a failed test or the loss of a boyfriend or girlfriend.

Teenagers' capacity to resist and cope with unwanted stress can vary greatly. Some become overwhelmed easily by outside pressures, while others endure them without ill effects or are even stimulated by the challenge. Still others develop healthy frustration tolerance, learning to remain flexible and take daily irritants in stride. Transient stresses usually pose no threat to physical or mental health. The most successful parents are protective, but willing to explain things to their children. They set rules, but they talk, too. Being able to talk honestly and respectfully with your child is perhaps the best protection against stress.

The ability to manage stress is especially necessary in a youngster's life, since so much of the teenager's existence involves continual change, clarification of values and forced choices. The adolescent years have traditionally been considered a turbulent period because of rapid emotional and bodily changes, adding to the teenager's perception of being out of control with his life. But teens can learn to manage their response to stress better. Help your teenager acquire good stress management skills. Learning the goals and principles of coping can help children draw vitality from stress and use it constructively. Be alert for the symptoms that show your child is experiencing stress. Watch closely for stress signs that show the child is not coping well, and then get help if you feel you need assistance. Your school counselors, family doctor and your child's pediatrician are all potential sources of help. A number of books can teach you how to help your teenager learn how to manage stress.

School Is Your Teen's First Job: Be A Mentor

16

 We all want our teenagers to experience school success. The first step is to help our children assimilate the value of becoming *learners for life*. How can we help our teens remain curious about the world around them?

THE DESIRE TO LEARN BEGINS AT HOME: PARENTS ARE TEACHERS

You help your child develop the desire to learn when you show that you value learning for the sake of being aware and informed. Talk with admiration about friends or acquaintances who share information and stories of interest based on what they have experienced or learned. Help your children want to know more about themselves, others, the world and the universe.

Your modeling teaches a joy, curiosity and love of learning. Your teenagers will follow in your footsteps. When they see you as an ongoing learner, reading the newspaper, books and magazines, they are more likely to assimilate the same actions. Discuss what you are learning. Talk about the importance of getting an education. If you show your teenagers that education is important to you, it will become important to them as well. When you subscribe to magazines and newspapers and read and discuss stories of interest, you show by example the fun and importance of learning. When you attend evening courses at the local university or discuss conferences you attended for the company you work for, you set an example of the importance of learning. Showing an interest in your teen's school and his homework sends the message that you care about your child's learning, and he should too. You're conveying the message that school is purposeful, learning is important.

How is that school experience molding your children? Do you know? Are you involved? Are they learning as you had hoped they would learn? Are you an active participant in their school life?

12 Things You Can Do To Help Your Child Have A Good School Experience

You want your teenager to have a positive, rewarding experience in school. You want him to feel challenged by school, but not overwhelmed by it. You want your teenager to feel confident that he can do the work required of him in order to pass classes and get through school. For many teens school is an intense and frustrating experience. Help your teenager develop skills in managing his world of work.

WHAT YOU CAN DO TO HELP

1. Show Your Teen How To Get Organized

Your teenager needs the appropriate tools to do the job: a quiet study area safe from interruption, equipped with a good light, a desk and a bookcase, pencils, paper, maybe a computer and standard supplies. Set up a file and explain how to use it. This filing cabinet can be the standard kind, or it can be as simple as a large cardboard box divided with inserts separating files in terms of contents ("Great articles: save for future book reports;" or separate by subject area or more complex headings, such as "English exams;" "English notes to use for studying for the semester exam;" "English papers handed back" and so on).

Next, get a large month-at-a-glance wall calendar to record work assignments and school-related activities. This reminds your teen to focus on particular projects and assignments, and when he's free to schedule social activities. It instills the feeling of being a serious student.

He should have his own work space, not a shared space. It doesn't have to be large, just a space he can associate with doing homework. Not having a place of their own to work, or the proper tools, is a big reason why many children don't want to do their homework.

2. Enforce Boundaries On Study Time

There should be no TV or Walkman, and no phone calls during study time. Phone calls can be made after homework is finished. If your child needs to clarify an assignment by talking to a fellow student, two to three minutes is sufficient. You want to teach your child the power of uninterrupted concentration. Explain to her why this is a good practice to get into.

3. Agree On A Regular Study Time

Whether you decide this time should be right after school or after the evening meal, keep it consistent when possible. This routine helps your child get in the habit of doing his homework consistently every day.

4. Take A Specific Interest In Your Teen's Schoolwork

Ask specific questions based on what you know is being taught. Rather than asking, "How was your day?" to which she will reply, "Fine," ask about what she is learning. Say something like,

- "Do you feel you are making an improvement in math?"
- "What contributed to your poor grades?"
- "What is your favorite subject? Why?"
- "Was an A a mark of achievement or was the test too easy?"
- "Did you get the D because you didn't understand the material or because you weren't prepared?"

Remember, school is tough for A students too. Your attitude is all-important. Children do as their parents do, not as they say. If you get excited about a new course or focus of study, your teen will also. A brief conversation shows your teen that her education is important to you and can influence how she does in school.

5. Determine What Skills Your Child Needs

Use clues from report cards, teacher conferences and aptitude tests to become familiar with your child's strengths and weaknesses so you'll know where you can help. Is he lacking a particular skill that is holding him back? Can you obtain special tutoring for a problem area? Is there a physical problem, perhaps with eyesight or hearing? Is there a particular learning disability?

6. Ask About Your Teen's "Co-workers"

Who are her friends at school and why? How much time do they get to be together in favorite school activities? Do they eat lunch together? Who are good students and why? Who are not such good students and why? Has she noticed that she's a better learner when she feels like a friend, and a better friend when she's feeling successful in school? What are her thoughts about this realization?

7. Talk To Your Teenager About Her Teachers

Does your teen like her teachers? Why or why not? What teacher(s) does your teenager find exciting and why? In many cases, children choose a career based on a *special* teacher. Who is this *special* teacher for your teen?

8. Teach Time-Management Skills

Most teenagers never seem to have enough time outside of school to cope with assignments, friends, extracurricular activities and family, with time left over for themselves. Even during the school day, one of the greatest pressures on your youngster is time. Show your child how you set priorities, how your management of time allows you to do the things you want to do. Break long-term projects down into manageable parts so she can begin on them, and not wait until the last minute to do something she won't be able to complete in a short period of time.

9. Help Your Child With Homework

When children become students, parents often have to become "students" again too. Helping your teen with homework can be very frustrating for both parent and child. Some parents are unable to help their teenagers with homework. If you are unable to help your teen, for whatever reason, find outside help. College students enjoy working with students younger than themselves. Teenagers often want tutoring to prepare for college entrance exams. Find out — from the schools, from the newspaper, from friends — what outside resources are available. Many public libraries have volunteers who will read to children, or tutors to do one-on-one sessions. These are often free. If your child needs special help because they have learning disabilities (such as dyslexia), the schools can probably recommend specialists. There's someone out there who can help, no matter what the problem.

10. Follow Your Teenager's Progress

Your teen's report card tells you how he's doing overall. However bad grades don't suddenly appear. If you've been watching his weekly reports, grades on papers and tests, you should have some idea of how he is doing. Even if your adolescent's report card isn't as good as you would like, look for something positive — a grade raised in history or a teacher's comments on how hard your child is working, and show your teen how pleased you are with his success, just as you are concerned with his less successful efforts. If you ground your child because of a bad report card, or if you yell and tell him he is lazy or stupid, you're not doing anything to help his grades. In fact, you're probably making the situation worse.

11. Meet The Teacher

Meet your teen's teacher at the beginning of the term. Many parents feel uncomfortable about contacting their child's teacher, and even more anxious if the teacher calls to request a meeting. The teacher may still be associated with the parent's own childhood when the teacher was a strong authority figure. But most teachers are parents, too, and often come to parent-teacher conferences with their own apprehensions and uncertainties about how they will be viewed by you, the child's parents. Understanding the perspective will help make your relationship with the teacher productive and enjoyable. If you have specific questions or think there's a problem, make an appointment with the teacher immediately.

12. Help Your Teen Cope With School Stress

School can be a stressful experience. Today children have a tough academic load, sports, social activities and a half dozen other activities, all demanding their time and attention. Your teenager's academic well-being is affected by her ability to prevent or deal with stress. Should your teenager view academics as the only source of her discomfort, she will not achieve success there.

Our teens will need to have social skills that enable them to deal confidently and competently with their peers. How good are your adolescent's assertiveness skills? Does your teenager know how to stand up for herself? Can she handle herself when being bullied by others? Talk with her about the best ways to handle stress situations assertively.

And remember, not every child is going to be a straight-A student. Some students will honestly work as hard as they can just to get C's. Parents need to help their children feel capable academically regardless of their grades. It's this *attitude* of capability, more than I.Q. or opportunity, that determines your child's willingness to do other things. Children with an attitude of "I can do it!" are willing to go the extra mile. Because they have that attitude, they usually make it to the finish line. With an increased sense of confidence, your child expects to do well and actually does better. In turn, positive experiences build your child's image of her competence. Each success stimulates your child's efforts, and she soon has a storehouse of positive reminders of her being capable, a "can-do" person. Books such as *Teach Your Child, A Parent's Guide* can help you help your teen tackle school successfully. This resource and others are listed in the reference section in the back of this book.

Let your teenagers know you are pulling for them to do their best. Applaud their school successes and help them understand their failures. This approach allows them the security to take the risks that lead to making the most of their school experience.

APPENDIX A:

How To Find A Therapist

You can find a therapist in several ways. Ask friends who have been through counseling to give you the names of those who have helped them. Look in the Yellow Pages under "Psychologists" or "Family Counselors." Your Employee Assistance Program, counseling referral service, church or synagogue can give you the names of qualified professionals. Concerns about cost shouldn't keep you from getting help. Health insurance policies usually cover psychological services. Check your policy. (If in doubt, ask your agent directly.) Universities and colleges often have psychiatry or psychology departments that run counseling centers at a very low cost, as do YMCAs and community agencies. Many therapists work on a sliding-scale basis. Counseling comes in all price ranges; you'll find many counselors who are willing to work with you.

Guidelines for choosing a therapist:

- Is she a licensed psychotherapist who is respected by the professional community and general public?

- Does the therapist have a pleasant disposition, a sense of humor and appear to be functioning well in his own personal life?
- Do you feel safe, comfortable and at ease with the therapist?
- Is the therapist willing to explain her approach to your problem, as well as goals and probable length of treatment?

In addition to helping you through the current crisis, a good therapist will also help you learn new skills that you can continue to use in the future.

APPENDIX B:

WHERE TO GO FOR HELP

Many organizations, some with toll-free 800 phone numbers, provide helpful information.

DRUGS

(800) COCAINE (toll free) is the National Drug Abuse Hotline and a confidential drug abuse treatment, referral (including local referral) and information service. They provide help for drug abusers and other concerned individuals.

National Institute on Drug Abuse, P.O. Box 2305, Rockville, MD 20852.

ALCOHOL

Alcoholics Anonymous, General Service Board, New York, NY 10016. Alcoholics Anonymous is an international fellowship of men and women who share the common problem of alcoholism. Family members of alcoholics can receive help through groups associated with Alcoholics Anonymous, mainly Al-Anon and Al-Ateen. Al-Ateen, Al-Anon Family Group Headquarters, P.O. Box 182, New York, NY 10159-0182. Local AlAteen chapters are listed in some telephone directories, or contact a local Al-Anon group for more information.

National Clearinghouse for Alcohol Information, (301) 468-2600. NCAI is a service of the National Institute of Alcohol Abuse and Alcoholism. The clearinghouse collects worldwide information on studies and programs pertaining to prevention, training, treatment and research aspects of alcohol abuse and alcoholism, and shares this knowledge with interested professionals as well as with the general public.

HIV/AIDS

The following organizations offer information concerning HIV disease or other sexually transmitted diseases. In addition, you might check with your local health department, crisis hotlines, or HIV/AIDS centers. If you have trouble finding a service, call the National AIDS Hotline which can provide you with information on a wide variety of services available in your area. National AIDS Hotline: (800) 342-2437 (English); (800) 344-7432 (Spanish); (800) 243-7889 (Hearing Impaired). AIDS Hotline for Teens: (800) 234-TEEN.

FAMILY STRESS

Check the telephone directory or contact the United Way organization in your area for the Family Services Agency nearest you. These organizations offer a variety of counseling services.

CHILD ABUSE

National Child Abuse Hotline, (800) 422-4453. The National Child Abuse Hotline handles crisis calls and provides information and referrals to every county in the United States. The hotline, a program of Childhelp USA in Woodland Hills, California, also provides literature about child abuse prevention.

STEPFAMILIES

Stepfamily Association of America, (301) 823-7570. The national Stepfamily Association provides information about local chapters and issues a newsletter. Local chapters offer classes, workshops and support groups for blended families. Some classes, workshops and services are free.

CRISIS CENTERS

Crisis Hotline: Crisis counseling and information is available 24 hours-a-day, seven days a week, (800) 352-0386 (in California); (800) 421-6353 elsewhere.

YOUTH RUNAWAY

National Runaway Switch Board: (800) 621-4000. For the name of a runaway or teen crisis shelter in your area write: National Youth Work Alliance, 1346 Connecticut Avenue, N.W., Washington, D.C. 20036.

SUICIDE PREVENTION

Almost every state has one or more suicide hotlines and suicide prevention centers. Check with your local phone operator for the hotline number in your area.

OTHER ORGANIZATIONS THAT CAN HELP

Big Brothers/Big Sisters of America. Families under stress and single parents can find extra support and occasional respite from parenting responsibilities through this program. Under the direction of professionally trained staff, volunteers support families by working with children in need of additional attention and friendship. Call the national office of the local agency listed in the telephone book.

Family Services of America (FSA). FSA is a membership organization of agencies that deals with family problems serving more than a thousand communities throughout the United States and Canada. Member agencies serve families and individuals through counseling, advocacy and family life education.

National Coalition Against Domestic Violence: (202) 293-8860. The coalition is a membership organization composed of independently operated shelters for battered women and their families, as well as individuals. To locate a shelter in your area, contact the coalition in Washington, D.C.

Parents Anonymous (PA). PA is a self-help program for parents under stress and for abused children. There are no fees, and no one is required to reveal his or her name. Group members support and encourage each other in searching out positive alternatives to the abusive behavior in their lives. To locate a PA in your area, call toll-free outside California, (800) 421-0353; inside California, (800) 352-0386.

Adults Molested As Children United (AMACU). Parents United developed AMACU, a self-help program for adults who were sexually abused as children. Members work through weekly therapy groups to resolve the problems and conflicts that the sexual abuse has caused in their lives. To find a local AMACU group, or for referrals to local sexual abuse treatment specialists, contact the office in San Jose.

The National Center for Missing and Exploited Children. The center assists families, citizens' groups, law enforcement agencies, and governmental institutions with information that could lead to the location and recovery of a missing child, (800) 843-5678.

Child Find, Inc., 7 Innis Avenue, New Palz, NY 12561, (212) 245-6200 or (914) 255-1848. For the name of a runaway or teen crisis shelter in your area, write: Crisis Centers: National Youth Work Alliance, 1346 Connecticut Avenue, N.W., Washington, D.C. 20036.

National Anorexic Aid Society (NAAS), 1925 E. Granville Rd., Columbus, Ohio, (614) 436-1112.

Incest Survivors Anonymous, P.O. Box 5613, Long Beach, CA 90805-0613. Support groups and literature based on a 12-Step program. Send a business-size, self-addressed stamped envelope for meeting information, with a note saying you are a survivor. Packet, $15.

Survivors of Incest Anonymous, P.O. Box 21817, Baltimore, MD 21222-6817; (301) 282-3400. Support groups, 12-Step literature. For group directory, send self-addressed business envelope with 58 cents postage. Newcomer packet, $5 (free if you can't afford it).

Survivors United Network, Kempe Children's Foundation, 3607 Martin Luther King Blvd., Denver, CO 80205. Founded by Marilyn Van Derbur and family. Phone (303) 355-1133 or (800) 456-4673. Volunteers give information and referrals.

VOICES (Victims of Incest Can Emerge Survivors) in Action, P.O. Box 148309, Chicago, IL 60614; (800) 786-4238. National network for incest survivors, literature, referrals, conferences, newsletters.

Incest Resources, 46 Pleasant St., Cambridge, MA 02139. Literature, tapes, newsletter. Send self-addressed business envelope with 58 cents postage; ask for IR fliers.

$\int$UGGESTED READINGS

Anderson, Eugene, George Tedman, and Charlotte Rogers. **Self-Esteem For Tots To Teens.** New York: Meadowbrook/Simon and Schuster, 1984.

Anglund, Joan Walsh. **A Friend Is Someone Who Likes You.** New York: Harcourt and Brace, 1985.

Baron, Jason D. **Kids And Drugs.** New York: Putnam, 1983.

Bautista, Belyisezar. **How To Teach Your Child: A Parent's Guide.** Farmington Hills, MI: Bookhaus Publishers, l991.

Bedley, Gene. **The ABCs Of Discipline.** Irvine, CA: People-Wise Publications, 1979.

Bennett, William. **Schools Without Drugs.** Washington, D.C.: U.S. Department of Education, 1989.

Bensman, J. and R. Lilienfield. "Friendship And Alienation." *Psychology Today.* October 1979.

Bergstrom, C. **Losing Your Best Friend: Losing Friendship.** New York: Human Science Press, 1984.

Bessell, H. and T. Kelly, Jr. **The Parent Book.** Rolling Hills Estates, CA: Jalmar Press, 1977.

Betancourt, J. **Am I Normal?** New York: Avon, 1983.

Bingham, E. Edmondson and S.J. Stryker. **Choices: A Teen Woman's Journal For Self-Awareness And Personal Planning.** El Toro, CA: Mission Publications, 1985.

_____ **Choices: A Teen Man's Journal For Self-Awareness And Personal Planning.** El Toro, CA: Mission Publications, 1985.

Blume, J. **Are You There, God? It's Me, Margaret.** New York: Dell, 1970.

Bodenhamer, Gregory. **Back In Control: How To Get Your Children To Behave.** Englewood Cliffs, NJ: Prentice-Hall, 1983.

Bonny, H. and L. Savary. **Music And Your Mind.** San Francisco: Harper & Row, 1973.

Booraem, Curtis, John Flowers and Bernard Schwartz. **Help Your Children Be Self-Confident.** Englewood Cliffs, NJ: Prentice-Hall, 1978.

Bradley, B. **Where Do I Belong? A Kid's Guide To Stepfamilies.** Reading, MA: Addison-Wesley, 1982.

Branden, Nathaniel. **Psychology Of Self-Esteem.** Los Angeles: Bantam Books, 1969.

Briggs, Dorothy Corkille. **Your Child's Self-Esteem.** New York: Dolphin Books, Doubleday & Company, 1975.

_____ **Celebrate Yourself.** Garden City, NY: Doubleday, 1977.

Burkhart, K. **Growing Into Love: Teenagers Talk About Sex In The 1980s.** New York: Putnum, 1981.

Chesnut, Lynnann. **My Mom Doesn't Look Like An Alcoholic.** Deerfield Beach, FL: Health Communications, 1991.

"Children Having Children: Teen Pregnancy In America," *Time.* December 9, 1985: 78-90.

Clems, Harris and Reynold Bean. **Self-Esteem: The Key To Your Child's Well-Being.** New York: Putnam, 1981.

Coles, R. and G. Stokes. **Sex And The American Teenager.** New York: Harper Colophon Books, 1985.

Coopersmith, Stanley. **The Antecedents Of Self-Esteem.** San Francisco: W.H. Freeman, 1967.

Crockenberg, Susan and Barbara Soby. "Self-Esteem And Teenage Pregnancy," in *The Social Importance Of Self-Esteem.* Berkeley, CA: U.C. Press, 1989.

Crow, Lester and Alice. **How To Study.** New York: Collier Books, 1980.

Csikszent, Mihalyi and Reed Larson. **Being Adolescent: Conflict And Growth In The Teenager.** New York: Basic Books, 1984.

Davis, Lois and Joel. **How To Live Almost Happily With Your Teenagers.** Minneapolis: Winston, 1982.

Dayton, Tian. *Daily Affirmations For Parents: How To Nurture Your Children And Renew Yourself During The Ups And Downs Of Parenthood.* Deerfield Beach, FL: Health Communications, 1991.

Deal, T. and A. Kennedy. **Corporate Cultures: The Rites And Rituals Of Corporate Life.** Reading, MA: Addison-Wesley, 1982.

Diet, Nutrition and Cancer. Washington, D.C.: Committee on Diet, Nutrition and Cancer, Assembly of Life Sciences, National Research Council, National Academy Press, 1982.

Dinkmyer, D. and G.D. McKay. **Raising A Responsible Child.** New York: Simon & Schuster, 1973.

DiPrete, Thomas, Chandra Muller and Nora Shaeffer. **Discipline And Order In American High Schools.** Washington, D.C.: National Center for Education Statistics, 1981.

"Do You Know What Your Children Are Listening To?" *U.S. News & World Report.* October 28, 1985.

Dobson, James. **Preparing For Adolescence.** Santa Ana, CA: Vision House, 1978.

Dodson, Dr. Fitzhugh. **How To Discipline With Love.** New York: Rawson Associates, 1977.

Dreikurs, Rudolf, M.D. **Children: The Challenge.** New York: Hawthorn, 1964.

Dyer, W. **What Do You Really Want For Your Children?** New York: William Morrow and Company, 1985.

Elkind, D. **All Grown Up And No Place To Go.** Reading, MA: Addison-Wesley, 1984.

Ephron, D. **Teenage Romance.** New York: Ballantine, 1981.

"Family Fitness: A Complete Exercise Program For Ages Six To Sixty-Plus." *Reader's Digest* (Special Report) 1987: 2-12.

Feingold, Norman S. and Nora Reno Miller. **Emerging Careers: New Occupations For The Year 2000 And Beyond.** Baltimore: Garrett Park Press, 1989.

Fensterheim, Herbert. **Don't Say Yes When You Want To Say No.** New York: Dell, 1975.

Fox, Emmet. **The Sermon On The Mount.** New York: Harper & Row, 1938.

_____ **Alter Your Life.** New York: Harper & Row, 1936.

_____ **Power Through Constructive Thinking.** New York: Harper & Row, 1938.

Gardner, R. **The Boys and Girls Book About Stepfamilies.** New York: Bantam Books, 1982.

Gernsbacher, L. **The Suicide Syndrome.** New York: Human Science Press, 1985.

Getzoff, Ann and Carolyn McClenahan. **Stepkids: A Survival Guide For Teenagers In Stepfamilies.** New York: Walker and Company, 1984.

Giovacchini, P. **The Urge to Die: Why Young People Commit Suicide.** New York: Macmillian, 1981.

Gomes-Schwartz, B. "Child Sexual Abuse: The Initial Effects." *Library of Social Research* 179, 1990.

Goodman, E. "The Turmoil of Teenage Sexuality," *MS.* July 1983: 37-41.

Gossop, M. "Drug Dependence and Self-Esteem." **International Journal of Addictions** 2, 1976.

Halpern, S. **Sound Health: The Music That Makes Us Whole.** San Francisco: Harper & Row, 1984.

"Has Rock Gone Too Far?" *People.* September 16, 1985: 47-53.

Haynes-Klassen. **Learning To Live, Learning To Love.** Rolling Hills Estates, CA: Jalmar Press, 1985.

Helfer, R., and C.C. Kempe, eds. **Child Abuse And Neglect: The Family And The Community.** Cambridge, MA: Ballinger, 1976.

Hirshberg, Charles and Denise Stinson. "Baytons Boys Do the Right Thing." *Life.* September 1991: 24-32.

Hyde, Margaret O. **Parents Divided, Parents Multiplied.** Louisville, KY: Westminster/John Knox Press, 1989.

James, Muriel and Dorothy Jongeward. **Born To Win.** Menlo Park, CA: Addison-Wesley, 1971.

Jampolsky, Gerald G., M.D. **Teach Only Love.** New York: Bantam, 1983.

Kalb, Jonah and David Viscott, M.D. **What Every Kid Should Know.** Boston: Houghton Mifflin, 1974.

Keegan, Andrew. "Positive Self-Image — A Cornerstone Of Success." *Guidepost.* February 19, 1987.

"Kids and Cocaine: An Epidemic Strikes Middle America." *Newsweek.* March 17, 1986: 58-63.

Klagsbrun, Francine. **Too Young To Die.** New York: Houghton-Mifflin, 1981.

Krantzler, M. **Creative Marriage.** New York: McGraw-Hill, 1981.

Lansky, D. and S. Dorfman. **How To Survive High School With Minimal Brain Damage.** Minneapolis: Meadowbrook, 1989.

"Latchkey Children: The Fastest Growing Special Interest Groups In The Schools." Special Research. *Phi Delta Kappa.* March 1986.

LeHaye, Tim. **The Battle For The Family.** New Jersey: Revell, 1982.

Leite, John S. and J. Kip Parrish. **Successful Parenting: A Common Sense Guide To Raising Your Teenagers.** Deerfield Beach, FL: Health Communications, 1991.

LeShan, E. **What's Going To Happen To Me? When Parents Separate Or Divorce.** San Francisco: Four Winds Press, 1978.

Lewis, Helen Coale. **All About Families — The Second Time Around.** Atlanta: Peachtree Publishing Ltd., 1980.

Mack, John and H. Vivienne Hickler. **The Life And Suicide Of An Adolescent Girl.** Boston: Little, Brown and Co., 1981.

Maris, R. "The Adolescent Suicide Problem." **Suicide And Life Threatening Behavior,** 15:2, 1985: 91-109.

Maslow, Abraham. **Toward A Psychology Of Being.** New York: D. Van Nostrand, 1962.

McCabe, Margaret E. and Jacqueline Rhoades. **How To Say What You Mean.** Los Angeles: ITA Publications, 1985.

McCubbin, H. and C. Figley. **Stress And The Family.** New York: Brunner/Mazel Publishers, 1983.

Miller, Gordon Porter. **Teaching Your Child To Make Decisions.** New York: Harper & Row, 1984.

Newman, Mildred and Bernard Berkowitz. **How To Be Your Own Best Friend.** New York: Random House, 1973.

O'Gorman, Patricia and Philip Oliver-Diaz. **Breaking The Cycle Of Addiction: A Parent's Guide To Raising Healthy Kids.** Deerfield Beach, FL: Health Communications, Inc., 1991.

O'Gorman, Patricia and Philip Oliver-Diaz. **12 Steps To Self-Parenting For Adult Children.** Deerfield Beach, FL: Health Communications, Inc., 1991.

Palmer, Pat, **Liking Myself.** San Luis Obispo, CA: Impact, 1977.

Peal, Norman Vincent. **You Can If You Think You Can.** Pawling, NY: Foundation for Christian Living, 1974.

Pelletier, K. **Mind As Healer, Mind As Slayer.** New York: Delacorte, 1977.

Pfeffer, C. "Intervention For Suicidal Children And Their Parents." **Suicide and Life Threatening Behavior.** 12:4, 1982: 240-248.

Postman, N. **The Disappearance Of Childhood.** New York: Delacorte Press, 1982.

Richards, Arlene Kramer and Irene Willism. **Boy Friends, Girl Friends, Just Friends.** Atheneum, NY: McClelland & Stewart, Ltd., 1979.

Rolfe, Randy. **Adult Children Raising Children: Sparing Your Child From Co-dependency Without Being Perfect Yourself.** Deerfield Beach, FL: Health Communications, Inc., 1991.

Rutter, Michael, et al. **Fifteen Thousand Hours: Secondary Schools And Their Effects On Children.** Cambridge, MA: Harvard University Press, 1979.

Samples, B. **Openmind/Wholemind.** Rolling Hills Estates, CA: Jalmar Press, 1987.

Sanderson, Jim. **How To Raise Your Kids To Stand On Their Own Two Feet.** New York: Congdon & Weed, Inc., 1978.

Satir, Virginia. **Peoplemaking.** Palo Alto, CA: Science & Behavior Books, Inc., 1972.

Seyle, Hans. **Stress Without Distress.** New York: Lippincott, 1974.

_____ **The Stress of Life.** New York: McGraw-Hill, 1976.

Sheehy, Gail. **Pathfinders.** New York: Morrow, 1981.

Sheinkin, D. **Food, Mind and Mood.** New York: Warner Books, 1980.

"Shelters And Streets Draw Throw-Away Kids." *New York Times.* June 3, 1983.

Silberstein, W. **Helping Your Child Grow Slim.** New York: Simon & Schuster, 1982.

Simpson, Bert K., Ph.D. **Becoming Aware Of Values.** La Mesa, CA: Pennant Press, 1973.

Skager, Rodney. **Prevention Of Drug And Alcohol Abuse.** Sacramento, CA: California Attorney General's Office, 1988.

Skoguland, Elizabeth R. **To Anger With Love.** New York: Harper & Row, 1977.

Smith, Manuel J. **When I Say No I Feel Guilty.** New York: Bantam, 1975.

Stainback, W. and S. Stainback. **How To Help Your Child Succeed In School.** Minneapolis: Meadowbrook, 1988.

Statistical Abstracts of the United States. Washington, D.C.: U.S. Department of Commerce, Bureau of the Census, 1990.

Steffenhagen, R.A. and Jeff D. Burns. **The Social Dynamics Of Self-Esteem.** New York: Praeger, 1987.

Syed, Husain and T. Vandiver. **Suicide In Children And Adolescents.** Spectrum Publications. 1984.

"Teenage Fathers." *Psychology Today.* December 1985: 66-70.

"Treating Troubled Teens." *Newsweek.* January 20, 1986: 52-54.

Viscott, David, M.D. **The Language Of Feelings.** New York: Pocket Books, 1976.

Visher, Emily B. and John S. Visher. **How To Win As A Stepfamily.** New York: Dembner Books, distributed by W. W. Norton & Co., 1982.

Wahlross, Sven. **Family Communication.** New York: Macmillan, 1974.

Wallerstein, Judith and Joan B. Kelly. **Surviving The Break Up.** New York: Basic Books, Inc., 1980.

Warren, Neil Clark. **Make Anger Your Ally.** Garden City, NY: Doubleday, 1983.

Weiss, Laurie. **An Action Plan For Your Inner Child: Parenting Each Other.** Deerfield Beach, FL: Health Communications, Inc., 1991.

Winn, Marie. **Children Without Childhood.** New York: Pantheon Books, 1981.

Wood, A. "Stepparents: How To Deal With Them." *Seventeen.* February 1983.

Wyckoff, Jerry and Barbara Unell. **Discipline Without Shouting Or Spanking.** Minneapolis: Meadowbrook, 1988.

Youngs, Bettie B. **Stress In Children: How To Recognize, Avoid And Overcome It.** New York: Avon, 1985.

_____ **A Stress Management Guide For Young People.** Rolling Hills Estates, CA: Jalmar Press, 1992.

_____ **Friendship Is Forever, Isn't It?** Rolling Hills Estates, CA: Jalmar Press, 1992.

_____ **Goal Setting Skills For Young People.** Rolling Hills Estates, CA: Jalmar Press, 1992.

_____ **The 6 Vital Ingredients Of Self-Esteem And How To Develop Them In Your Child.** New York: Rawson/Macmillan, 1991.

_____ **You & Self-Esteem: A Book For Young People.** Rolling Hills Estates, CA: Jalmar Press, 1991.

_____ **Self-Esteem And The Professional Educator.** Rolling Hills Estates, CA: Jalmar Press, 1991.

_____ **Keeping Your Children Safe: Promoting Physical, Emotional, Spiritual and Intellectual Well-Being, Ages 2-20.** Louisville, Kentucky: Westminster John Knox Press, 1992.

_____ **Getting Back Together: Creating A New Relationship With Your Partner And Making It Last.** New York: Bob Adams, Inc., 1990.

_____ **The 6 Vital Ingredients Of Self-Esteem And How To Develop Them In Your Students.** Rolling Hills Estates, CA: Jalmar Press, 1992.

Zelnick, M. and J. Kantner. "Sexuality, Contraception and Pregnancy Among Young Unwed Females." **U.S. Research Reports, Commission on Population Growth and the American Future** 1 (Washington, D.C.: Government Printing Office, 1990).

ABOUT THE AUTHOR

Bettie B. Youngs, Ph.D., Ed.D., is an internationally known lecturer, author, counselor and consultant. Her work has been known in more than 60 countries for more than two decades, earning her a reputation as a respected authority in the field of personal and professional effectiveness. She has earned national acclaim for her work on the effects of stress on health, wellness and productivity both for adults and children, and for her work on the role of self-esteem as it detracts from or empowers vitality, achievement and peak performance.

Dr. Youngs is a former Teacher-Of-The-Year, professor at San Diego State University, and Executive Director of the Phoenix Foundation. She is the author of 14 books published in 23 languages, as well as a number of popular audiocassette programs.

As a member of the National Speakers Association, Dr. Youngs addresses audiences throughout the United States and abroad, meeting with nearly 250,000 people each year. She serves on the board of the National Council for Self-Esteem and is a frequent guest on radio and television talk shows. Her consulting firm provides instruction and professional development to business, industry and school districts nationwide. To contact Dr. Youngs, write or phone:

Bettie B. Youngs & Associates
Instruction & Professional Development
3060 Racetrack View Drive
Del Mar, CA 92014
(619) 481-6360

Other Books By . . .
Health Communications

ADULT CHILDREN OF ALCOHOLICS (Expanded)
Janet Woititz

Over a year on *The New York Times* Best-Seller list, this book is the primer on Adult Children of Alcoholics.

ISBN 1-55874-112-7 $8.95

STRUGGLE FOR INTIMACY
Janet Woititz

Another best-seller, this book gives insightful advice on learning to love more fully.

ISBN 0-932194-25-7 $6.95

BRADSHAW ON: THE FAMILY: A Revolutionary Way of Self-Discovery
John Bradshaw

The host of the nationally televised series of the same name shows us how families can be healed and individuals can realize full potential.

ISBN 0-932194-54-0 $9.95

HEALING THE SHAME THAT BINDS YOU
John Bradshaw

This important book shows how toxic shame is the core problem in our compulsions and offers new techniques of recovery vital to all of us.

ISBN 0-932194-86-9 $9.95

HEALING THE CHILD WITHIN: Discovery and Recovery for
Adult Children of Dysfunctional Families — Charles Whitfield, M.D.

Dr. Whitfield defines, describes and discovers how we can reach our Child Within to heal and nurture our woundedness.

ISBN 0-932194-40-0 $8.95

A GIFT TO MYSELF: A Personal Guide To Healing My Child Within
Charles L. Whitfield, M.D.

Dr. Whitfield provides practical guidelines and methods to work through the pain and confusion of being an Adult Child of a dysfunctional family.

ISBN 1-55874-042-2 $11.95

HEALING TOGETHER: A Guide To Intimacy And Recovery For
Co-dependent Couples — Wayne Kritsberg, M.A.

This is a practical book that tells the reader why he or she gets into dysfunctional and painful relationships, and then gives a concrete course of action on how to move the relationship toward health.

ISBN 1-55784-053-8 $8.95

3201 S.W. 15th Street,
Deerfield Beach, FL 33442-8190
1-800-851-9100

Health
Communications, Inc.®